Aesthetics and Politics of Space
in Russia and Japan

Aesthetics and Politics of Space in Russia and Japan

A Comparative Philosophical Study

Thorsten Botz-Bornstein

LEXINGTON BOOKS
A division of
ROWMAN & LITTLEFIELD PUBLISHERS, INC.
Lanham • Boulder • New York • Toronto • Plymouth, UK

Published by Lexington Books
A division of Rowman & Littlefield Publishers, Inc.
A wholly owned subsidiary of The Rowman & Littlefield Publishing Group, Inc.
4501 Forbes Boulevard, Suite 200, Lanham, Maryland 20706
http://www.lexingtonbooks.com

Estover Road, Plymouth PL6 7PY, United Kingdom

British Library Cataloguing in Publication Information Available

Library of Congress Cataloging-in-Publication Data
Botz-Bornstein, Thorsten.
  Aesthetics and politics of space in Russia and Japan : a comparative philosophical study
/ Thorsten Botz-Bornstein.
    p. cm.
  Includes bibliographical references and index.
  ISBN 978-0-7391-3068-1 (cloth : alk. paper) — ISBN 978-0-7391-3070-4 (electronic)
  1. Space. 2. Aesthetics. 3. Political science. I. Title.
  BH301.S65B68 2009
  111'.850947—dc22   2009025939

Printed in the United States of America

Contents

Acknowledgements

Work on this book, sometimes sporadic, sometimes more intense, stretched over a period of more than ten years. What is perhaps not unusual in terms of time is unusual in terms of space, as I was working within a variety of geographical contexts. My thanks go to all those people who have helped and influenced me in "local villages" as diverse as Helsinki, St. Petersburg, Paris, Kyoto, and Hangzhou.

I also would like to thank the following journals for having granted the permission to reprint revised versions of their articles: *Theandros: The Online Journal of Orthodox Christian Theology and Philosophy* for 'Virtual Reality and Virtual Irreality: On Noh-Plays and Icons' that was published in 2004 in its issue 2: 2; the *Japan Review* for 'The I and the Thou: A Dialogue Between Nishida Kitarō and Mikhail Bakhtin' that was published in 2004 in its issue Nr.16, 251-275. An earlier version was also included in my *Place and Dream: Japan and the Virtual* (Rodopi, 2004); *Environment and Planning D: Society and Space* (Pion Limited, London) for 'Philosophical Conceptions of Cultural Space in Russia and Japan: Comparing Nishida Kitarō and Semën Frank' that was published in 2008 in its issue Nr. 26: 5. 842-859; *Asian Philosophy* for 'From Community to Time-Space Development: Trubetzkoy, Nishida, Watsuji' that was published in 2007 in its issue Nr. 17: 3, 263-282; *Philosophical Frontiers* for 'Russian and Japanese Philosophies' that was published in 2008 in its issue Nr. 3: 1.

Schrader: In Japanese art there is a concept of *mono no aware*, sweet sadness, the pleasure of endings, of autumn and seeing a dying leaf.

Sokurov: For Russia, sweet sadness and pleasant farewells are not possible. On the contrary, in the Russian sense of elegy, it's a very deep, vertical feeling, not a delighting one. It gets you deeply, sharply, painfully. It's massive.

Conversation between Paul Schrader and Alexander Sokurov

Introduction

In the present book I examine the parallels between Russian and Japanese philosophies and religions by revealing a common concept of space in Russian and Japanese aesthetics and political theories. I show points of convergence between the two traditions regarding the treatment of space within the realm of identity (both individual and communal), and in formulations of the relationship between regionalism, localism and globalism.

Before starting an analysis of space, I establish in Chapter One, Japanese and Russian philosophies as phenomena that clearly have a common scope, which I define as follows: both philosophies analyze the relationship between faith and reason, as well as the critique of secularism. Concepts like "organicity," "person," and "totality" are central in both traditions. Among the most popular philosophical themes discussed by Russian and Japanese philosophers are reflections on the problem of personalism and philosophical developments of "intuition."

In Chapter Two, I offer an analysis of space as it is understood in Russian and Japanese aesthetics. Both traditions (1) strive to effectuate a shift in the mental awareness of the spectator in order to establish a realm

ix

outside the physical framework of space-time as well as of matter and (2) tend to define spatial experience as determined by a strong psychological component. I illustrate this by comparing two of these cultures' most classical aesthetic expressions: Russian icons and Japanese Noh-plays. Though the former are pictorial and the latter theatrically enacted, both turn out to be highly compatible on several levels: both require a high degree of formalization and regulation; both maintain an interesting anti-relationship with realism; and both meditative characters make aesthetic experience the central theme of a religious art.

The reflection on Noh-plays and icons permits me also to untangle the relationships between the virtual, the dream, the imaginary, and reality. The virtual environment, according to Michael Heim, "pulls its users with a power unlike that of any other medium—unless we include the religious rituals and sacred dramas that once provided the context for art works" (Heim 1998b: 55). This is also the effect of Noh-plays and icons. First I analyze the virtual, the dream, and the imaginary, on the utmost abstract, linguistic level. The "virtual" is reflected against that aspect of life, which French philosophers of the 1950s used to call the "existential" one. I am inclined to call the virtual aspect of life the "dreamlike" one and show that both Noh-plays and Russian icons include such a virtual space.

I continue the analysis of cultural similarities between Japanese and Russian conceptions of space through a comparative analysis of the Japanese notion of *basho* and the Russian notion of *sobornost'*. In the hands of NISHIDA Kitarō and Semën Frank, space becomes in a very interesting way dynamic. This concerns also the notion of community. While Western philosophy has persistently attempted to interpret the community through metaphysical terms like self, will, and spirit, Japanese and Russian philosophers overcome the idea of individual 'I's as materialized "objects." For them, procedures like *Einfühlung* or intuition are inefficient because they do more than transform the other, from the point of view of the 'I,' into an object.

From there it is not a long way to reflections on inter-subjectivity, self-reflection, and style that are developed in Chapter Four dealing with Nishida and the Russian literary critic Mikhail M. Bakhtin. Having shown, in Chapter Two, that space is also an aesthetic phenomenon, I now examine aesthetic space within the framework of a more formal aesthetics. Bakhtin serves as an interesting example because, unlike Frank's, Bakhtin's reflections on "dialogical space" extend into contemporary (postmodern) thought: Bakhtin deals with style as a basis for a theory of civilization.

In Chapter Five, I return to the communal aspect of spatial experience and examine how Russian and Japanese philosophers transformed the traditional notion of communal space (that has always been seen as an organic time-space unity) into a sophisticated element better described as "time-space development." Important here are the theories of Nishida, Watsuji, Trubetzkoy, and the Eurasianists. Nishida's idea that "nations transcend themselves while remaining true to themselves and construct a single multi-world," or the concept of an East-Asia in which all nations should eventually "transcend themselves and construct their own distinct world" can be interpreted as a culturological means of overcoming of cultural egocentricity and as the suggestion of a philosophical system of convergence. In this way Nishida's system comes amazingly close to Trubetzkoy's. Also for the Eurasianists, the state organization had at its center a personal god and the "symphonic personality" of Russia-Eurasia represented a non-egoistic, communal consciousness. Towards the end of the chapter I associate both Nishida's and Eurasianist ideas with neo-Darwinian versions of the theme of evolution as it has been developed by Henri Bergson, Gilles Deleuze and Felix Guattari. The Eurasianists' combination of spatial-temporal "undifferential entities" can be seen as such "postmodern" elaborations of space similar to Deleuze and Guattari's rhizomes. All these systems are determined by neither evolutionary linearities nor abstract models of unity and are able to develop their own internal dynamics.

Russia and Japan

Before engaging in the comparative discourse, it should be established that both objects of research, Russian and Japanese cultures, are really comparable. Russia is a huge continental power containing a large variety of ethnic, religious, and social types while Japan is a relatively homogenous island nation. In terms of geography, Russia and Japan do not seem to have much in common, except the fact that both countries developed in the periphery of larger cultural areas (Byzantium and China respectively). Even in socio-economic terms many people will be skeptical that these two countries have much to share. Economic development has turned Russia first into a communist superpower and then into a realist, semi-totalitarian capitalist state that intrigues few people in terms of life-style. Though Japan has presented itself often as a "contradiction of advancement and backwardness, or exotic primitivism conjoined with hi-tech supremacy,"[1] it is certain that its modern culture, which developed hand-in-hand with a techno-digital revolution and with a pervasive consumerism, transformed the archipelago, as has said Fran Lloyd, into "an exemplar of the unreal, a society of endless floating signs, of simulation and pastiche."[2]

In spite of these discrepancies, people have observed various similarities—some of which date back to pre-modern times—that are supposedly responsible for Russia's and Japan's parallel development as "successful latecomers" to the club of modern countries. In the 1960s, Hugh Seton-Watson explained to all reformers of Africa and Asia that what is "more beneficial to them than the ritual invocation of "Asianism" or "négritude" is the "the study of Russian and Japanese experience [of reform]."[3] From a certain point of view, both countries' approaches towards modernization appear to be similar because, according to Marius Jansen, both had "responded strikingly to the challenges posed by the prior development of science and technology in the North Atlantic world."[4] It is in Russia and in Japan that the old precepts of "spirit and technology" could be reformulated in the 1920s not in terms of romantic, revisionist exaltation, but rather in the manner of a modern social theory. More precisely, the combination of "Russian spirit" and "Western technology," practiced at the time of Peter the Great, echoes the Japanese slogan *wakon yōsai* (Eastern spirit—Western science). This practice has been current since the beginning of the Meiji restoration and could, in the 1920s, serve as a starting point for reflections not only on how to become "Western" but also on how to escape Europeanization.[5] According to the Eurasianist Nicolai Trubetzkoy, Peter the Great has been fully aware of Russia's distinctive cultural character but he first wanted to implant European technological thinking. Once this was done however, Russia's spirit would have to be maintained (Trubetzkoy himself suggested adopting the achievements of Romano-Germanic culture without adopting its endemic 'egocentrism').[6]

Philosophy in Russia and Japan

The present book does not attempt to compare the two countries' cultures or economical or political organizations, but their respective philosophies. As a matter of fact, Russia and Japan are not only successful reformers but also the first "non-Western" countries that develop a *philosophy*—in the "Western" sense—of their own and *on a larger scale*. Still it seems that, in spite of this striking parallel, no comparative research has been done on these two philosophical traditions. Studies on "Nishida and Heidegger" are numerous while topics like, say, "Nishida and Berdiaev" or "Watsuji and Trubetzkoy" have never been taken up for examination. This is more so surprising because the comparative potential of such studies is obvious, be it simply for historical reasons. In Russia, the Eastern Orthodox Church passed by, for example, those Neo-Platonic dichotomies like 'body' and 'mind' that are, not coincidentally, assumed by the Western Church as well as for Western metaphysics (cf. Lopatin 1913). Also in Japan these notions had never been taken for granted. This is one of the reasons why in both countries an ambiguous "Western" philosophy could adopt similar forms.

Talking about "philosophy" in Japan and Russia creates, of course, an exceptional situation. Philosophy is not indigenous to either country. Indeed "Japanese philosophy" and "Russian philosophy" are products of modernization. In premodern Japan (before the Meiji period), Japanese thought was religious, influenced often by metaphysical Buddhist motives and a Confucian ethical system. The Western idea of the "philosopher" as an independent thinker was almost absent, and if it existed, it was marginal and not influential. Since the Meiji Restoration, however, there has been an abundant introduction of Western philosophy into Japan, though traditional components continued to occupy an important place. NISHI Amane (1829-1897), the father of Japanese philosophy, introduced Comte's positivism and Mill's utilitarianism and coined a large number of philosophical terms in the Japanese language, among which is also the term "tetsugaku" (philosophy). Nishi insisted on the philosophical "superiority" of the West[7] and attempted to destroy Japan's Confucian basis; however, his absorption of Western thought remains often superficial. Following generations of philosophers, Japanese thinkers undertook an amazing adoption and assimilation of Western ideas into the native Japanese system. They seldom did this without thoroughly reworking these ideas and adapting them to the needs of Japanese culture. The Kyoto School of philosophy, centered around NISHIDA Kitarō, especially formulated these problems. In particular, Buddhism had a strong influence particularly on Japanese elaborations of philosophical aesthetics and psychology. The overall result of these convergences is a philosophy that is Japanese and at the same time comparable with its Western counterpart.

"Russian philosophy" as a notion poses similar problems. It is difficult to say with certainty when Russian philosophy started—a problem discussed in the first chapter of the present book—but it is certain that it started relatively late. Roughly, it is right to say that since the writings of the Slavophiles, Russia emerged as the first non-Western nation to challenge Eurocentric philosophical models. Paradoxically, this philosophical "particularism" coexisted with "universalistic" tendencies, which, often formulated through religious considerations, continued to be dominant in Slavophilism as well as in Russian philosophical thought in general. Kireevsky's critique of the rationalism predominant in European philosophy (a critique that sometimes reads like an anticipated antagonism of analytic and continental philosophy) or of "Eurocentric reason," for example, is interesting in itself. His critique of Leibniz' excessive "ratiocination" ('*rassudochnost*'),[8] or his idea of (fully reasonable) "interior harmony" that should be opposed to the "formal harmony" or the law (ibid.) are reminiscent of certain contemporary Western ideas.[9] From there on, mostly through Russian nihilism and names like Herzen and Solov'ëv, Russian philosophy has been able to conquer a marginal place in the European philosophical landscape.

One of the objectives of the present book is to sketch the cultural similarities between Russia and Japan by concentrating on their philosophies and on some decisive stances in their intellectual history. C. T. K. Chari's comparative article published in *Philosophy East and West* in 1952 is probably the first explicit attempt ever made at interpreting Russian ontology by using certain models from East Asian thought. Chari draws on the medieval mystical heritage of the Eastern Church and encourages research into the Russian *Weltanschauung* that would, in his opinion, give easier access to Eastern thought for Westerners. Chari points to Solov'ëv's 'All-Unity' as a phenomenon reminiscent of Swami Vivekananda's *Hymn of Samādhi* in which "The 'I' is paralleled by the 'Thou' in me" (231). Unfortunately Chari shows surprisingly much interest in "paranormal or supra-normal phenomena" including parapsychology (a temptation, which perhaps already forecasts post-perestroika Russian research into this part of Russian thought).

Towards a New Ethnophilosophy?

It is necessary to mention a further aspect of the preceding considerations. The present book can also be read as a reflection on the place of philosophy within a "globalized" world. Can or must philosophy be linked to a "local" culture?[10] However one turns the problem around, it is clear that the existences of "Japanese philosophy" and "Russian philosophy" question the authority of "general" truths and forces us to integrate "local discourses" into the overall construction called "global philosophy" or World Philosophy. The philosophies dealt with in this book did not develop in isolation from life but represent intellectualized forms of practice as they emphasize the existential outlook of philosophy as well as the values that are based on a certain system of beliefs, politics, and aesthetics.

One of the negative undertones clinging to the term "globalization" is linked to it being seen as a uniformizing and flattening power that eliminates existing cultural differences. However, there is an important side effect of globalization represented by those movements acting against it, stressing the importance of "localization" or "regionalization." These approaches, when formulated in a radical fashion, have to face the reproach of relativism, and of enclosing themselves in a cultural sphere supposedly inaccessible to others. The Russian and Japanese examples discussed in this book show that a "middle course" is possible. The part and the whole, individual and communal identity, as well as other dichotomies do not need to be construed as such, but appear in a new light once one accepts to consider the main ideas of these non-Western philosophies. Finally, a note on how to use this book. Not every reader will be equally versed in the Japanese and the Russian histories of ideas. Anyone desiring to acquire some knowledge about the basic Russian and Japanese terms beforehand (especially about the political context of Pan-Asianism on the Japanese side and Eurasianism on the Russian side) is recommended to first read the "Explanation of Terms" at the end of the book. Other technical terms like *basho* or *sobornost'* are explained in the text at the moment they first appear.

Japanese names appear in Japanese order, which is to say that surnames are followed by given names, except when an individual is better known internationally with his or her name reversed. Because not all readers of this book will be acquainted with this, for example, those more familiar with Russian philosophy, I decided to capitalize all Japanese surnames the first time they appear in the text. Note, too, that macrons have been dropped from common Japanese words.

Notes

1. Kumiko SATO: "How Information Technology has (not) Changed Feminism and Japanism: Cyberpunk in the Japanese Context" in *Comparative Literature* 41: 3, 2004, 335.
2. Fran Lloyd (ed): *Consuming Bodies: Sex and Contemporary Japanese Art* (London: Reaktion Books, 2002), 9.
3. Hugh Seton-Watson: "Russia and Modernization" in *Slavic Review* 20: 4, 1961, 588. Seton-Watson does not forget pointing out that "no other modernizing state has ever made such a bad job of national education as Imperial Russia, nor such a good job as Japan" (ibid).
4. Marius B. Jansen: "On Foreign Borrowing" in A. Craig (ed.): *Japan: A Comparative View* (Princeton: Princeton University Press, 1979), 18.
5. In Japan, such ideas have been current since the beginning of the Meiji restoration, but they could, in the 1920s, serve as a starting point for reflections on how to escape Europeanization. The slogan *wakon yōsai* had actually first been launched in the 1840s by Sakuma Shōzan.
6. "Europe and Mankind," 78. The Tsar died before the latter act could be accomplished.
7. See Thomas R. Havens: *Nishi Amane and Modern Japanese Thought* (Princeton: Princeton University Press, 1970), 129.
8. Ivan Kireevsky, *Collected Works I* (Moscow: Gerchenzon, 1911), 194.

9. Kireevsky is convinced that "Rome reserved the monopol of judgment to its hierarchy" and the result was as follows: "The people should not think, it should not understand the liturgy . . . but only listen to it without understanding and obey without discussing (ibid., 229)." Like this was formed an "unconscious mass" of people that only consume religion.

10. The problems of "ethnophilosophy" in a contemporary context are discussed in a volume that I edited (with Jürgen Hengelbrock) entitled *Re-ethnicizing the Minds? Cultural Revival in Contemporary Thought* (Amsterdam, New York: Rodopi, 2006).

Chapter One

The Historical Foundations of Russian and Japanese Philosophies

Modernization in Russia and Japan

Is it possible to compare Russian and Japanese philosophies? And why should one do so? First, looking at how "philosophical events" and publications are distributed over the time axis, one could conclude that the temporal difference between Japan and Russia is simply too large and that comparisons are impossible. In Russia, "modernization" began with Peter the Great (1672-1725), paralleling the Tokugawa seclusion. In both countries, reforms led to the strengthening of the inner situation of the bureaucracy and of the military. However, in Russia, a *philosophical* critique of modernization processes would be produced only more than a hundred years after Peter's death. The reason for this is that in the eighteenth century there simply was no Russian philosophy able to formulate such a criticism. In Japan the situation was different. Even though modernization began there only around 1855 (and officially only as late as 1867), philosophical criticism and intellectual comment developed very quickly. 1867 is the date of the Pan-Slavist congress in Moscow and the date of the official beginning of the Meiji reformation in Japan (see time-

1

line at the end of the book) but the vigor of philosophical expressions is not reflected by these dates.[1]

This is at least one way of comparing both traditions, and it clearly establishes a temporal parallelism. Another way of seeing both countries' development is, as does Marius Jansen, to state that they began modernization at the same time. The Meiji Reform and the Great Reforms in Russia (liberation of peasants as well as several judicial reforms under Alexander II) began both in the 1860s and from there on one can note striking signs of development (Jansen 1979: 18).

Jansen's scheme makes sense, but, even though Japan and Russia have generally been recognized as "late modernizers" for just these reasons, one should not forget that the political development of Eastern Europe and Japan was far from being on the same level. The aforementioned time gap between Peter the Great and Meiji is responsible for these differences. The decisive point is that comparisons of the Meij Reform and the Great Reforms in Russia are only partially correct because the Meiji revolution was conservative and not progressive. This means that individualism (let alone democracy) was not among the main issues discussed by policy makers in the Japan of the 1890s.[2] In Europe (including Russia in this case) the situation was different because "modernization" had different meaning there than in Japan. Europe had by that time definitely relegated into the archives of history Romanticism, sentiment, and idealism, and was working towards a more enlightened "science" that would soon influence all domains of society. In other words, politics was no longer determined by idealist principles of ethics and truth but by scientifically measurable quantities or by "material forces." However, as usual, the coin has two sides. The newly acquired scientific way of dealing with politics also entailed a critical attitude towards democracy. Movements like Pan-Slavism (which was a phenomenon of the 1860s) cannot be understood without taking into account this ambiguous tendency uniting scientific thought and romanticism.

It is impossible to find a parallel double-faced phenomenon in Nineteenth Century Japan. Even at the beginning of the twentieth century the constellation is of an entirely different kind: here aggressive nationalism fostering pragmatic and cynical political methods coexists with a newly adopted intellectual attitude that is eager to discover ways of expressing Pan-Asian feelings through Western *idealist* concepts (cf. Okakura's *Ideals of the East*).

The Development of Russian
and Japanese Philosophies

In Russia, intellectual criticism of modernization took form relatively late because Russian philosophy had to be developed first. True, the Japanese had no "philosophy" either; however, when looking at the degree of sophistication with which Okakura defines his "Ideals of the East" in 1902, only 35 years after the Restoration, and at Nishida's *Zen no Kenkyū* inaugurating, nine years later, a true Japanese tradition of philosophy, it appears as if Russia's intellectual Pan-Slav machine had difficulties getting started. (Eastern European Pan-Slavism was perhaps philosophically more interesting at the beginning but declined later.)

Next, there is a difference not only in politics but also in learning. True, in principle, both countries started to absorb Western learning at the same time (in the 1770s), but the conditions under which the learning took place were not the same. Russia had direct access to Western culture while Japan had been closed since 1640. The question is: how could Japan catch up so quickly? An indirect reason is certainly that in Japan, "modernization" represented an official policy adopted by the government, which means that critical reflections of this policy were mainly made from outside the government. In Russia, on the other hand, both Slavophiles and Modernizers stood outside the government. Within the mixed discourse of modernization/anti-modernization that is so typical for the Russian 1840s and 1850s, a more streamlined philosophical conception of Pan-Slavism could evolve only very slowly.

If we consider Peter Chaadaev, who vacillated between Modernization and Slavophilism, as the "first original philosopher of Russia" (Mikhail Epstein), we might be tempted to think of NISHIDA Kitarō as his Japanese counterpart, because with his *Zen no Kenkyū* he arises, in 1911, as "the first original philosopher of Japan."[3] However, this parallelism is inappropriate, because the intellectual output of Slavophilism after Chaadaev is, in terms of philosophical quality, not comparable with that of the Kyoto School after Nishida.

It seems to be more accurate to establish a date around 1902 when Okakura's *Ideals of the East* inaugurated the "Asian Spiritual Renaissance," and 1901, when the Religious-Philosophical Society of St. Petersburg was founded by symbolist writers and idealist philosophers who claimed to inaugurate the "Russian Religious-Philosophical Renaissance." Intellectually, this Russian group was extremely removed from westernizing thought (Herzen's "nihilism" could not find their favor), but it did keep a link with Slavophilism: the "essence of Russianness" remained a favored subject in their discussion.[4]

In Russia, once the more paternalist style of the Slavophiles is overcome, any hybrid forms of imperialism, culturalism, and hidden imperialist intentions will *not* make their way forward to a first class intellectual plan. In Japan this tendency exists. At some point Japan falls back on the level of early Slavophiles by producing the genre of "Cultural Particularism" for which a part of the Kyoto School of philosophy remains famous. This concerns especially those students of Nishida (among them NISHITANI Keiji) who sought to influence national policy, and finally to justify a Pan-Asianism that implemented leadership instead of partnership.

With which Japanese phenomenon then can the Russian "pre-philosophical" phase be compared? With regard to the curious mixture of modernization and traditionalism that Russian thought developed after Chaadaev, it appears reasonable to compare the Russian 1840s and 1850s with KITA Ikki (1886-1957) and ŌKAWA Shūmei (1883-1937). Kita's "Japanese socialism" is indeed more reminiscent of Alexander Herzen's Russian version of socialism than of any of the philosophies developed by Kita's Russian contemporaries. Herzen (1812-1870) was against all empty abstraction of progress, though also against revolutionary violence. Attacking all sorts of systems and dogmas, he was against oppression of human beings by reference to idealized abstractions such a freedom, progress, and the common good (for Lenin, Herzen even remained the founder of the revolutionary movement). Also the rightwing thinker ŌKAWA Shūmei sympathized with Bolshevik Russia and admired Lenin, which suggests a comparison with Nicolai Chernyshevsky (1828-89). Being convinced that Russians should learn from the West, Chernyshevsky continued the Westernizing line, though at the same time he remained close to the Slavophiles.[5]

If we look at the cultural development of Russia and Japan in that way, the above mentioned time gap appears much smaller: only fifty-six years lie between Herzen's *From the Other Shore* and Kita's *Theory of National Polity and Pure Socialism*. The Russian Slavophiles, on the other hand, appear to be the conservative ingredient of Pan-Slavist thought that can be paralleled with Japanese "Paternalists" like NITOBE Inazo, TOGO Minoru, MOCHIJI Rokasaburo, and NAGAI Ryutarō (some of whom were involved in the creation of chairs of "Colonial Studies" in Tokyo in 1908). The respective contemporaneity of KITA Ikki and Japanese colonialists on the one hand, and Slavophiles and Modernizers on the other, justifies this parallelism.

What about the philosophical phase in Russia? I am inclined to let the "philosophical phase" of Pan-Slavism begin with Danilevsky's *Russia and Europe* or with the first writings of Solov'ëv (who was then still influenced by Kireevsky). Solov'ëv was the first to diagnose a crisis in Western *philosophy* and, similar to Nishida, he attempted what Western philosophy had so far been unable to do: to bring together religious and philosophical truth. The Slavophiles, though philosophical, keep a reactionary undertone in general. The Modernizers, though also philosophical, tend to see philosophical problems of identity, national culture and so on, in the light of social engineering and not of spiritual, psychological, and cultural transformation.

If we admit this scheme for Russia, its philosophers appear to have an advance of thirty to forty years with regard to Nishida's *Zen no kenkyū*. However, the Japanese caught up quickly. Indeed, they caught up so quickly that one can speak in 1920, in terms of complexity and profundity, of an eminent parallelism between Russian and Japanese reflections.

Common Themes of Russian and Japanese Thought

Both Japanese and Russian philosophies are engaged in analyzing the relationship between faith and reason as well as in the critique of secularism. Concepts like "organicity," "person," and "totality" are central in both traditions. Among the most popular philosophical themes discussed are reflections on the problem of personalism and philosophical developments of "intuition."

All-Unity

Comparative studies of the subject of All-Unity in Russia and Japan can very well pass under the heading: "Absolute Unity: Totalitarian or not?" As totalitarian can be considered the philosophies of Danilevsky, Karsavin, and—with some restrictions, as we will see below—Watsuji, while others, like S. L. Frank or Nishida tend to depict All-Unity as an unsolvable philosophical conundrum.

In general, the idea of All-Unity is more "eastern" than "western." As mentioned, C. T. K. Chari points to the proximity between classical Russian ontology and East Asian thought[6] claiming that Solov'ëv's 'All-Unity' is reminiscent of Swami Vivekananda's *Hymn of Samōdhi*. Though we do not find concepts like those which hold that "the whole universe is manifest in every atom" (Okakura on the "science" of the Asanga and Vasubandhu period)[7] in Russian philosophy, a certain metaphysics of All-Unity (*vseyedinstvo*) is central to a range of Russian philosophers such as A. Khomiakov, L. P. Karsavin, V. Solov'ëv, Lev Lopatin, Evgeni Trubetzkoy, Pavel Florensky, Sergei Bulgakov, Semën

Frank, and Nicolas Lossky. Thoughts about All-Unity, often discussed in proximity with the quest for harmony of faith and reason, are not simply philosophical protests against the ecclesiastical "egoism" of Protestants who are said to affirm a "multitude without unity," but most often represent direct attempts to overcome the entire intellectual machine of Western metaphysics by Eastern Orthodox means.

As mentioned in the introduction, the Eastern Orthodox Church passed by several Neo-Platonic dichotomies that are binding for Western metaphysics and All-Unity as a philosophical subject did not develop along the same lines in both cultural spheres. In a schematic way one can say that in Western philosophy the subject of All-Unity has never been assumed as a philosophical end but has been transformed, by Spinoza, Bruno, Eckhart, Hegel, and others, into sophisticated dialectical, cosmological, or monadological systems.[8]

In Japanese philosophy, "All-Unity" does not appear as an explicit notion but is implicit in many of the reflections of the Kyoto School, especially in Nishida's. Contrary to Spinoza, Bruno, Eckhart, and Hegel, who were eager to annul the tension between the whole and the part whenever they encountered the idea of All-Unity, Nishida's reflections about the whole and its parts as they exist in a "place" (*basho*), maintain and even emphasize a contradiction.

The idea of *basho* came to Nishida when analyzing the notion of *chôra* as it occurs in Plato's *Timaeus*. Appearing as diametrically opposed to the Aristotelian substance (*ousia*), *basho* represents a new ontological category summarizing Nishida's personal, Japanese version of the Western intuition. *Basho* is an existential place in which the objective world establishes itself. Nishida's treatment of place as something containing negativity has an effect on the treatment of the conceptualization of All-Unity or Oneness. *Basho* is not (like Hegel's "nation") an organically defined whole but a horizon determined by self-negation through the Buddhist idea of nothingness. Though literally, *basho* means "place," it is rather a "negative space" in which things do not simply "exist" but in which they are "local," i.e., in which they "are" in a concrete way.

For Buddhism, Nirvana, as an ultimate state of being, is nothingness. Illusions (the veil of appearance) need to be negated in order to arrive at ontological truth. Correspondingly, for Nishida, reality is nothingness, a conception that is "in sharp contrast to the basic Western notion that reality is to be considered as being" (Piovesana 1997: 117). It is in this sense that Nishida writes about his idea of the "One" or All-Unity: "What I mean by the self-determination of absolute nothingness, even though I said that it is the all-encompassing basis of all self-determinations of universals, does not simply mean Plotinus notion of the 'One.' My notion of the self-realization of nothingness is not at all the idea of religious *ekstasis*."[9] Nishida sees All-Unity as an original unity of things and the Absolute One is absolute only because it is the self-negation of itself.

It needs to be pointed out that this is very different from Watsuji's more "totalitarian"—or more Hegelian—totality "in which parts are synthesized into an organic whole and in which parts are proper to themselves" (Naoki SAKAI). In Watsuji's view—and what earned him much criticism—this totality is able to depict the emperor as a "living totality."[10]

The Myth of Uniqueness

Large parts of Russian philosophy deal with the *samobytnost'* (originality) of Russian culture and read like a Russian adaptation of Japanese *nihonjinron*. According to ANNO Tadashi, the "resurgence of discourses on the 'nation' and its alleged 'uniqueness' has been "one of the most conspicuous developments in the intellectual history of both Japan and Russia since the 1960s" (Anno 2000: 329). Norbert Elias remarked that for the English and the French, the question 'What is really French?' and 'What is really English?' had long ceased to be a matter of discussion while "What is really German" had not been laid to rest by the Germans of the nineteenth century (Elias 1978: 6). In the case of Germany it has obviously been the lack of national identity that sparked these discourses. What could be the reason in Russia and in Japan?

It has been pointed out that one of the reasons for the parallel between Russian and Japanese particularist attitudes is the common use of ancient written works for the establishment of identity and nationalism. The Japanese *Kojiki* (the earliest historical record of Japan) and the Russian *Primary Chronicle* (a medieval Kievan Rus historical work) both represent (mythical) starting points of cultural traditions.[11] Marius Jansen writes that both mythico-historical works rely "on the written and cultural tradition of an ancient empire . . . combined with a need for national identification and distinction and this is resolved through the ascension of a special origin and a mission for the fledgling state" (Jansen 1979: 30).

In Japan, there is a kind of nativist thinking or culturalism deeply involved in items like the Japanese "pantheistic love of nature" that is said to linger at the bottom of Japanese culture in the form of a unique and unchanging essence. This thinking can also be encountered in academic philosophy.[12] It is through ranges of cultural reductivism, particularism, and determinism that "social, economic and political phenomena are often seen as symptoms of immanent culture," according to KOSAKU Yoshino (1992: 10). While the idealized presentation of Japanese culture in popular writings is dismissed by serious scholars, numerous genuinely philosophical projects dig into the Japanese identity in order to formulate particularly Japanese approaches. By contrasting typically Japanese intellectual models with conventional Western ones, one hopes to produce insights into subjects that are of wider interest. NISHITANI Keiji's or KIMURA Bin's works are examples of the latter category.[13]

Also Russian philosophy is marked by recurrent allusions to its cultural uniqueness, many of which evolve along lines that separate east and west.[14] Since the mid-1960s, a new Russophilism began to supplant neo-Leninism (Anno 2000: 330), borrowing from older Russian discourses on the *russkaia ideia*.[15] The idea that the European mind is violent and should be contrasted with a "Slavic mind" that is cooperative, tolerant, and selfless is expressed by Nicolai Danilevsky (1822-1885) as well as by Alexei Khomiakov (1808-1860).[16] While Chaadaev (1794-1856) still contented himself with reproaching Russia for its absence of any spiritual tradition, his outspoken anti-messianic cultural critique of Russia[17] was quickly replaced with the Slavophiles' "locally minded particularism" (Suvchinsky)[18] that attempts to establish Russia as a superior culture.

Russian philosophy itself arose from the insight that "Western formulas were not applicable to us; [that] in Russian life there was some kind of particular beginning foreign to other people; here development proceeded by another law, as yet undetermined by science" (Yuri Samarin).[19] The style of philosophizing as well as the ideological direction not only of the entire Slavophile project but of much of Russian philosophy in general, are marked by a constant wondering about the character of Russian culture. Still in 1922 Gustav Shpet could write that "Slavophile problems are the only original problems of Russian philosophy."[20]

There is a Slavophile concept of the "chosen people"[21] that affirms "the idea of God that placed Rus' higher than any other state and that the center of world history had shifted to Russia" (Barabanov 1992: 30). In spite of this, in general, Russian philosophical styles are less narcissistic than those of the Japanese *nihonjinron*. Having been led by the intention to find a philosophy appropriate for Russian culture, Russian philosophy was able to preserve some of its cultural particularity by clinging to this "Slavophil" project only in the largest sense, which prompted V. V. Ivanov to say that "Russia has preserved the spiritual strength that distinguishes it from most big countries."[22] The reverse of the coin is that such discourses might also turn out to be the major obstacle for Russian mature philosophizing in the twenty-first century. Valentin Bazhanov maintains that "Still many obstacles are on the path. The main one . . . is to underscore Russian exceptionality and uniqueness, to insist on the originality of Russian culture."[23]

Another point needs to be mentioned in the context of the subject of uniqueness. In spite of both countries' ambitions to create a strong national identity, it is obvious that in both cases an almost natural tendency towards imitation is predominant. The cultural critic TAKEUCHI Yo-shimi reproached Japan with being a "slave nation" that successfully imitates its master without noticing that its success is a failure (see post-face of the present book).[24] Seventy years earlier, FUKUZAWA Yukichi (1835-1901), referring to Japan, stated that "even if they did imitate the West, [what Japanese modernization achieved] could not be called civi-lization" since "the mere existence of 'Western styles' is no proof of civilization."[25] Criticism of Japan like Takeuchi's is directed to the same cultural situation that has been characteristic in Russia where, as accord-ing to Mark Raeff, people "did not learn about 'high' culture of the West European artistic and scientific elites, but . . . absorbed the applied tech-nology of the 'consumer-oriented' popular culture."[26] Trubetzkoy's vi-sion of Russia comes closest to the modernized Japan criticized by Fu-kuzawa and Takeuchi:

> The latest fad and 'last word' from Europe (mechanically adopted and clumsily realized) will stand side by side with specimens of pitiable, shabby provinciality and cultural backwardness. All of this—with its spiritual emptiness concealed behind conceited self-adulation, shrill salesmanship, and bombastic phrases about national culture, originality, and so on—will be simply a pathetic surrogate, not a culture but a cari-cature.[27]

The topic of imitation will be further developed in Chapter Five.

Personalism

Personalism is a philosophical movement that developed numerous branches on almost every continent of the earth. It establishes the person as the ultimate explanation for being and combats all attempts at objecti-fication of subjective life, be it that of a society, of a culture, or of a per-son. Though influenced by religious motives and theological tradition, Personalism inherited also much from Hegel and his emphasis on dialec-tical movement toward wholeness. With regard to the Russian and Japa-nese authors discussed here, Personalism can also appear to be a product of the philosophical culture described above that centers its reflections simultaneously on All-Unity and cultural uniqueness.[28]

The subject of personality occurs strikingly often in modern Russian and Japanese philosophy.[29] Robert Bellah identified the "type of fusion of culture, society, and personality which seems to be present in Japan" with a "normal feature of primitive society and archaic cultures [that] was found quite generally in the bronze age monarchies which existed throughout the civilized world until the first millennium BC."[30] Bellah's attempt to discredit the "culture-and-personality" school appears as questionable if one considers that "personality" is only an old-fashioned word for what is today more commonly called "self" and whose relevance in compounds like "self-awareness" and "self-realization" almost nobody would question (cf. Lebra 1992: 105). In Japan and Russia the personalist theme recurs as a kind of remedy against a modern strain of thought which tends to disintegrate the personality by rationalism. ABE Jirō,[31] Watsuji,[32] and Nishida[33] are personalist philosophers as much as Danilevsky, Kireevsky, Pavel Florovsky,[34] Berdiaev, Karsavin, and Nicolai Trubetzkoy. The project that these philosophers advance is not so much that of defining personhood as an evidence of individual thought (opposed to functionalist views that interpret the person in terms of agency) but, paradoxically, to discover a hidden, immediately functioning principle that unifies the individual and his/her environment *in personality*. Rejecting the Kantian notion of a "universal self," ideas like the Eurasianist "symphonic personality," Khomiakov's "free unity," Danilevsky's "collective personality"[35] or Nishida's "concrete personality"[36] are attempts to produce an integral, collective, supraindividual and internalized vision of the human mind that transcends pure ratiocination.

Berdiaev holds that personality, though still being something social, is not determined by society.[37] Nishida's project to "actualize individual aspirations beyond society" (ARIMA Tatsuo[38]) bears similarly contradictory traits. Nishida defines experience as something which precedes the individual (which is thus not determined by society), though the self which is formed through this experience is supposed to be social. Also Nishida wants to prevent what Berdiaev saw as an imminent danger of modernity: that "personality is submerged in the general, man is socialized, determined by natural laws, true communication of persons becomes impossible, and only mediated approximations through concepts are left."[39]

A further apparent contradiction contained in these philosophies is that "personality" is laid out as a closed system (in the most extreme case an "autarky" [*pravitel'nitsa*] for the Eurasianists)[40] but that it is at the same time supposed to be compatible with supra-national perspectives. A closer look shows that the contradiction is only apparent because what is at work is rather a sophisticated interlocking of individuality with All-Unity. In every society personalism is necessary for the emergence of human individuality; but individuality is not "egocentric;" rather it is determined by communality that can be defined in a supra-individual and supra-national fashion.

Similar to the Eurasianist elaboration of *pavitel'nitsa*, Nishida links personalist philosophical ideas to the old Japanese notion of "national polity" (*kokutai*).[41] The important point is that he suggests that *kosei* 個性 (personality)[42] as the manifestation of Japan's cultural characteristics should remain open to the world. Quoting from Nishida's diary, YUSA

Michiko writes that "[the *kokutai*] should harbor within itself the universality of the human spirit and history."[43] This is not an appeal to abstract universalism in the form of a categorical imperative because that would be, once again, contrary to the idea of personality. Like the Slavophiles who strongly opposed "universal uniform law, universal equality, universal life, universal justice, and universal prosperity,"[44] Nishida writes in the article "On the National Polity:" "We human beings are born as creative elements of the creative world. The life of our self, expressing unique personality lies herein."[45] And later: "This is the reason why that which is uniquely creative as a historical individual is truly personal. Such a merely formal imperative, on the contrary, is rather the negation of true individual personality." Kant's kingdom of ends "only expresses the abstract form of the self-determination of the creative universal (84)."

Immediacy: Bergson and Fichte in Russia and Japan

In both Russia and Japan various forms of philosophical intuitionism have developed outspoken reflections on the subject of immediacy. Some of them are used in order to design philosophical models of human communities. Kireevsky's and the Slavophile's *narodnost'* (= "nationhood" as opposed to *obshestvo* = "society") is supposed to establish a natural immediacy between members of a society. In Japan, Nishida defines a "place" (*basho*) in which interaction between self and object is *immediate* because prior to any subject-object distinction. (Concepts like "seeing without a seer" and "active intuition" are in agreement with these attempts). Later Nishida extends these reflections on models of intercultural communication.

In Russia, "intuitionist" philosophies moved to the centre of philosophy during the first three decades of the twentieth century. Since Solov'ëv's death, an "intuitionist school" evolved around its founder Nicolas Lossky (1870-1965). Lossky suggested a system of logic based on intuitionism,[46] an attempt paralleled by Nishida's efforts to give "intuitionism a logical foundation in terms of a completely original logic of place."[47]

Most obviously, Bergson's intuitionist philosophy is highly compatible with these approaches. While Bergson's idea of intuition does not necessarily overlap with that of Lossky, it remains a fact that both Lossky and Nishida attempt to grasp reality through intuition *immediately* in all its originality. While Bergson declares that we need intuition in order to overcome models of typically spatial understanding or of spatial logic, Lossky tries to show that understanding itself is intuitive and able to grasp reality.[48]

However, Bergson's intuition is also highly compatible with Buddhism. SAIGUSA Mitsuyoshi found that Bergson bears a "close resemblance to the so-called *yuishin-ron* (idealism) exposited in such sections of the Buddhist canon as the Sarvāstivādin of Mahāyāna Buddhism."[49] In *Intuition and Reflection in Self-Consciousness* (1913-1917)[50] Nishida extensively uses Bergson's models of internally unified and immediate experience (*durée pure*). At the same time, Nishida criticizes Bergson because his focus on time and intuition still does not overcome the object-subject dichotomy.[51] Nishida holds that intuition is not abstract and dissociated from actual facts but takes place within a real socio-historical world or a "place." Within intuition, general and particular truths are not opposed to each other.

Lossky's intuitive logic brings forward similar points. For Lossky there is a universal consciousness in which subjects participate and real objects are present in the consciousness.[52]

In both Russia and Japan an idealist conception of a non-objectified consciousness as sole reality produced what can be called a Bergsonian interpretation of Fichte. "Experience as consciousness" or "consciousness as experience" is a topic that can be rendered in terms of Bergson's *élan vital* as much as of Fichte's *Tathandlung*.[53] *Tathandlung* can be translated as a "creative act" through which the 'I' establishes its own identity. In this activity there are no established facts, no substances and no being, but only the auto-productive activity of the *Tathandlung* itself. The *Tathandlung* is a self-producing, self-evident certainty that cannot be found but can only be reconstructed.

The above parallels must be considered as surprising because there are no concrete links between Fichte and Bergson. As a matter of fact, Bergson hardly ever took notice of Fichte. (In a lecture manuscript on Fichte, Bergson puts forward Fichte as an example of an outdated philosopher whose mistakes Bergson's own brand of "spiritualist positivism" is going to avoid).[54] At the same time it is possible to perceive Bergson's critical reading of Fichte as a quasi Neo-Platonic interpretation of Fichte's intellectual intuition as a kind of "pensée pure" and the *Tathandlung* as an unthinkable One.[55]

A quasi-Bergsonian reading of Fichte that concentrates on consciousness as a temporal phenomenon seems to have inspired not only Nishida but also Lossky, Berdiaev, and Lossky's student Georges Gurvitch.[56] Fichte's metaphorical way of establishing (absolute) knowledge, intuition, and action is reminiscent of Bergson as much as other representatives of French and Russian spiritualist intuitivism. The *Tathandlung* itself aspires wholeness (unity) and organicity (since Absolute Knowledge is organic).[57] As it hovers (*schwebt*) between being and non-being (WL, 51), Absolute Knowledge is knowledge neither of something nor of nothing (WL, 14).

Nishida's intellectual intuition (or "acting intuition" (行為的直観, *kōiteki chokkan*)[58] is a reinstatement of his earlier developments of pure experience and can appear, as it eludes the cognitive moments of the Kantian intuition, as Fichtian; and Fichte's *Tathandlung* remains Nishida's grounding concept between 1917 and 1927."[59]

In Russia, Berdiaev develops a notion of personality that comes close to Fichte's "Absolute Self."[60] Gurvitch is fascinated by Fichte's synthesis of individualism and universalism[61] that is, of personalism and transpersonalism, which leads him to an extensive study of Fichte's idea of the concrete-ideal.[62] For Gurvitch, Fichte's "concrete ethics" bears an anti-intellectualist trait because ethic purity is irrational and opposed to theoretical reason (see *Fichtes System*, 65). Gurvitch understands Fichte's philosophy as the development of a primordial intuition that he opposes to Kantian formalism.[63]

These parallels, though spelled out in a succinct fashion, are supposed to provide a background for the following studies of space, community, and style in Russia and Japan.

Notes

1. William Naff has reflected upon the question if the Meiji revolution and the Russian revolution should be equated. He notes the remarkable "attempts made by [two] leading nations during the past century and a half to reconstitute themselves." Furthermore he draws attention to similarities between a Russian and a Japanese novel. TōSON Shimazaki's (1872-1943) *Before Dawn (Yoake no mae)* was written in the 1920s on Meiji Revolution. Naff compares this with Mikhail Sholokhov's (1904-1984) *The Quiet Don*, written between 1928 and 1940 on the Russian revolution. William Naff: "Toson's *Before Dawn*: Historical Fiction as History and as Literature" in White, 92.
2. Cf. John D. Pierson. *Tokutomi Sohō 1863-1957. A Journalist for Modern Japan*. (Princeton: Princeton University Press, 1980): "No sense of individual duty or calling or responsibility. Unwilling to deviate from established norms of the groups and *community*, they were concerned mainly with adhering to formalities and with maintaining appearances" (207). "Students were told that individualism and nationalism are incompatible" (212).
3. In the words of NAKAMURA Yūjirō: "Nishida, le premier philosophe original au Japon" in *Critique* 39: 32-54, 1983. See also John Maraldo "Tradition, Textuality, and the Trans-lation of Philosophy: The Case of Japan" in Heine, Steven and Charles Wei-hsun Fu (eds), *Japan in Traditional and Postmodern Perspectives* (Albany, NY: SUNY Press, 1995) on Nishida's status as Japan's first philosopher.
4. Another Japanese phenomenon paralleling more or less the foundation of the Religious-Philosophical Society of St. Petersburg could be the foundation of Inoue Enryō's "Philosophical Institute" in 1887. INOUE Enryō (1858-1919) studied at the main temple of Pure Land Buddhism, earned a degree in philosophy at Tokyo Imperial University. He opposed the Westernization of Japan and

the conversion of officials to Christianity. He founded his institute to promote the study of Buddhism. As part of his campaign to rid Japan of superstitions associated with folklore and mythology, he established the Ghost Lore Institute in Tokyo. One could also mention the vigorous defender of Buddhism, MU-RAKAMI Sensho (1851-1929) who was working on an intellectual recovery of Buddhism that had been suppressed by the Meiji Enlightenment. Which led to Japan's more intense attempts, during Taihō and early Shōwa, to accentuate its role as the "disseminator of Buddhism to the world, especially between the world wars. This also had a certain "Pan-Asian flavor." Cf. Jackie Stone: "A Vast and Grave Task: Interwar Buddhist Studies as an Expression of Japan's Envisioned Global Role" in J. Th. Rimer: *Culture and Identity: Japanese Intellectuals During the Interwar Years* (Princeton University Press), 217. Meiji New Buddhism, on the other hand, tended to see Japan as "the sole heir to the spiritual and ethical heritage of the East precisely at a time of heightened imperial ambitions and military adventurism." (Robert Sharf: "The Zen of Japanese Nationalism" in *History of Religions* 33: 1, 1993, 5.)

5. Chernyshevsky was in favor of collectivism, an unacceptable point for the conservative Slavophiles.

6. C. T. Chari: "Russian and Indian Mysticism in East-West Synthesis" in *Philosophy East & West* 2: 2, Oct. 1952, 226-237.

7. OKAKURA Kakuzō in *Ideals of the East* (New York: 1905) on the Asanga and Vasubandhu period: "That the whole universe is manifest in every atom; that each variety, therefore, is of equal authenticity; that there is no truth unrelated to the unity of things; this is the faith that liberates the Indian mind in science (110)."

8. See Dieter Henrich (ed) *All-Einheit: Wege eines Gedankens in Ost und West* (Stuttgart: Klett-Cotta, 1985). See also my article "All-Unity Seen Through Perspective or the Narrative of Virtual Cosmology" in *Seeking Wisdom* 2, 2005.

9. NISHIDA Kitarō. 私と汝 (Watashi to nanji; I and Thou) [1932], NKZ 6: 341-427. Quoted from ARISAKA Yoko: *Space and History: Philosophy and Imperialism in Nishida and Watsuji* (Riverside: University of California Press, 1996), 80.

10. Naoki SAKAI *Translation and Subjectivity. On Japan and Cultural Nationalism* (Minneapolis: University of Minnesota Press, 1997), 66.

11. The *Kojiki* was completed in 712 but purportedly records the events dating back to 660 BC and the creation of the Japanese Imperial line. The Primary Chronicle was compiled in Kiev about 1113 and gives an account of the early history of the eastern Slavs.

12. Peter Dale finds 700 *nihonjinron* titles published between 1946 and 1978. 25 percent of these were published between 1976 and 1978. P. Dale: *The Myth of Japanese Uniqueness* (New York: St. Martin's Press, 1986), 15.

13. See NISHITANI Keiji's *Religion and Nothingness* (Berkeley, Los Angeles and Oxford: University of California Press, 1982) and KIMURA Bin's works: Kimura, Bin. 1972. 人と人のあいだの病理 [Hito to hito no aida no byori]. (Tokyo: Kobundo 1972). German trans. by E. Weinmayr: *Zwischen Mensch und Mensch Strukturen japanischer Subjektivität*. Darmstadt: Wissenschaftliche Buchgesellschaft, 1995; 分裂病の現象学 [Bunretsubyō no genshōgaku; Symptomatology of Schizophrenia] (Toyko: Kobundo, 1975); 時間と自己 [Jikan to jiko; Time and I] (Tokyo: Iwanami, 1982); *Ecrits de*

psychopathologie phénoménologique (Paris: Presses Universitaires de France, 1992). The anthropological writings of IRIE Takanori, who suggests an "Edoization" of the world in order to combat Western "rationalism," are examples for the former category. There is an apparent resemblance with Russian thinkers like Dugin or Gumilev. For Irie see Tessa Morris-Suzuki 1995, 774ff.

14. For a good account of the "uniqueness" of Russian philosophy see Evert van der Zweerde's chapter "What is Russian About Russian Philosophy" in Botz-Bornstein & Hengelbrock (eds) 2006.

15. Anno points out that "Leninism was a successor to the 'populist' version of Russian nationalism—for Leninism combined the claim of superiority of Soviet Russia over the capitalist West (transvaluation) with the populist theme of antipathy toward Westernized elites of tsarist Russia" (2000: 337).

16. Recurrent in Danilevsky's *Россия и Европа* [Russia and Europe] (1867) for example 57-58. Also Khomiakov holds that Slavs have communal qualities while Germanic peoples are conquerors and exploiters.

17. Petr Chaadaev: "Nous ne vivons que dans le présent le plus étroit, sans passé et sans avenir, au milieu d'un calme plat." Chaadaev: *Sotchineniia i pismi* (Moscow: Mysl, 1978), 78. Quoted from Alexandre Koyré: *La Philosophie et le problème national en Russie au début du XIXe siècle* (Paris: Gallimard 1976), 22.

18. Pierre (Petr) Suvchinsky: 'L'Eurasisme' in Eric Humberclaude: *(Re)lire Souvtchinski* (Paris: La Bresse, 1990), 66.

19. The Slavophile Samarin relates this about his professor of history, Pogodin, who decided to take the at that time unusual turn towards an appreciation of Russian culture. [He declared that] Slavophilism itself is unable to exist without the conviction that Russian thought is different from any other culture in the world, (Quoted from Jelena Milojkovic-Djuric: *Panslavism and National Identity in Russia and in the Balkans 1830-1880: Images of the Self and Others* (Boulder, CO: East European Monographs, 1994), 55. Cf. Scanlan who affirms "that Slavophilism distinguishes *Russian* thought from that of any other culture; this is the basis of the philosophical *uniqueness* of Slavophilism." James Scanlan: "Slavophilism in Recent Russian Thought" in Scanlan (ed): *Russian Thought After Communism: The Recovery of a Philosophical Heritage* (Armonk, NY, London: M. E. Sharp, 1994), 35.

20. From Scanlan 1994, 36.

21. Michael Boro-Petrovich: *The Emergence of Russian Pan-Slavism 1856-1870* (New York: Columbia University Press, 1956), 46. Cf. also Solov'ëv: "Mais le danger de ces doctrines religieuses est le messianisme. Dès l'instant où l'on déclare qu'un seul peuple est appelé à réaliser la vérité, on quitte le domaine chrétien pour rentrer dans la tradition juive. La Russie n'échappera pas toujours à ce danger." *Conscience de la Russie* (Paris: Plon, 1950), 15.

22. Ivanov "Afterword" in Scanlan 1994, 405.

23. Valentin Bazhanov: "Philosophy in Post-Soviet Russia (1992-1997): Background, Present State and Prospects" in *Slavic and East European Thought* 51: 3, 1999, 240. Cf. Marina Bykova who detects the superiority complex in Russians even today, "insofar as Westerners supposedly cannot grasp the depth and complexity of the Russian soul." "Nation and Nationalism. Russia in Search of its National Identity" in Zweerde & Steunebrink: *Civil Society, Religion, and*

the Nation: Modernization in Intercultural Context: Russia, Japan, Turkey. Amsterdam & New York: Rodopi, 2004, 29.

24. TAKEUCHI Yoshimi: *What is Modernity? Writings of Takeuchi Yoshimi* (New York: Columbia University Press, 2005), 99.

25. FUKUZAWA Yukichi: *An Outline of a Theory of Civilization* (trans. by D. Dilworth and G. C. Hurst), (Tokyo, Sophia University 1973), 16.

26. Marc Raeff: *Political Ideas and Institutions in Imperial Russia* (Boulder, CO: Westview Press, 1994), 292.

27. Nicolai S. Trubetzkoy: "The Ukrainian Problem" in *The Legacy of Genghis Khan and Other Essays on Russian Identity* (Ann Arbor: Michigan Slavic Publication, 1991), 260. It is interesting to mention here Solov'ëv's attempts to "reconcile" Russian and Western cultures, a reconciliation that he perceives on a religious basis in the largest sense and which alludes to a kind of slave attitude identical with the one criticized by LU Xun and Takeuchi: "Interior and true reconciliation with the West is not a servile submission to Western forms but a free agreement, a profound acceptance of the spiritual principle on which is built the Western world." Vladimir Solov'ëv: *Conscience de la Russie* (trans. J. G. Egloff) (Paris: Plon, 1950), 60.

28. In the case of some Russian philosophers the idea of personality flows immediately out of their philosophy of All-Unity. This is especially true for L. P. Karsavin who has been working much on personality as a cultural phenomenon. Cf. Julia Mehlich: "Die philosophisch-theologische Begründung des Eurasismus bei L. P. Karsavin. *Studies in East-European Thought* 52 1-2, March 2000. It is also true for Vernadsky (see Chapter Five) who wrote: "I have a sensation of being an inseparable part of some *alive* huge entity, individual parts of which are laboring and beating in some other places, but which are all united with an indissoluble strong chain . . .; in [reference to] society, the brotherhood is a distinct singular *personality*." Russian Academy of Sciences Archive *fond* 208, *opis* '3, *delo* 429, *listy* 141, 142. Quoted from Borisov 1993, 427.

29. Japanese aestheticians like ONISHI Yoshinori read the Austrian personalist philosopher Friedrich Kainz (1897-1977) who wrote *Personalistische Ästhetik* in 1932. See UEDA Makoto's article in Rimer 1990.

30. Bellah 1965, 592.

31. For ABE Jirō's personalism see Dilworth 1974.

32. See Sakai's explanation of Watsuji's distinction between person and personality: "Therefore, person is partly being (*yū*) as opposed to personality (*mu*). Yet, person and personality are always combined in the human being as *jikaku sonzai* or the being aware of itself. Sakai quotes Watsuji: "The 'I' who is conscious of the objectified 'I' according to the form of inner sense, that is, according to the 'I' in itself, is nothing but the I of the 'I think,' that is, the subjective ego. Furthermore, the 'I think' is empty, without any content, and is the 'transcendental personality,' but is never a 'person.' Therefore, person is neither simply identical to the 'I' as an object nor identical to the subjective 'I' (*shukan ga*). [WTZ vol. 9, 332-33]. From Sakai 1997, 82.

33. See Nishida: 実在の根底としての人格概念 ("The Concept of Personality as the Foundation of Reality)" NKZ 14, 133-174.

34. Pavel Florensky opposes the "Western" logic of things and attempts to create an epistemology of consubstantial (gr. *homoousios*) persons. Cf. *The Pillar and Ground of the Truth* (Princeton University Press, 1997).

35. "Each type has a character. Its collective personality, style of life, particular process of development result from the character's inevitable unfolding." Danilevsky 1867, 50.

36. Cf. Jacinto Zavala: "The early Nishida wrote about thee characteristics of God's personality in the essay "Kami no jinkakusei 神の人格性" [The Personality of God, NKZ 15: 354ff] in which, just as in *Zen no kenkyū*, we can see the influence of John Richard Illingworth's *Personality: Human and Divine* (1894) .... But the late Nishida's view of God is not a mere regression to an earlier stage. After his middle period, in which he talks primarily about absolute nothingness even in reference to religion, Nishida viewed the absolute as personal in nature, both with regard to Christianity (which he saw as personalist) and Shin Buddhism. In his exposition he goes back again to Kant for the characteristics of personality (NKZ 11: 388). He mentions that personality is unique in history and does not repeat itself, that it is creative, and that it has will and freedom . . ." Zavala: "The Bodily Manifestation of Religious Experience and Late Nishida Philosophy" in *Zen Buddhism Today* 15, 1998, 42.

37. From Edie et al. *Russian Philosophy III*, 156-157.

38. ARIMA Tatsuo: *The Failure of Freedom: A Portrait of Modern Japanese Intellectuals* (Cambridge MA: Harvard University Press, 1969), 6.

39. Quoted from "Nicolas Alexandrovich Berdiaev" in Edie et al. *Russian Philosophy III*.

40. Cf. Antoshchenko on the Eurasianist autarky: "Meaning the well-being of the group of peoples inhabiting this particular autarkic world, and provided peoples with the same level of life while preserving the variety of their national cultures." Alexander Antoshchenko: "On Eurasia and the Eurasians: Studies on Eurasianism in Current Russian Historiography" http://www.karelia.ru/psu/chairs/ PreRev/bibleng.rtf.

41. See below more on *kokutai*.

42. Nishida uses *jinkakusei* on other occasions. See note on Jacinto Zavala.

43. Cf. YUSA Michiko: "Nishida and the Question of Nationalism" in *Monumenta Nipponica* 46: 2, 1991 207.

44. Peter K. Christoff, *An Introduction to Nineteenth Century Russian Slavophilism. A Study in Ideas*, Vol. 1: A. S. Xomiakov. 'S-Gravenhage: Mouton, 1961, 280.

45. Nishida: '哲学論文集第四補遺' (Tetsugaku ronbun shū dai yon hoi; Fourth supplement to the philosophical article) [1944] in NKZ 12: 397-425. Engl. transl.: "On the National Polity" in D. A. Dilworth, V. H. Viglielmo and Augustin Jacinto Zavala (eds) *Sourcebook for Modern Japanese Philosophy* (Westport, CT: Greenwood, 1998: 78-95), 78.

46. In the preface of the German translation of his *Logika* (1922) Lossky declares to represent "Intuitivist Idealism." *Handbuch der Logik* (Leipzig: Teubner, 1927).

47. Cf. ABE Masao: "Nishida's Philosophy of Place" in *International Philosophical Quarterly* 28: 4, 1988, 356.

48. See *Интуитивная философия Бергсона* [The Intuitive Philosophy of Bergson]. Moscow., 1914

49. SAIGUSA Mitsuyoshi: "Henri Bergson and Buddhist Thought" in *Philosophical Studies of Japan* 9, 1969, 79-101, 80.

50. 自覚に於ける直観と反映 (Jikaku ni okeru chokkan to hansei). NKZ 2. Engl. trans.: *Intuition and Reflection in Self-Consciousness*. Albany, NY: State University of New York Press, 1987.

51. "But Bergson's duration, too, belongs to the world of objects, and is based on an a priori. In absolute free will, which moves freely from one a priori to another, no fact can leave any trace whatever . . . . If we speak of absolute will as determining itself in an act, we have already objectified it." (163).

52. The reader is invited to compare these two passages by Lossky and Nishida respectively because they show how the idea of a certain form of intuitivism is born out of similar experiences. Both Nishida and Lossky are born in 1870, and refer to an experience that can be dated to approximately the same date (Lossky indicates 1898). In an autobiographical passage in his *Sensory, Intellectual and Mystical Intuition* (1938) Lossky tells how, while driving through St. Petersburg in a cab one foggy autumn evening "I was thinking that there are no sharp boundaries between things, when suddenly the thought flashed into my head: 'Everything is immanent in everything.' I sensed at once that the riddle was solved, that the elabration of this idea would provide the the answer to all questions that disturbed me." (Quoted from James Scanlan's entry on Lossky to the *The Routledge Encyclopedia of Philosophy*, ed. E. Craig. London and New York: Routledge, 1998, 833-838). Nishida writes about the time when he was a high school teacher in Kanazawa: "I have had the idea that true reality must be actuality as it is, and that the so-called material world is something conceptualized and abstracted out of it. I can still remember a time in high school when I walked along the streets of Kanazawa absorbed in this idea as if I were dreaming." (善の研究 Zen no kenkyū; Study of the good) in NKZ (NISHIDA Kitarō Zenshū [Complete Works], Tokyo: Iwanami, 1965-66) Vol. 1: 1-200. Engl. trans. by ABE Masao and Charles Ives: *Inquiry into the Good* (New Haven: Yale University Press, 1990), 7.

53. On Nishida's Fichte interpretation see: John Maraldo: "Translating Nishida" in *Philosophy East & West* 39(4), 1989,479-480; David Dilworth: "Nishida's Early Pantheistic Voluntarism" in *PEW* 1970: 20.

54. Within the context of the university curriculum Bergson had been obliged to design a lecture course for the level of *agrégation* on Fichte. Cf. Jean-Louis Vieillard-Baron: "Bergson et Fichte" in Ives Radrizziani (ed.): *Fichte et la France* (Paris: Bauchesne, 1997). Bergson's lecture has been published as *Fichte* (Presses Universitaires de Strasbourg, 1988).

55. Cf. Jean-Christophe Goddard: "Bergson: Une lecture néo-platonicienne de Fichte" in *Les études philosophiques* 4, 2001, 465-479, 471.

56. The French sociologist Georges Davidovitch Gurvitch (1894-1965) was born in Russia, studied Law and Philosophy in Petrograd from 1912 to 1917 and was Assistant Professor at Petrograd University during 1918. According to Lossky, he had been attracted in his youth by "transcendental-logical idealism," which brought him in contact with Russian Neo-Kantian philosophers. He worked in Tomsk until his emigration to Prague and lived in France from 1921 on, and is today recognized as an eminent French sociologist of Russian origin.

57. Fichte: *Darstellung der Wissenschaftslehre aus dem Jahre 1801* (Berlin: Veit, 1845), Sämmtl. Werke II, 22.

58. Nishida: '歴史的世界においての個物の立場' [1938] (Rekishiteki sekai ni oite no kobutsu no tachiba; The Position of the Individual in the Historical World) in NKZ 9: 69-146, 112.

59. Cf. David Dilworth in his postface to Nishida's *Last Writings: Nothingness and the Religious Worldview* (Honolulu: Hawaii University Press, 1987), 128.

60. See Piama Gaidenko: "The Philosophy of Freedom of Nicolai Berdiaev" in James P. Scanlan (ed): *Russian Thought After Communism: The Recovery of a Philosophical Heritage* (Armonk, NY, London: M. E. Sharp, 1994).

61. Georg Gurwitsch (Georges Gurvitch): *Fichtes System der Konkreten Ethik* (Tübingen: Mohr, 1924).

62. Gurvitch's Russian contemporaries excelled in existential analyses of the concrete-ideal foundations of the world. See Lossky's review of Gurvitch's book: "Fichtes konkrete Ethik im Lichte des modernen Tranzendentalismus" in Logos 1926.

63. See Alexis Philonenko's comment on Gurvitch in *La Liberté humaine dans la philosophie de Fichte* (Paris: Vrin, 1966), 33ff. For Gurvitch's later sociology these Bersonian themes remained important, as shows a quotation from his important study on time and society: "Pour préciser ce que nous comprenons sous le terme de temps, dans l'optique où nous nous plaçons, il suffit de le décrire tantôt comme une coordination, tantôt comme un décalage de mouvements, coordination et décalages qui durent dans la succession et se succèdent dans la durée." *La Vocation actuelle de la sociologie* Vol. II, (Paris: PUF, 1969), 329.

Chapter Two

Space in Noh-Plays and Icons

Introduction

This chapter on Japanese Noh-plays and Russian icons defines space as a unique phenomenon that is important not only for aesthetics but also for those social and politial subjects that will occur in the subsequent chapters of this book. I begin the comparison of Noh-plays and icons by introducing some reflections on Virtual Reality. What will turn out to be the "virtual" character of Noh-plays and icons, leads to considerations of their most decisive component: their existence and being in terms of space. However, first it is necessary to establish the virtual with regard to its linguistic meaning.[1]

The virtual is essentially distinct from the simulated. While the latter represents an unreal place aiming at the simulation of an already existing reality, the virtual establishes an autonomous reality supposed to be lived *like a reality* and independent of any resemblance it could have with a preexisting reality. In other words, the virtual represents a *total* reality annulling all interferences between interior and exterior, and, in this way, any play of simulation or dissimulation. Its particular effect of *reality* and *authenticity* is acquired by an integration of the spectator into a virtual place by trying neither to simulate nor to dissimulate outside reality. This means that the virtual does not try to produce an *actuality*, but exists *beyond* the distinction between the actual and the non-actual.

Thereby the virtual is also distinct from the *imaginary*. Popular vocabulary that designates as virtual every "imaginary" space created by computers is misleading. As a matter of fact, the creation of Virtual Reality or cyberspace is not a matter of creating an artificial space in the same way in which one would create an imaginary universe but it aims at manipulating ontology. In other words, Virtual Reality is not just a second imagined reality, but exists as a world of its own, obeying its own ontological laws. It is certainly tempting to use the distinction between an imaginary universe and an entirely autonomous, virtual one for establishing the difference between Virtual Reality and the reality of art. "Art" can be (or for some people even *should* be) apprehended by means of ontology; it is clear that this "ontology" cannot be the same for reality and for Virtual Reality.

The problem of the virtual and art will be discussed below in the context of immersion. Here, however, I am eager to introduce the "Eastern" way of seeing the virtual and its relationship with aesthetics. As a matter of fact, some specialists of East Asian art explain that in the East, art is always *necessarily* virtual. For OHASHI Ryōsuke, for example, Japanese culture attempts to attain a vision of the *real world* as something virtual *by means of an aesthetics of the virtual*. According to him, in Japanese culture the paradox which makes the imagined "non-real" more existential than the "virtual real" disappears.[2] Art is a virtual reality as it exists not only for itself but also permits us to recognize the virtual character of *all* reality. Also François Cheng affirms that, "since [aesthetic] sensation cannot be limited to sense-perception, beauty is this potentiality and this virtuality towards which strives all being (Cheng 2006: 41).[3]

In Western aesthetics one would hesitate to call a work of art "virtual." Though the reasons for this hesitation are multiple, the most essential point is certainly the following: Western art, as much as Western philosophy, is mainly preoccupied with *reality*. "Reality" is not necessarily the "reality out there" but can also be the *reality of art* which is also seen as "real," as "something" that has been imagined and which is therefore different from "real" reality, but which is still not "virtual." Or, seen the other way round: A work of art creates a kind of reality which, even though it may be immersive and provide a certain amount of "authentic" experience, is conceived as an *imagined* reality and not as virtual.[4]

Despite the level of sophistication of its discourses, Western aesthetics concerns itself largely with the opposition of "reality" to an imagined "non-reality" which is then seen as more or less "real." Within this aesthetic tradition, the "virtual" has rarely been a topic worthy of discussion.

True, Western philosophy also recognizes the nature of "reality" as that of "Being" and develops, through the discipline of ontology, sophisticated approaches attempting to transgress the static opposition of reality and (imagined) non-reality. In "Being," imagination and reality can coexist, and therefore any imagined "non-reality" can obtain the status of Being. What is absent in Western philosophy of art and aesthetics, however, is the idea of *reality* as opposed to that of the *virtual* since this opposition does not fit into the existing framework. What would the virtual "be"? Since it does not exist in the form of Being, it cannot be a matter of ontology, at least not of the same ontology through which both reality and art are examined. Any persistence to adopt the virtual as a subject for aesthetics, on the other hand, would have dramatic consequences: it would oblige us to grant the status of Being to a quantity which, by definition, *does not exist in terms of Being.*

"Western" and "Non-Western" Models of Representation

One of the purposes of this chapter is to describe ontological alternatives to the "virtual" that exist in branches of aesthetics developed outside the mainstream of Western philosophy. For this purpose I chose to analyze the aesthetics of Japanese Noh-plays and Russian icons. What might appear curious at first will nevertheless turn out to be efficient. Though these two art forms share no historic links and are even different kinds of media, a simultaneous examination of their treatment of the phenomenon of *representation* will show the shortcomings of the Western idea of the virtual. I justify the fact that Noh-plays and icons are, through their common ideas about the virtual, conceptually linked, through mainly three points:

1. Both icons and Noh-plays create a presence that exceeds simple appearance. The creation of this presence requires a high degree of formalization and regulation, as well as the shunning of individual creativity.
2. Both icons and Noh-plays maintain an interesting anti-relationship with Western-European "realism" that allows them to appear "virtual."
3. The "meditative" character of icons as well of Noh-plays makes (aesthetic) "experience" the central theme of (religious) art.[5]

The first two points concern the particular form of "presence" obtained in Noh-plays and icons, a presence that necessitates extreme "formalization" as well as a well-defined attitude towards anti-realism. It has been said that the Noh-play creates a "reality of its own," providing a paradoxical "reality effect" which is simultaneously opposed to realism. Within certain limits, the Noh-play represents an "ideal image of reality"; however, this "ideal image" is not simply the *representation* of an idea, but arises out of continuous acts of severe formalization. According to KAWATAKE Toshio, instead of as a realist or idealist *representation*, the Noh appears as a "stylized presentation, [which] gives nevertheless convincing impression of something that is real and natural" (Kawatake 1990: 45). What is in question is an entire Japanese aesthetic tradition of visual and performing arts aspiring to create "a sense of reality without realism" or for which, as said KUSAHARA Machiko, "realism is not necessarily the best way of achieving the sense of reality" (an observation which leads her to an appreciation of virtual pets in Japanese culture).[6]

Similar things can be said about the icon. The icon, as a Christian art, treats the human person as a *corporeal* and at the same time *spiritual* being. For icon painters it has always been out of the question to present the human being within a concrete cultural and historical context, as was common, for example, for Renaissance artists. Still, icon art is not *abstract* but is firmly linked to the concrete: like the Noh, the icon strives to create a certain kind of "spiritual concreteness." However, this spiritual concreteness will be realized only through tradition, meditation, and rules that have been well elaborated by preceding generations of painters. For this reason, for Noh artists just as for icon painters, nothing is left to imagination, intuition or abstraction, but the reality of artistic representation remains a strictly *formal* one.[7]

Before entering into more detailed philosophical examinations let me show that the parallelism in question is perhaps not as surprising as it appears to be as there are parallels between Japanese Zen-aesthetics and the "Byzantine" aesthetics of Old Russia. Since their exact location could, of course, only be undertaken in a separate chapter, here I will only draw a brief sketch of what I consider as most striking. Like in Japan's Zen culture (by which the Noh is influenced), in Old Russia, *aesthetics* also occupied a large part of the place that Western-Christian culture usually assigns to *philosophy*. Moreover, in both Eastern cultures, this aesthetics was supposed to examine "expressions of the spiritual."[8] The Japanese are usually, as Kawatake has put it, "more concerned with five senses than with logic or reason" (Kawatake: 88). Similarly, the Old Russians "abhorred abstract ideas" (Bychkov) as long as they were not immediately linked to concrete artistic manifestations.

We arrive here at the third one of the three points mentioned which concerns the meditative character of Noh-plays and icons and their connection with asceticism. As a matter of fact, "simplicity" became the keyword for Japanese as well as Old Russian aesthetics. With regard to the Orthodox tradition, this fact is often forgotten in the West. However, not only did Andrei Ryublev and his generation of artists meditate in front of icons but the icon's purpose itself was to transfer its contemplator to a meditative state of mind.[9] The phenomenon of "simplicity" in connection with "meditation" leads to an important notion. In Old Russia, aesthetic simplicity obtained through meditation could create the feeling of the *sublime* (Bychkov 1992: 27). In general it was found that any lack of clarity fails to inspire awe and is thus unable to create the feeling of the sublime. Complicated structures "unnecessarily and dangerously complicate the relationship between the sublime figure and the venerating beholder" (Onash & Schnieper 1997: 277). The sublime as a meditative form of simplicity, required a certain amount of asceticism as well as a formal regulation because it was believed that, as an author from antiquity wrote, "sublimity is the resonance of the magnitude of soul" (quoted from Onash & Schnieper 277). The sublime represented thus an "unconditional and ritually sanctified solemnity" (278).

The most striking parallel pattern in Japanese aesthetics is, of course, the phenomenon of *yūgen,* which represents the most essential element of the Noh aesthetics. This notion of *yūgen,* which is translated as "mystery and depth," is also often related to the notion of the "sublime." As becomes clear especially in the writings of Yoshinori Onishi,[10] this notion maintains a close relationship with a formal quantity that can, in Western terms, be best defined as *style. Yūgen*'s function is to provide a description of nature that has "eliminated the distance between poetic description and object or topic and poet, rejecting the superficial psychological capturing of a subject" (Konishi 1985: 204). In other words, through *yūgen,* objects appear with an utmost degree of simplicity, which, in spite of the directness of the artistic expression (reminiscent of German *Einfühlung*[11]), is still *not realistic.* On the contrary, the effect of *yūgen* is, as has said Steven Heine, "nearly opposite to realism in that nature depicted in its primordial state completely mirrors the realization of authentic subjectivity."[12] Again, this still does not aim at the "idealized image" of subjective feelings. "Reality" is expressed in a "meditative" way, and this is true for icons as much as for Noh-plays. What this "meditative" representation (which is perhaps most reminiscent of some Western ideas about *style*) actually is will now be examined by viewing both Noh and icon through the phenomenon of the virtual.

Noh-Plays and East Asian Models of Representation

The Noh-play is a classical Japanese theatre form that emphasizes the unity of word, dance, music, and mystical experience and was developed especially in the fourteenth century by ZEAMI Motokiyo (1363-1443).

Before discussing Noh in detail, it will be useful to establish its position within a larger context of East Asian philosophy. This can best be done by locating its place within the above discussion of "Being" and the problem of the virtual.

At the beginning of the this chapter I claimed that Western aesthetics views reality in terms of Being and therefore has problems in assigning a proper "ontological" status to the phenomenon of the virtual. To say it straightaway, in East Asian art and aesthetics, as far as influenced by the Confucian, Taoist, or Buddhist tradition, the problem of incompatibility of the virtual and Being does not appear. As mentioned, East Asian aesthetics easily agrees that art is *in the first place* virtual (Ohashi 1999: 91ff). Of course, like in Western aesthetics, explanations are complex and varied. However, the reasons for the equation of artistic reality and virtual reality should not be sought in a different eastern concept of *Being*. On the contrary, the philosophical idea of Being as a quantity composed of reality and non-reality mediated through human experience is something that East and West share (in comparative philosophy, reflections on Being often turn out to be the most convenient ground for exchange and communication).

The reasons for the different attitudes towards the "virtual" in Eastern and Western aesthetics are rather to be looked for in the idea of *experience* that is valued differently in both traditions. Robert Sharf has noted that in their religious practice, East Asian religions put an emphasis on experience, an emphasis not found in the West (Sharf 1998: 94-98). For Sharf, Eastern religions are more *experientially rooted*, and phenomena like "intuition" or "purity of experience" are constantly highlighted. An essential part of Sharf's observations possibly applies to East Asian traditional *arts* as well.

A variety of things can be said concerning the problem of "experience" in Eastern art, but I prefer to refer here only to the most important reason for the "purity" that Eastern art and religion strive to cultivate in "experience." An essential *difference* between Western and Eastern art consists in the fact that the latter does not take the equation of reality and being for granted. Furthermore, in eastern intellectual traditions shaped by Taoism and Buddhism, there is a tendency to design "reality" as something that is essentially different from Being: Ultimately, reality is not seen as Being but as *Nothingness*. Here, nothingness is not understood as a lack of meaning potentially overshadowing the world of Being, but rather as the ultimate, immaterial ground of reality. *Any art or philosophy that brings this fundamental equation of reality with Nothingness to consciousness, will—indirectly—depict "reality" as virtual.* This means that through art, nothingness, though itself absolutely formless and invisible, can project itself into the visible world.

I will now try to reveal the particular notion of the "virtual" as it appears in the Noh-play by concentrating on the idea of "representation." It has been said that Japanese stage art does not represent but present (cf. Kawatake: 115). First this establishes a difference with western stage art, and second, it introduces the virtual into reflections on "representation." As mentioned, Japanese traditional theatre creates a reality of its own, and this lets its theatrical space appear as virtual. Compared to this, western drama appears as "realist." However, in no case does the western "realism" qualify Japanese theatre as "non-realist" in the sense that it would produce images that are simply "unbelievable," as they are too far removed from reality or "unlikely." On the contrary, in Japanese traditional theatre the level of presentation is even "purer" and more direct than in Western theatre, and therefore also more "real." As a matter of fact, "purity and "directness" are the components which bestow to Japanese theatre its "virtual" character. The reason for this is that the reality presented by traditional Japanese theatre, *represents* nothing, but is simply the *presentation* of reality itself. In this way Japanese theatre manages to found itself on Nothingness. Japanese theatre is thus not, like Western theatre, founded on the reality ("out there"), but it simply presents. Because of this constellation—and not because a certain "reality" would be represented in the most realistic way—an absolute "irreality" can, finally, be experienced as "real."[13]

The Icon

One generally considers wooden panels with paintings representing a holy person or one of the traditional images of Greek or Russian Orthodox Christianity as icons [Greek *eikon*: image]. This definition is, certainly, narrow, since even in the Byzantine Empire there existed other manifestations of figurative art (mosaics, statues in materials reaching from ivory to metal) which, from around the mid-eleventh century on, should also have been called icons (Talbot Rice 1974: 11). Yet, icons are not only of Byzantine-Russian origin; icons also existed in East Asia and were even essential for the spreading of Buddhism, which the Chinese often refer to as the "religion of images."[14] Buddhist "images" might be images in the most common sense of the word, but to them applies the "Buddhist condition" that Oscar Benl recognized as a working principle also for Noh-plays: Buddhism, especially Mahayana Buddhism, discourages "any attachment to colorful images of the world of appearance" (Benl 1952: 110). The image of the icon is thus no illustration of something, it is no symbol, and no metaphor, but "simply" the manifestation of something divine.[15] In this sense Buddhist icons, like their Byzantine cousins are supposed not to *represent* but to *be*.[16]

Given the abundance of philosophical literature on the subject, I am, in this chapter, mainly interested in the status of representation offered by *Russian* icons. The sacred art of old Russia distinguished itself from Greek-Roman, as well as from European Renaissance and post-Renaissance art in that it refused imitation or representation of the real world and of the psychological state of the human being. The church, together with its art, was supposed to "be" a "real world" following its own spiritual and material laws, enabling man to participate in the invisible world of the Holy Spirit.

We must recognize the status of the icon as something that is supposed to "be." Iconoclastic criticism of icons was directed against the belief in the image as a living entity. While the relevance of this criticism might no longer be felt as strongly as it once did, a related point contributes still today strongly to the "strangeness" of icons. Annulling the Cartesian distinction between the sentient and the insentient, the icon's claim to "present" and not to represent obviously challenges the modern understanding of images. Even more, the icon's state of "Being" as a pure *presentation* provokes theological, metaphysical, ontological, and semiotic confusion because it contradicts Platonic and Aristotelian models of reality by holding that something can be *concrete* and at the same time *true*. According to the Aristotelian-Platonic tradition by which modern science and philosophy are influenced, *concrete things* should first be dissolved into general *ideas* or conceptions before any statements about their reality in terms of *Truth* can be made. *Representation* in the icon, on the other hand, is not based on these models. Taking the cue from Dyonisos Areopagites instead of from Aristotle, the icon painter sees the world as a "cover" obscuring its true meaning or the essence.[17] The icon, since it presents the true meaning or the essence of the world, is thus not an idea or a concept but the direct "uncovering" revelation of the image of God (Weizmann 1993: 243). Or, as Greek theologians expressed it, it serves as the "deutorotypos of the prototype";[18] or, still more clearly: it is the *reflection of divine reality*.

First, it should be said that the icon illustrates the truest example of a religious picture as defined by Hans-Georg Gadamer: "Only the religious picture shows the full ontological power of the picture . . . . Thus the meaning of the religious picture is an exemplary one. In it we can see without doubt that a picture is not a copy of a copied being, but is in ontological communion with what is copied" (Gadamer 1975: 126). The icon is supposed to be not only the image of something invisible but the *presence* of an invisible reality.[19] In this sense the icon is a *presence*, without simply overlapping with the presence of "subjective reality." However, it is also not "unreal" either, and it is not simply an imagined or remembered fact.

The icon's way of representing is thus *symbolic* in the largest sense of the term: the symbol's representation is, in spite of its concreteness and materiality, not *reduced* but represents the *full sense* of the signified. Even more, through the influence of the signified, the signifier participates, as has said Egon Sendler, "in an opening towards the infinite" (Sendler 1981: 76). The iconic symbol tends thus, by its nature of representation, towards the "unsayable." In philosophical terms it becomes *transcendental*. The "reality" of the icon can also be called an *infinity reflected in the finite*.

Out of the above observations flows the point that constitutes for me one of most obvious parallels between icon and Noh-play: the absence of any *illusionism*. With regard to icons, few people have defined this more clearly than Lossky and Uspensky:

> The task of the icon in no way includes the creation of an illusion of the subject or even it depicts, for, according to its very definition, the icon . . . is opposed to illusion. When we look at it, we do not only know but also see that we stand not before the person or the event itself, but before its image, that is, before an object which, by its very nature, is fundamentally different from its prototype. This excludes all attempts to create an illusion of real space or volume (Uspensky & Lossky 1999: 41).

The kind of reality produced by the icon is neither an illusion nor an imitation of reality but can be called "virtual reality" in the true sense of the term. This applies for the icon as much as for the Noh-play. However, before examining this "virtual" input, the "Western" idea of virtual reality must be explored more completely.

The Western Idea of Virtual Representation

What can be said about the Western approach towards Virtual Reality? As a matter of fact, it is diametrically opposed to the traditional Japanese as well as to the Old Russian Virtual Reality. On the one hand, Western Virtual Reality tries to found its reality on "nothing" (this is why it is virtual); but on the other hand, it clings to "reality" as the primordial model it strives to imitate.

A typical phenomenon flowing out of this constellation is that of "immersion" as a means of producing an effect of "reality." This paradox seems to go widely unnoticed, though it is easy to recognize the absurd character of the overly abundant "it is just as if . . ." prefaces to descriptions of Virtual Reality, meant to be comparative yardsticks which illustrate that everything is "really virtual." At the moment Virtual Reality claims to be autonomous and self-sufficient, there should not be any room for "as if . . ."

The lack of consistency and undigested treatment of Virtual Reality in popular as well as specialized discourses has its root in a Western tradition of aesthetics that has yet to find much theoretical access to the idea of the virtual. Being "realist" in the sense described above, Western aesthetics and Western philosophy are so far unable to adopt the virtual as a term even remotely as important as that of "reality" or *"imaginatio."* Instead they focus on the *representation* of reality on the one hand, and on *Being* as an existential, and not necessarily representing mode of reality on the other. This, however, leaves no space for a simply "presenting" reality which, *as a reality*, neither represents nor exists in terms of "Being." Yet, this is the essence of virtual reality. In Western philosophical discourse, if the virtual appeared at all, it served as a contribution to formal classifications of beings like in the philosophy of Duns Scotus who claimed that things contain their manifold qualities not in reality but *virtually*. Or else it served the purpose of an absolute, Kantian, rationalism taking the virtual as its own ontological foundation, as is done in the philosophy of Bouterwek (1766-1828), who coined the term "Absolute Virtualism" as a kind of absolute intensification of the Kantian rationalist critique of idealism.[20]

When, quite unexpectedly, the virtual was discovered in the 1980s by Western thought, it appeared, curiously, not as a component of art but in the form of a quality sticking to a kind of non-existent space created by computers and through electronic communication. First, philosophy was conceptually rather helpless. There was almost nowhere to look for philosophical approaches that would systematically explain the nature of the virtual. Still, from the beginning it was clear that virtual reality was not simply a matter of illusion (similar to postmodern simulation) created by sophisticated technology. Though formally, Virtual Reality appeared to be very much like television, it also included a psychologically and ontologically disquieting quantity. Terms like "transcendentality" or "Absolute Spirit" quickly occurred and could not be eradicated since. To many, virtual space spontaneously appeared as something "spiritual."

My claim is that the phenomenon commonly known as "Virtual Reality" should be opposed to a more intimate type of Virtual Reality that does not aspire to create, as does the latter, a *second reality*, but that creates an *irreality*. Virtual Reality lacks the existential component that virtual *irreality* considers as its main purpose of existence.

Spirit and Emptiness: Noh, Icons, and Virtual Reality

First it must be said that in Eastern art the virtual is not destructive or negative for human culture, but that any search for a virtual quantity able to transcend purely realistic interpretations of the world, is conceived as a fundamental need for human culture. Already in this sense, the virtual element sought by eastern art is designed in a way entirely different from Virtual Reality flowing out of electronic communication. I will explain this through a more detailed comparison of Noh, icons, and Virtual Reality.

Also the reality of the Noh-play has been called an "Absolute Spirit" (Bohner 1959: vii), and the icon is supposed to be the manifestation of the Holy Spirit. As a matter of fact, Noh, icon, and Virtual Reality share aspirations that can be crystallized in the following three points:

1. All three create a space and a spatial experience that is determined by a strong psychological component, thereby effectuating a shift in mental awareness.[21]
2. They strive to establish a realm outside the physical framework of space-time and of matter.
3. They claim to need no ontological basis for the reality they create since they are able to provide this basis on their own.

Still, there are essential differences between two types of the "virtual." In the following paragraphs I will exemplify these differences with the help of an analysis of the virtual element in Noh-plays, from which the qualities revealed are also valid for icons.

First, what distinguishes the virtual reality of Noh-plays from common, technological Virtual Reality is that the latter follows the principal lines of Western aesthetics and attempts to establish an alternative kind of "virtual realism" by means of logic and reason. Zola's approach of capturing "life itself" is based on the "reasonable" approach of attempting to reproduce reality. It is opposed to "Romantic" ways of grasping the world based on personal feelings and other subjective components. However, even when reality is perfectly "represented" to the point that it appears as absolutely real, the fact to represent something cannot escape subjectivism. What Zola can be reproached with represents also the weakest point of computerized Virtual Reality. Reality cannot be equated with verisimilitude.

Second, there is a difference on the psychological level. In the Noh-play the three points mentioned have a beneficial effect on man's psychological condition. Computerized virtual reality, on the other hand, though based on these same characteristics, is unable to let these characteristics work in the service of a relief of existential angst and materialist loneliness. Instead, Virtual Reality creates what Michael Heim has termed a "hyper world" that is "hyper-active" in the psychopathological sense of making people "agitated, upset, [and] pathologically nervous" (Heim 1998: 172).

Heim's points are interesting for the present discussion. Heim has done extensive work on the philosophical constellations underlying the phenomenon on Virtual Reality as well as on its social and psychological effects. In one article he opposes the quietness and serenity inherent in the Japanese Tea Ceremony to the "culture of explosion" and of speed produced by Virtual Reality. He elaborates some of the typically Japanese qualities of the Tea Ceremony as patience, ceremonial gentleness, refined rhythmic sensibility, and suggests redesigning "virtual experience" according to this model. Heim's idea is original and daring but, curiously, he fails to consider the moment of "virtuality" inherent in the Tea Ceremony itself that provides the essential impetus for the "shift of perception" produced by this Japanese art form.

Space

Because of its particular spatial quality, I prefer to stick to the Noh-play and leave the Tea Ceremony aside. Some people conceive of Virtual Reality as an empty space able to grant its inhabitants a potentially high degree of self-expression (Laurel 1991: 95). Because this space is removed not only from everyday matter but from matter as such, an apparently absolute freedom remains unaffected by coincidences linked to the impact of material "reality." Therefore, in cyberspace, any action can reach an exceptionally high degree of necessity. Things function here very much like on an empty theatre stage. Peter Brook has shown that when the stage is empty, even the slightest action occurring within this empty space adopts an absolute character (Brook 1968). Similarly, for many people the idea of "cyberspace" is fascinating because the elements created within this empty space can, theoretically, acquire a state of "absoluteness."

We are here close to the Noh-play not only because the stage of the Noh is extremely sober and appears as rather "empty,"[22] but also because the space of the Noh-play is determined by a Buddhist concept of "emptiness" or Nothingness. Emptiness or Nothingness projects us into a realm that is *absolutely* free of everyday matters. As mentioned, Mahayana-Buddhism (by which Noh is influenced) recommends the abandonment of all "images" inscribed in the sphere of appearance. However, neither Mahayana Buddhism nor Noh would hold that the access to the "other" sphere (that is more "real" than the shadows on the Platonic cavern wall) would lead to the true knowledge of reality. For Mahayana Buddhism as well as for Noh, the alternative of *appearance* is *"emptiness."*

It becomes particularly clear here how much Western theatre as well as cyberspace remains linked to the Platonic philosophical tradition. However strong their tendencies towards "emptiness" may be, in the end they must fill the empty space with "something" (be it at least an idea or a concept) in order not to be infinitely boring.

Noh-Space

In contrast to cyberspace, Noh is anxious to keep its theatrical space absolutely empty. Only the persisting state of emptiness guarantees this theatrical space the status of a form of "reality" that I have termed above "virtual irreality." This constitutes the main difference between Noh-space and cyberspace: the purpose of the Noh-play is not to install, within its "empty" space, "real" things in order to create a reality, not even a virtual one. On the contrary, the reality of the Noh is supposed to *remain* empty in the sense that the "things" it presents are shadows of the nothingness which normally has no form but has become visible within this virtual sphere of *irreality*. In other words, the space containing these "shadows" is *virtual* because it is not supposed to represent anything, *not even a newly invented reality*. Or, in more concise technical terms: the Noh-play *presents* emptiness, while computerized Virtual Reality *represents* reality within a realm of (extra-temporal, extra-spatial) emptiness.

However abstract this may be, more concrete observations will show that the Noh-play refuses to produce a reality and that it therefore remains within the virtual space of "irreality." An essential point is that in Noh performances, the actors are willingly shown within a realm *outside* the stage, in the so-called "mirror room" in which they prepare for their on-stage appearance. The players reach the stage over a kind of bridge or catwalk called *hashigakari* situated west (left hand side) of the main stage. More famous than the *hashigakari* is the *hanamichi* which is used in Kabuki theatre and which serves the same function as the *hashigakari* in Noh. The *hanamichi* has been especially called a "bridge of dreams" as it links "this world" with the "other world." The significant point is that the public can see the actors arriving from the mirror room world to the world of the stage.[23]

This refers us to the subject of illusion as it has appeared in the analysis of icons. Surprisingly for Western observers, the *hanamichi* or *hashigakari* custom negates any effect of illusion. This is consistent, because "illusion" is not what is going to be presented. The only thing that *is*, is the presentation of an irreality for which "reality issues" like identity, immersion, or participation do not exist. The use of the *hanamichi* signifies thus the conscious acceptance of otherness, separation, and dislocation. This means that "virtual irreality" created in Noh thwarts all attempts of identification, be it those related to reality and those related to illusion. What remains is the paradoxical coexistence of unreal-consciousness and self-awareness providing an aesthetico-existential experience able to distill a non-materialized, "virtual" atmosphere within human experience.

Icon Space

Most works on "icons and space" concentrate on the phenomenon of perspective. I have no intention of discussing this phenomenon here in detail but will directly place it in the context of the aforementioned ideas on the "virtual space" of icons and Noh-plays.

Icons have, in general, no or only little spatial profundity. They often manifest "strange," unstable, forms of architecture and of landscapes, and objects often appear as if seen from two sides at the same time. Obviously, what is lacking in icons—at least of those up to the seventeenth century—is the *linear perspective* used by Western-European painters since Renaissance.[24]

Of course, in perspective and non-perspective paintings the respective internal relationships of *representation* are different. Linear perspective shows the represented object from a central point of view of an individual as if s/he were looking through a window. Linear or central perspective rationalizes and homogenizes space because, as Erwin Panofsky has said, it does not accept a given space as it is, but produces space through construction (Panofsky 1991: 30). While Western aestheticians tended, for some time, to disqualify iconic art as "unable" to create perspective (Gombrich 1960: 125), at least since Panofsky and Francastel it has become commonplace to admit that the Western art of representation is in no way superior to the non-perspective one of icons. Both ways are acceptable styles of representing reality.

The point I am interested in here is that the lack of perspective frees representation of any "illusionism." Perspective is subjective and individual, and creates an individualist and rational *illusion* of profundity and of three-dimensional bodies. Of course, this strategy is precisely meant to be "realist," a strategy which icons attempt to transcend in order to transform space into a "virtual" phenomenon.[25]

"Virtual Perspective" in Icons and Noh

An interesting point linked to the phenomenon of perspective is the "theatrical effect" of icons. Boris Uspensky has drawn attention to the parallel treatment of space by *traditional* Russian theatre and icons. He notes that both apply unusual patterns that regulate the position of the actor in theater, or of the painted person in an icon. In traditional Russian theatre

> the actor always sits with his face toward the audience, and may even, as a result of this, have his back turned toward the person with whom he is speaking at the moment; upon leaving the stage, the actor completes a full circle, even though he can often reach the door by a much shorter route, and so on (Uspensky 1976: 62).

Uspensky sees in the geometrical-perspectival deformation of theatre space a parallel with icons in general. About the fresco *The Adoration of the Magi* from the St. Therapont Monastery, for example, he notes that

> the Virgin and Child regard the viewer . . . . On the other hand, the faces of the Magi are also turned toward the viewer, although they must obviously be turned towards the Virgin, whereas their bodies . . . are turned toward the Virgin, which allows us to reconstruct their actual position in space (60).

It goes without saying that the same "methods" are also used in Noh-play. In Noh, the actor often speaks facing the audience, though his interlocutor might be behind their back. This effect is even more important in the more humorous *Kyōgen*-plays[26] where the effect observed by Uspensky in icons is very common. When starting a dialogue, the *Kyōgen* actors face each other, but will soon turn their faces towards the audience and present the rest of their speech.

It is well known that in historical Japan, perspectival construction of representation was, while not absent,[27] not well developed. Even today theoreticians of architecture and urbanism do not cease pointing out that the feeling for perspective in Japan is not as much developed as it is in the West.[28] In this sense, the discovery of a common lack of "perspectival thinking" in Japanese and Russian traditional art is not surprising. What is interesting, however, is that in Noh-plays a kind of a-perspective perception has some formalization.

This happens through the introduction of a secondary actor (*deuteragonist*) called *waki*. The *waki* is a "bystander" who has no particular role to play with regard to the action's plot, but whose permanent and silent presence next to the *waki* pillar (*wakibashiro*) on the front of the right stage (which is named after him as the *waki*-stage or *waki-jōmen*) is important. Normally the *waki* comes in, briefly presents himself, sits down and says, for example, that he has been or will go on a journey. Occasionally he may interfere in the play by giving comments or explanations. However, what is much more important than the actual dramatic input he delivers is the fact that though his existence the play can be perceived *as seen through him*. The events on the stage are events that *he* experiences. Yet, interestingly, the *waki* does not view these events himself but rather stays fixated on the audience.

The result is not only that the *waki* appears as the intrinsic producer of the time of the play (he condenses the time of the "real" event). He also produces a *space* that is no longer real space (seen from the realistic perspective of the audience), but a space that has lost its *actual* reality. Still this space is not simply subjective or psychological because the *waki* is not a narrator. A virtual character of this reality is obtained through the use of a peculiar a-perspectival model of space, which denies the existence of any *logical* or *linear* link between the *waki* and the events happening on the stage.

Virtual Dream Space

Some of the philosophico-aesthetic considerations enabling icons to create a special nature of space do overlap with the nature of Noh-space. These considerations concern the production of space and a virtual phenomenon strongly opposed to illusionism but philosophically linked to the phenomenon of *dream*. Vladimir Lossky has said that the avoidance of illusionism also excludes the creation of an illusion of "real space or volume." What is thus the nature of this space which is not "real?" First there are, as we have seen, particular devices concerning perspective. However, this is not all. Icon-space can be called virtual for the same reasons as can Noh-space. Like the *hashigakari* in the Noh-play, which creates a place in which otherness, separation, and dislocation are accepted instead of pushed towards ontological *identification*, the icon is part of a liturgical place created by the liturgical action. In other words, the environment created by the liturgical action is, like the Noh-space, a "border-region" functioning as a transitional space between the visible and the invisible. Only in this way can it be conceived as a "window to celestial realms" (Bychkov: 25) where "artistic symbols are perceived as 'real symbols'" and the represented, as well as the symbolized, and the signified "'express [themselves] in reality'" (ibid.).[29]

To find an appropriate aesthetic term for this phenomenon one can say that the reality represented in the icon is not unreal but real and simultaneously *transfigured*. Of course, particularly during the Thirteenth,

Fourteenth, and Fifteenth Centuries, through the use of mystical colors, non-realist devices like the dematerialization of human figures, and fleeting brush techniques creating "phantom-like appearances," icon painters managed to suggest a state of sublime "irreal" representation. Through these techniques, icons also came close to the representation of dream. However, still more contributive to the creation of this dreamlike effect was the conception of space that, through its subjective and variable character, can *itself* be conceived a category of the sublime.[30] Icon-reality is not actual reality but independent of actual time and space. The state of transfigured reality is arrived at only through the production of a paradoxical in-between that affirms reality as much as ideality. Onasch and Schnieper have written about one of the main difficulties of icon painters:

> In their portraits of Christ, however, icon painters had the task of reproducing the ideal image—that is, of combining the sublimity of this divine Person with his true humanity. At the same time, the beauty of the humanity redeemed by him was supposed to shine forth in the beauty of his image (Onash & Schnieper: 121).

This reality is "virtual" in the true sense of the word; it also comes close to dream reality. The "in-between" manifests itself on several levels. The icon represents a "real" world that is perceived as real and not as an illusion, because it is the "reflection of a world where there are no dimensions" (Sendler: 104). In principle, it is a world cut off from sensory enjoyment which nevertheless "uses all visible nature" (Lossky) in order to express the spiritual reality it desires to express. This is why it comes so close to dream, which is an "in-between": it is absolute *clarity* while at the same time independent of earthly logic. Few comments make the link between icon and dream clearer than the "Icon" entry of the *Grove Dictionary of Art*:

> The appearance of visible objects and the three-dimensional world is altered and adapted so that, as in a dream, another reality is discerned in which the logic of sense perception is suspended. The sacred events are not located in earthly space and time. Icons do not convey the rhythms and energy of ordinary life; instead there is an absence of agitation: angels, saints and apostles enact scenes against a background of silence and eternity.[31]

The parallel between dream and icon with regard to clarity and logic has also been addressed by Leonid Uspensky and Lossky who explain that

for to transmit the invisible world to sensory vision demands not hazy
fog but, on the contrary, peculiar clarity and precision of expression,
just as to express apprehensions of the heavenly world the holy Fathers
use particularly clear and exact formulations (Uspensky & Lossky: 21).

With regard to space this shows the following: the particular conception of space that is often attributed to strange constellations of persons
and of architectural elements is not simply a matter of dimensions, perspective and geometry. True, the icon-space has "lost its dimensions" (cf.
Zeami who said about Noh-space: "Bring Above and Below into one").[32]
However, the production of space follows, if examined more closely, the
rules of Virtual Reality. The dreamlike effect suggested by this architecture is firmly grounded on philosophical convictions about the world as
something "virtual," which is the contrary of an illusion. As soon as the
understanding of dreamlike, virtual, iconographic language gets lost (as
happened after the end of the seventeenth century), representation almost
automatically turns towards illusion. Now "architecture becomes logical
and there ensues a fantastic, fairy-tale profusion of purely logical architectural forms" (Uspensky & Lossky: 40).

Secularized and Non-Secularized Virtual Reality

I want to claim that the latter *illusion-like* spatial representation of a
"fantastic," though at the same time "purely logical" world widely
overlaps with what we today call "Virtual Reality." It could also be
called a "secularized virtual reality." P. A. Michelis found that the "infinity" as it was thought by Renaissance was not a religious infinity but
represented the "materialized infinity" of science (Michelis 1964: 201).
The same can be said about today's Virtual Reality. The computer continues with utmost efficiency the Renaissance tradition of "materializing infinity" by turning virtual irreality into virtual reality. Appearing as
the prototype of a "window to celestial realms," the computer seems to
reinstate Renaissance laws of perspective in an almost caricatural way
(objects are obligatorily seen from a fixed point as if through a window,
and from there the view goes towards "infinity").
    For icons, alternatively, the picture is not a window through which
the human spirit can penetrate until "arriving" at a represented reality.
The irreality of the icon is rather a place of active presence able to "re-
ceive" the spectator. Only with this in mind can we understand Vasily
Kandinsky (whose art is influenced by icon painting) and his statement
that "for many years I sought the possibility of letting the beholder 'take
a walk' in the picture, of forcing him or her to a loss of self in a kind of

fusion with the picture" (Kandinsky quoted from Onash 281). What sounds today like a visionary statement about computerized Virtual Reality, should rather be understood as its contrary. "Taking a walk in the picture" is more like a dream experience in which the status of reality is founded on nothing but itself, so much, in fact, that the criteria of reality or non-reality become irrelevant. This state of experience neither is, and nor will ever be reached by computer simulation.

Baudrillard's example of people who are insinuated audio-visually into Renoir's *Dejeuner sur l'herbe* in the form of a virtual reality shows this.[33] The insinuation permits them to virtually experience the impressionist atmosphere of the painting. However, can this really be called an *aesthetic* experience? The same question can be asked concerning the already mentioned digital pets, which communicate a strong sense of reality *through interaction* but which do not necessarily communicate a sense of *aesthetic* reality. While Marie-Laure Ryan, in her book on immersion and interaction, postulates that the "ultimate goal of art" is "the synthesis of immersion and interactivity,"[34] my point is that even an interactive visitor of a virtual theme park will remain "lost" in a fictional world as long as this world does not obtain the cultural status of authenticity. The most "authentic" status any platform like a VirtuSphere can obtain is that of being "as real as the real world." The realistic immersion of the whole body obtained with the help of graphics, sound, and touch (and to a lesser degree of smell and taste) might be technically perfect, but what we get immersed in will never be a cultural world but a synthetic one. The explorer of the virtual world, as she is walking through the VirtuSphere[35] (the house she intends to hire or Fifteenth Century Florence), is not received by an active cultural presence as does the icon or Kandinsky's painting but by a system whose only objective is to cheat her senses. Our full presence in the world, as writes Michael Heim, "comes not only from manipulating things but also from recognizing and being recognized by other people in the world" (Heim 1998b: 23). "Involvement" means that "someone . . . watches what we do and responds to our actions" (ibid).

Also art is not cheating but rather working towards the stimulation of an altered state of consciousness in which "active" and "passive" are—like in dreams or games—of another order. Ryan's "immersion vs. interactivity" syndrome addresses this point but reaches, in fact, not to the bottom of the problem. It is true that, as Ryan states, "[t]he major objection against immersion is the alleged incompatibility of the experience with the exercise of critical faculties," and that the "semiotic blindness caused by immersion" can be solved through interaction (12). However, the passive attitude of the virtual visitor who is entrapped in an artificial reality is different from the dream experience described by Kandinsky. The same is true for Asian theater. The idea is not to produce a reality that is retrieved through interactive experience but to plunge the spectator in an "in-between" of the real and the unreal. In CHIKAMATSU Monzaemons' puppet theatre *Ningyō Jōruri*, for example, the artistic quality does not flow out of interaction and immersion but out of a created interspace "between unreal and real being" as writes Ohashi (2000b: 54). It is the "interspace between the unreal in the sense of the non-real void and the real" which makes art aesthetic. This interspace, which is inconceivable in the real world, represents the "higher reality" (58).

For the same reasons, Vladimir Lossky would likely identify our contemporary computerized Virtual Reality as "a mixing of Church image and worldly image," in which "symbolical realism, based on spiritual experience and vision, disappears through the absence of the latter and through losing its link with Tradition." This results in the replacement of "transfigured reality" by "idealized reality" or simply by "reality as an idea," that is by the expression of "different ideas and opinions connected with this reality" (Lossky, ibid.).

Virtual Reality and the Presentation of Style

All this becomes particularly obvious with regard to the production of style. Like in icons, in Noh also there are cases of representation of non-being, expressed through the coexistence of *dream-consciousness* on the one hand, and *conscious self-awareness* on the other. First, there is the aforementioned aesthetic quality of *yūgen* which, according to Richard Pilgrim, "functions as a scrim, a haze, or dream through which the numinal is vaguely sensed . . . point[ing] beyond itself to a sense of reality veiled by, and not confined to, the phenomenal world" (Pilgrim 1976: 294). Pilgrim's definition of *"yūgen* as dream" contains perhaps a little too much "veils" and "haze." It is true that Noh undertakes a "deepening the feeling of *yūgen* by avoiding overly realistic depiction" (Komparu 1983: 160). However, as for the icon, the *dream* produced must be clear and simple, not foggy and complicated, if it strives to be sublime (or to manifest *yūgen*).

The non-materialized, virtual atmosphere of Noh can also be seen as that of dream. This aesthetic insight led not only to the development of *yūgen*, but also to that of the *mugen* type of Noh, a type directly aimed at the presentation of fantasy, of phantasm, or of dream. Here, the above-mentioned paradox is explicated. The "bridge" between stage and mirror room will be used, in this dream-type Noh, even more intensely. The virtual reality produced through Noh-like dream irreality is obtained by radically renouncing the status of reality as such—including that of a *dream reality*—and by placing the Noh-dream into an "in-between" of reality and non-reality.

Through this mechanism all Noh types, not only the *mugen* Noh, can acquire a dreamlike character. This does not mean that they represent elements that the observer would likely classify as a dream. Rather, they present something non-material: a style. Furthermore, the presentation of this style is mediated only *through* the style of the Noh. When style appears (since it has no "reality" that it could represent) as a reality that presents nothing but itself, the Noh-play becomes an event that adopts a fundamentally virtual character. This is neither realism nor anti-realism but a kind of virtual irrealism in which "imitating and becoming" have been united. Virtual Reality here is not a matter of seeing but of feeling. "Feeling" is not understood as the subjective experience imposed upon the human consciousness or even upon the unconsciousness through the effects of, for example, the cultivated realism of the "culture of explosion." On the contrary, the Noh-actor (as well as the spectator) are, as says YAMAZAKI Masakazu, "carefully warned against indulging in his own emotions as well as using a technique to manipulate them" (Yamazaki 1984: xlii). The feeling that arises through the confrontation with a virtual irreality is rather a "normal" feeling that at times turns towards the *unheimlich* since we approach an irreality through the same psychological state in which we normally approach the real.

The dream thus becomes *one* experiential quality with the help of which we can—metaphorically—capture the character of this virtual irreality. The quality of *style* is yet another one. Finally, it is only through stylized *presentations* (which are *presentations of style*) that Noh captures an impression of reality, which appears *natural* even on the deepest layers of its aesthetic existence. In no case does it create a second reality representing things that would exist only "here" and not "elsewhere." In this way Noh attains a moment of virtuality.

Conclusion

The present chapter demonstrates that both the Noh-play and the Russian icon capture the "beauty of life" (including all existential moments that are also contained by ordinarily life) not directly, through realistic *representation*, but indirectly, through their *styles of representation*. What is presented is not a *presence* but rather what Derrida would most likely call an *écriture*. In Noh "the written, mute-optical element has priority," wrote Hermann Bohner.[36] And, significantly, in Russian language one does not say that an icon is "painted" but that it is "written."

It is tempting to suggest that the images of Virtual Reality have an essentially "phonological" character. By this is meant that Virtual Reality lacks the "silent" stylistic capacity that Noh and icon have. With regard to style, Virtual Reality chooses a process diametrically opposed to that of Noh or the icon: It stylizes an existing reality and is therefore the *representation* of a stylized reality. Alternatively, style for the Noh-play as for the icon, is not simply an outspoken stylized form, or, as Yamazaki asserts, it is not "a fiction" (xxiv). Noh and icon simply (silently) *present* style in the form of a virtual world. There is no manipulation of stylistic form, or of time and space, but virtual reality presents itself *as a whole* within which experience is "neither contradictory nor disjoined" (Komparu 1983: 77). Style does not exist because some reality has been stylized; and "purity" (of experience or expression) does not exist because something "impure" has been purified.

This is inexplicably linked to the particular character of the stylistic reality transmitted through a paradoxical fusion of two opposing states of human consciousness: *dream* and *reality*. As a matter of fact, style is never "really" existent, but has a profoundly non-realistic nature. Expressed differently, style is always of virtual quality, virtually (and silently) present in the sphere of reality, but perceivable only through a state of consciousness elaborated in accordance with the style about to be perceived. A "realistic" consciousness will not see this style. A "sleeping," non-realistic consciousness blinded by illusions will not see it either. The sphere *between* sleep and being awake is, of course, dream. For this reason, the style-perceiving consciousness in Noh-plays and icons is developed along the lines of a consciousness that is dreaming. Computerized Virtual Reality must be seen as "realistic" for the same reasons. However, in Virtual Reality the spiritual style so essential to Noh-plays and icons, cannot be transmitted.

Notes

1. I follow here explanations that I have developed in 'Virtual Reality and Dream: Towards the Autistic Condition?' in *Philosophy in the Contemporary World* 11: 2, 2004.

2. See Ryōsuke Ohashi: "Phänomenologie der Noh-Maske" in his *Japan im interkulturellen Dialog* (München: Iudicium 1999), 91ff. The sinologist François Jullien locates an aesthetic quality in traditional Chinese painting that he names "insipidity" (*fadeur*) which represents a "beyond" appearing as a "virtual" quality, providing a "special type of intuition of existence." François Jullien: *Eloge de la fadeur: A partir de la pensée et de l'esthétique de la Chine* (Paris: Livre Poche, 1991).

3. "La sensation ne saurait se limiter à son niveau sensoriel, et la beauté est bien cette potentialité et cette virtualité vers lesquelles tend toute être."

4. This is different from possible worlds theory for which reality is the sum total of the imaginable. Though also PW distinguishes between the actual and the non-actual, Virtual Reality in the way Granger and I define it, is the reality, which exists *beyond* such a distinction.

5. Onasch and Schnieper write: "Even at home, Orthodox believers are accustomed to singing appropriate seasonal hymns softly before the icon. . . . Here, without surrender of the self, the "vagabond" spirit of the Westerner can find peace. It is helpful to gaze at an icon in conjunction with the text of a hymn, what we call "meditation," that is, the encircling of the true center. By doing so, we may experience what it is like to participate in the Eastern Church's praise of Christ." *Icons: The Fascination and Reality* (New York: Riverside, 1997), 103.

6. KUSAHARA Machiko: "The Art of Creating Subjective Reality: An Analysis of Japanese Digital Pets" in *Leonardo* 34: 4, 2001. I follow pages 299 to 300.

7. Special Manuals or Pattern Books were considered binding for icon artists. The so-called "*gramota* of the three patriarchs" (confirmed by the Tsar) established a strict hierarchy among icon painters and their respective works. The most important category of iconographers were considered the *znameniteli* which were also responsible for the overall geometrical structure, the sketches and supervision of the final work.

8. Cf. Bychkov: ". . . dass es wohl angebrachter wäre, für Rußland nicht von einer Philosophie—im traditionellen Sinne des Wortes—, sondern von einer *Ästhetik* zu sprechen, worunter jedoch nicht eine Wissenschaft nach der Art von Winckelmann und Baumgarten, sondern ein *System von besonderen Ausdrucksformen des Geistigen* sowie ein nichtutilitäres, *kontemplatives* Verhältnis zwischen Subjekt und Objekt zu verstehen ist." "Die Eigenart des russsischen ästhetischen Bewußtseins im Mittelalter" in *Ostkirchliche Studien* 41: 1, 1992 (22-33), 23.

9. Bychkov points out that the use of Old Russian icons as objects for meditation by Daniil and his pupil Rublev was not unusual at that time. "Die Eigenart . . ." 27. It is worthwhile to mention here another form of meditation practiced in the sixteenth century, aimed at the experience of what a Church Father called "superluminescent darkness." *Gold* was conceived as a kind of absolute

"non-color," supposed to negate all other colors. The particular form of meditation pursued by these monks consisted in fixating on a pure gold background until the point when all other colors would disappear. The gold background was experienced as a kind of "absolute Nothingness, "as "the blackout of all objects, including the world of color." Konrad Onasch & Annemarie Schnieper: *Icons: The Fascination and Reality* (New York: Riverside, 1997), 287.

10. The Japanese aesthetician Onishi (1888-1959) published the article "On yūgen" in 1938 (*Shiso*, May-June) and a book called "Yūgen and aware" in 1939 (*Yūgen to aware*, Tokyo, Iwanami Shoten). The book represents one of the first attempts to systematize and Japanese traditional aesthetic concepts in a Western way and suggests essential parallels between the Japanese *yūgen* and the Western *sublime*. Lipps' concept of *empathy* (see note 12) is important for his developments on *yūgen*. See Makoto Ueda: "Yūgen and Erhabene: Onishi Yoshinis attempt to Synthesize Japanese Western Aesthetics" in T. Rimer: *Culture and Identity: Japanese Intellectuals During the Interwar Years* (Princeton: Princeton University Press, 1990)

11. Theodor Lipps' aesthetics of *Einfühlung* has been treated in Japan since right after its publication (1906) by Shimura Hōgetsu. Also the book *Aesthetics* (*Bigaku*, Tokyo, Iwanami Shoten), published by the Japanese aesthetician Jirō Abe (1883-1959) in 1917, drew heavily on Lipps.

12. Steven Heine: *A Dream Within a Dream* (New York: Lang, 1991), 88. Cf. Jin'Ichi Konishi who writes: "The contemplative expressive approach involves the bracketing of a poet's individual impressions and drawing near to the very essence of the subject. Once the essence has been regained, the poet will recommence grasping forms manifested on a more superficial level of awareness." "Michi and Medieval Writing" in *Principles of Classical Japanese Literature*, 204.

13. My definition of Irreality accords with Michael Heim's definition of irrealism as "[t]he view that 'world' is a plural concept. According to irrealism, each world is a variant of related worlds, and each world makes its own context and rules of intelligibility. . . . This is irreal because it undermines the uncritical affirmation of a single world. Irrealism parallels Heidegger's existentialist notion of world in *Being and Time*" (Heim 1998b: 216).

14. Robert H. Sharf: "Prolegomenon to the Study of Japanese Buddhist Icons" in R. Sharf and E. Horton-Sharf (eds.): *Living Images: Japanese Buddhist Icons in Context* (Stanford: Stanford University Press, 2001), 3. Interesting is the quotation from Sharf on Esoteric Mandelas which "did not serve as aids to ritual visualization, nor could they have; the mandelas are better viewed as living entities necessary to ensure the efficacy of the rites performed in their presence" (9).

15. It needs to be pointed out that, more than their Byzantine counterparts, East Asian icons are linked to relics whose presence, in Buddhist religion, was seen as pure and simple. A relic is, like an icon, non-representing.

16. Robert Sharf affirms that also the *honzon* (Buddhist icon) "is not merely a representation of god but the god itself. "On the Allure of Buddhist Relics" in *Representations* 66 Spring 1999, 84.

17. The sixth century Greek Christian writer Dionysios Areopagites probably influenced Eastern and Western medieval Christian theology more than any other writer. He elaborated a system of divine light important for the production

of icons. As noted by Sendler, his theory inverses the structures of representation because the object represented (beaming with light) comes to the contemplator instead of the contemplator sending beams of light to the object. The icon's "inverted perspective" as well as other models of perspective that appear as unfamiliar to us today, might be related to this model (Cf. Sendler, 140). Areopagite's works in translation are contained in *The Divine Names and Mystical Theology* (Milwaukee: Marquette University Press, 1980).

18. Cf. Sendler: "Tandis que le Christ selon saint Paul est la visible 'image du Dieu invisible' (col. 1 15), l'icône, comme le disent les théologiens grecs, est 'deuterotypos du prototype" [meaning the 'second existence of the prototype']." *L'Icône: Image de l'invisible. Eléments de théologie, esthétique et technique* (Paris: Desclée de Brouwer, 1981), 8.

19. The Russian icon's similarity with its East Asian cousins becomes obvious once again. The icon creates a "place of presence" similar to the East-Asian *mandale* which Sharf has named a "locus of the divine." Robert H. Sharf: "Prolegomenon to the Study of Japanese Buddhist Icons" in R. Sharf, E. Horton-Sharf (eds.): *Living Images: Japanese Buddhist Icons in Context* (Stanford: Stanford University Press, 2001), 18.

20. Bouterwek was a professor of philosophy at the University of Göttingen and a contemporary of Hegel. His "Absolute Virtualism" left traces in Schopenhauer as well as in French tradition of "spiritualist positivism" that paved the way for Bergson. On Bouterwek see the first Chapter of my book *Virtual Reality: The Last Human Narrative?* (Amsterdam, New York: Rodopi 2009).

21. One might object that this is true for all works of fiction. However, the imagination that feeds fiction does not *necessarily* manipulate basic spatial components (though it can do so, as, for example, in dream art).

22. It is necessary to note that in ancient times Nohs were never played inside buildings but outside, and that an empty space stretching around the stage was still essential at the beginning of the twentieth century. Cf. Noël Peri, *Le Nô* (Tokyo: Maison Franco-Japonaise, 1944): "Né d'ancêtres accoutumés en plein air, et sur une estrade ouverte aux regards de tous les côtés, le nô semble ne pouvoir se passer d'espace libre autour de lui. Ce serait lui faire violence de le diminuer que de l'enfermer dans une enceinte trop strictement délimitée, sur une scène trop exactement close" (31).

23. Kabuki is a more popular entertainment including, like Noh, music and dance. In Noh the bridge is separated from the audience (like the main stage) through a gravel surround while in Kabuki such a separation does not exist and audience and actors share the same world.

24. From the seventeenth century on Russian icons began being influenced by Western styles of representation and used more and more Western models of perspective.

25. Byzantine art declined at the end of the so-called "Paleologian period" (1261-1453) just because "Western-style realism" had started to enter its aesthetics. As writes Kurt Weizmann: "While the East thought greater abstraction, western European art, from the beginning of the Gothic period, developed in the direction of naturalism that was incompatible with the spiritual concept of the icon." Kurt Weizmann: *The Icon* (London: Evans, 1993), 9.

26. Kyōgen is a comic interlude played during the Noh.

27. In Chinese and Japanese drawing between the twelfth and seventeenth century one can find a highly developed art of linear perspective. See the hanging scroll by Du Jin: *Enjoying Antiquities* (fifteenth century, National Palace Museum of Taipei) and Tosa Mitsunobu's *Legends of the Founding off Kyomizu Temple* (handscroll, sixteenth century, Tokyo National Museum).

28. Cf. Günter Nitschke: "From Ambiguity to Transparency: Unperspective, Perspective and Perspective Paradigms of Space" in *Supplement of Louisiana Revy* 35, June 1995: "It is an unperspective or preperspective paradigm of space which unconsciously lingers in the minds of every average Japanese. The problem of how to identify a space in the third dimension did not arise in traditional Japanese cities since they did not develop a third dimension" (3).

29. A similar function has the so-called Iconostasis: "Separating the Sanctuary from the Nave (the Divine from the human) the iconostasis, just as did the ancient screen, points to their hierarchic difference, the importance and significance of the sacrament, which takes place in the Sanctuary. At the same time it indicates, like the ancient screen, the connection between the two worlds, heaven and earth, and it reveals this connection pictorially, showing in a concise form, on one plane, immediately before the eyes of the congregation, the ways of reconciliation between God and man . . ." Uspensky & Lossky, 67. It is also notable that some Orthodox theologians conceive of the Holy Spirit itself as of a "spatial event," as does for example father Boris Bobrinskoy, rector of the Alexandre Nevsky Cathedral, Paris, when writing: "Saint Basil parle de l'Esprit Saint comme de l'espace, dans un sens ascendant, de l'espace de l'adoration. L'Esprit Saint est le lieu—le milieu divin comme dirait Teilhard de Chardin—, de milieu dans lequel seul peut se faire, non seulement l'adoration, mais la vision. Il est cette luminosité sans laquelle il n'y aurait pas de transmission de l'objet lumineux vers notre égard. Voilà pour l'aspect ascendant." "Mais l'espace est aussi objet descendant, car l'Esprit Saint est non moins le lieu et l'espace de la sanctification. Donc, vous voyez: espace d'adoration, de contemplation, de vision et de communion bien sûr, espace de fortification. Donc l'Esprit Saint est ce lieu dans lequel s'opère cette relation de réciprocité et de dialogue" "L'Icône: Objet d'art ou de culte?" in: Saint Jean Damascène: *L'Icône: Objet d'art ou objet de culte?* (Paris: Cerf, 2001), 41 and 42.

30. Cf. Sendler who says about space that "de par sa nature, il appartient à la catégorie du sublime" (136).

31. "Icon" in *Grove Dictionary of Art* (New York: Macmillian, 1996), 76.

32. "上下一事" *Kwadensho* III. *Kwadensho* or *Fushikaden* (The Book of Flowers) is called the collection of Zeami's writings on Noh technique and aesthetics. Engl. translation T. Rimer (ed.): *On the Art of the Nô Drama: The Major Treatises of Zeami* (Princeton: Princeton University Press, 1984). See also Benl's German translation (note 18). For this quotation see also Bohner, 75.

33. Jean Baudrillard: *Art and Artefact* in N. Zurbrugg (ed.) (1997): *Jean Baudrillard: Art and Artefact* (London, Thousand Oaks, 1997) quoted from Ryan, 31.

34. Marie-Laure Ryan: *Narrative as Virtual Reality: Immersion and Interactivity in Literature and Electronic Media* (Baltimore: Johns Hopkins Press, 2001), 12. It is difficult to understand why Ryan adopts interaction and immersion as typical principles of art as if those would somehow stand *outside* the list of classical criteria of the virtual since Michael Heim postulated already ten

years ago as the three 'I's of VR: immersion, interactivity, and information intensity (Heim 1998b: 7).

35. The VirtuSphere (available since 2005) is a platform in the form of the sphere in which the visitor walks. The innovation consists in the fact that the floor moves and each virtual step is accompanied by a real one of the same dimensions. The visitor can physically navigate the virtual world with genuine human movement.

36. "Das Schriftliche, das stumme Optische behauptet den Vorrang" (Bohner, 15).

Chapter Three

Models of Cultural Space Derived from NISHIDA Kitarō and Semën L. Frank (*basho* and *sobornost'*)

Introduction

Nishida's notion of *basho* already appeared in Chapter One. The objective of the present chapter is to sketch the cultural similarities between Japanese and Russian conceptions of space through an examination of *basho* and the Russian notion of *sobornost'*. In particular, I will undertake a comparative analysis of the thought of the most important Japanese philosopher of the twentieth century, NISHIDA Kitarō (1870-1945), and Semën L. Frank (1877-1950) whom the historian of Russian philosophy Zenkovsky has put forward as "Russia's greatest Twentieth Century philosopher."[1] A comparison of both philosophers is appropriate because both engage in a modern philosophy of religion that maintains a critical distance with concepts of Western European Christianity. The originally Jewish Frank concentrates on Russian orthodox belief (to which he converted) and Nishida derives much of his most important insights from Zen-Buddhism.

However, first some words about the status of such a study on space and community. For many intellectuals it has become almost obligatory to declare the commitment to any kind of collective—be it a nation, a caste, or an ethnicity—to be false because it oppresses those that are inside the community as much as those on the outside.[2] Also, communitarianism is said to run the risk of creating an unacceptable relativism. I think that Russian and Japanese concepts of space and community that will be presented become interesting precisely because, paradoxically, their reflections of community carry implicit statements about the international order by which these communities are defined. This does not mean that organic communities are extended over continents. At stake is a much more sophisticated idea that also finds an echo in some of those thoughts that have most recently entered our contemporary agenda. Homi K. Bhabha writes in *The Location of Culture* that at present through "the emergence of the interstices—the overlap and displacement of domains of difference— . . . the inter-subjective and collective experience of *nationness*, community interest, or cultural value are negotiated."[3] For Bhabha, the most interesting contemporary questions about "communities" are those that ask how "subjects [are] formed 'in-between,' or in excess of the sum of the 'parts' of difference . . ." (Bhabha 1994: 2).

An "in-between" or "excess" produced through multicultural mixture as much as through our eminent prismatic reading of the world asks for a redefinition not only of homogenous national cultures but also for a reformulation of the notion of the community itself. And this also concerns the "supranational community." It is important to rethink the community by avoiding not only the "egocentric" essentialism but also the cooperative one.

Sobornost' is commonly associated with the Slavophile Alexei Stepanovich Khomiakov (1804-1860), but has also been elaborated by Sergei Bulgakov (1871-1944) and Nicolai Berdiaev (1874-1948). The untranslatable term can be rendered into English as "conciliarity" supposed to balance the relationship between authority and freedom. However, *sobornost'* is more than just a "community" linking several individuals together.[4] As a dynamic principle, *sobornost'* does not so much describe the individual's merging with or absorption by collectivity—as would do the *obshchina* (peasant community) so important for the Slavophiles—but rather an *Aufgehen*[5] of the individual in the collectivity. It is Frank who developed *this* potential of *sobornost'*.

In a similar way, Nishida's model of *basho* describes a very specific relationship between the individual and the community. In summary, one can say that, for Nishida, the "'together' of the most extreme differentiatedness"[6] is assembled through concepts like "discontinuous continuity" or "contradictory self-identity"—concepts which are definitely not part and parcel of Western analytical equipment. More precisely, *basho* (as much as Frank's *sobornost'*) eludes at least three Western social models:

1. It eludes the Hobbesian rationalist dichotomy between the self and the other because *basho* and *sobornost'* do not insist on the forces of alliances but on those of the community as a creative unity.
2. It eludes the Kantian model of a "peace federation" (*foedus pacificum*) developed by Kant in *Zum Ewigen Frieden*[7] because *basho* and *sobornost'* suggest "collective spheres" rather than groupings.
3. It eludes Rousseauian theories of the social contract by putting forward a paradoxical form of self-actualization that leads towards greater unity.

Sobornost'

Sobornost' already existed in the Old Russian tradition and is probably the most "original" concept of community that Russians can think of. Its origin is unknown. *Sobornost'* is a politico-religious notion that gives priority neither to Being nor to consciousness but *sobirat'* means simply "to bring together" and *sobor* means "council." The apostles of the Macedonians, Saints Cyril, and Methodius, are believed to have tried to render the meaning of the Greek *katholikos* (universal) through the Macedonian Slavic *sobornajai* (Christoff 1961: 146). Though Berdiaev affirms that in traditional orthodox doctrine one would find *sobornost'* with difficulty,[8] *sobornost'* is certainly representative of Old Slav Russian democracy present in the village community called the *mir*.[9] While in Russian literature allusions to *sobornost'* are rare before 1848 (Christoff: 139), the notion appears relatively frequently in the latter half of the nineteenth century as a philosophical tool helping to metaphysically underpin political, social, economic, and aesthetic positions that are believed to be particular to Russian culture. It has been reevaluated, especially by Khomiakov who described it as a "mystical unity of god and man" (Christoff: 126). After the First Slavic Congress in 1867, religious connotations of the *sobornost'* receded into the background. Through its rootedness in certain Russian *social* conditions, *sobornost'* could become a subject of sociological analysis. As a church of ecumenical councils it could be opposed to a monarchical ecclesiology.[10] As a social principle of the Russian peasant commune and the family[11] providing a vision of integration, peace, and harmony, it could be opposed to authoritarianism and to individualism. As the expression of a purified social consciousness, it could be opposed to the European (that is, "Roman") political consciousness (Christoff: 173) that has always been overdependent on juridical, administrative, and private laws.

Many of the politico-social reflections on *sobornost'* have been justified through substantialist ideas about the cultural difference of "the Slavic race" defined in opposition to the "Germanic race" with its entrenched penchant for limiting personal freedom by means of authority (while Germanic peoples need laws, Slavs manage "to limit the personal freedom of each member of the society through the moral authority of the unanimous will of all of its members"[12]). Paradoxically, while freedom and unanimity were seen as the real essence of Slavic life, in the end, racial, political, and religious conditions of Russia pushed *sobornost'* towards autarky. In the worst case, however, attempts were made to retrospectively impose religious elements upon certain social versions of *sobornost'*. Then *sobornost'* was declared to be a *sanctified* original peasant commune (*obshchina*).[13]

Vladimir Solov'ëv (1853-1900) rationalized *sobornost'* until it became a sort of All-Unity. He questioned especially the Slavophiles' simplistic identification of the Orthodox Church with the Russian people.[14] His critical adoption of this concept tends towards a philosophical anthropology that contradicts any egoistic self-enclosure of man.[15] When Hegelian language was used, moments of rationalization became even more obvious. Here *sobornost'* could be openly translated as All-Unity (as has been done, for example, by Ivan Il'in) (Christoff: 152). True, already in the Orthodox Church *sobornost'* represented an "organic synthesis of multiplicity and unity."[16] The difference is that the orthodox tradition claimed *sobornost'* as a *spiritual* unity of suprapersonal and atemporal nature that comes closer to a religio-aesthetic consciousness than to a political unity.[17]

Space in Russia and Japan

Sobornost' becomes interesting again through the thoughts of the "Silver Age" philosopher Semën L. Frank.[18] In Frank's philosophy, *sobornost'* loses all of its autochthonous character of *mir* or peasant commune. The Japanese equivalent of *mir* is *mura*, and both of them are traditional status societies and corporate entities that "distinguish between insiders and outsiders."[19] Frank's *sobornost'* is as far removed from the *sobornost'*/*mir* definition as Nishida's *basho* is from the *mura*.

Frank, who is often associated with Bulgakov and Berdiaev, was immensely fascinated by the works of the Slavophiles and Solov'ëv's

"Total Unity." However, in spite of this rootedness in the orthodox tradition, Frank, who was exiled in 1922 at the age of thirty-seven, produced a "modern" philosophy with a clearly European flavor. Frank's main focus is on the relationships between philosophy and psychology as well as on possibilities of bridging the gulf between thought and being. His biographer Philip Boobbyer writes that Frank's "purpose was to redefine freedom in a conservative context."[20] This purpose could also be attributed to Nishida. Another point that both have in common is that Nishida and Frank, who are only separated by seven years of age, engage in a sort of Bergsonian rationalist anti-rationalism which leads them towards conceptual redefinitions—or rather philosophical overcomings—of the idea of space and community in their respective traditions.

Much of what has been written on *sobornost'* before Frank is reminiscent of the thoughts of the Japanese communitarians and agrarians who opposed the social structure of custom to law and which H. Harootunian resumed like this: "Japanese 'native ethnology' upheld an image of the collective body that spoke, moved, and acted habitually, with necessary conscious intent . . . internalized reflex."[21] In other words, the communal body was believed to function like an automatic organism in which knowledge was part of an idyllic environment.[22]

Another Japanese traditional concept of communitarian space that Nishida had to overcome Nishida was *kokutai*. The above description of *sobornost'* might have led a careful reader to a perception of parallels between this traditional Russian notion and the Japanese theory of national polity, *kokutai* (国体). *Kokutai* has been Japan's main national ideology, and was dominant throughout all its modernization period up to the end of World War II. Between 1930 and 1945 *kokutai* was strongly associated with nationalism and thought control[23] and can therefore be compared on the Russian side not only with the idea of "Holy Russia" or Russian imperial theories of the "Third Rome,"[24] but also with the traditional notion of *sobornost'* as an organic-religious collectivism that has for so long been intrinsic in Russian culture and has also repeatedly been exploited by authorities.[25] However, the fundamental difference between the use that Nishida makes of *kokutai* in his 1944 article "On the National Polity" and the conception developed by orthodox nationalist during World War II, is that Nishida focuses on *kokutai*'s philosophical, religious, cultural character that, by its nature, cannot be grasped with the help of concrete, materialist notions.[26]

Basho

As mentioned in Chapter One, *basho* represents for Nishida a new onto-logical category summarizing his personal, Japanese version of the Western intuition. The notion appears for the first time in the collection of essays *From the Acting to the Seeing* (1927)[27] and denotes an existential place in which the objective world establishes itself. In his later work, Nishida sees *basho* also as a "place" of "history forming." The "place" forms a historical world that is not biological or material, but cultural, and science can only "objectify" this world by discovering intellectual objects,—that is, by reducing the world to *noemata*. In *basho* such an objectivation takes never place because here the world is seen as the self-determination of a socio-historical world, which always maintains an individual-general aspect. In a way, local culture "transcends itself." More interestingly, also intercultural space is here created through "self-negation,"[28] a problem that will be examined below along the lines of a comparative analysis of Nishida and Frank, and again in Chapter Four concerning Nishida and Bakhtin. Before doing this, however, it will be necessary to reflect these Russian and Japanese ideas against some of the most conventional *Western* ideas of space and community.

Space and Community

Jean-Luc Nancy has recently reminded us of the most generalized Western consciousness that is "always subject to the nostalgia of an ever more archaic and more lost community, mourning lost familiarity, fraternity, and conviviality."[29] Nancy's observation is especially true in the sense that this nostalgia longs primarily for "emotional" elements like familiarity and fraternity. It rarely yearns for the lost capacity of mutual scientific understanding, "lost democracy," or common forms of reasoning.

What comes first to mind when hearing of emotional ties that bind together individuals are not only Emile Durkheim's or Talcott Parsons's social theories about the collective consciousness,[30] but also Ferdinand Tönnies's (1855-1936) distinction between community (*Gemeinschaft*) and society (*Gesellschaft*). In principle, Tönnies theory provides a relatively simple organicist logic (later refined by Tönnies himself) about the formation of states.[31] While in Russia discussions of community and society thrived much earlier (mainly in the literary output of the Slavophiles), references to Tönnies are very frequent in Nishida and his Japanese contemporaries (see more on this in Chapter Five). However, Nishida does not reinstate Tönnies claim for community but uses Tönnies' contrasting notions in order to emphasize his idea of community as based on a "contradictory self-identity."

There is another way of addressing the topic of emotion and community. Nancy's allusions concord perhaps even more with a conception of the community that Kant suggests—though indirectly—in section 20 of the *Critique of Judgment* (1791) when defining the *sensus communis* (*Gemeinsinn*) as the human ability to judge according to the same "feeling" (sensus, *Gefühl*).[32] Kant's purpose is to establish aesthetic judgments as transcendentally valid: what *one* person judges to be beautiful must also be found beautiful by all the others because aesthetic judgments are universal. What is liked or disliked is determined by feelings rather than by concepts but these feelings have a universal character.

The idea of a "common subjectivity" is highly peculiar and does not even accord very well with Kant's own principles. In both his practical and theoretical philosophy, universal and transcendental qualities are supposed to be provided by reason and understanding. How can feeling (*sensus*) have a transcendental value? Has this ever been true? At least today, at a time of multicultural dialogues and confrontations, the transcendental validity of aesthetic judgments appears to be highly questionable. Whatever the answer is, it is true that aesthetic judgments cannot be purely individual either but must have *some*—even if limited—universal value in order to be genuinely aesthetic. Would it therefore not be best to understand the *sensus communis* as an aesthetic sense valid within and constitutive for a certain community? As mentioned, Kant's original idea is *not* to spell out transcendental qualities concerning the community; he was not trying to design a (Rousseauian) "general will" or even to submit the subjective will to the communal will. However, even though Kant speaks nowhere of the community in a spiritual-ethical-political sense, the reflection upon the "aesthetic sensibility" of individuals leads him to the formulation of something that is "common"—if not to *everybody*—then at least to a group of people. The conclusion must be that indirectly, for Kant, the aesthetic community is not a matter of common *reasoning* but of common judgments about taste and ethical matters and that these judgments are transcendental.[33] This means that *sensus communis* communicates common forms of cognition but the human attitude towards community is not based on reason and understanding. Kant makes clear that the *Gemeinsinn* is a matter of subjectivity that transcends the feeling of the single person in order to become *common*. This is why Heinz Kimmerle, in the introduction of his book on *sensus communis*, writes: "After the validity of the *sensus communis* has been limited in this way, there is no longer a universal *consensus*, but common judgments are related to the historical, social or cultural groups who agree on them" (Kimmerle 2000: 1).

By somehow blurring the sharp distinction between reason and feeling Kant insinuates that aesthetic judgments represent a partially constitutive component of the community. Japanese society represents perhaps by definition the ideal example of a community united through common judgments about taste. Roy Andrew Miller has written that in the seventeenth century, Japan, "in spite of civil unrest, was still united in what may be thought of as a fixed axis of basic taste" (Miller 1961: no page numbers).

Nancy notes that the community, since it is no absolute subject (self, will, spirit), is by its nature not inscribed in any logic of metaphysics. In spite of this, or indeed *because* of this, Western philosophy has persistently tried to interpret the community through precisely these metaphysical terms (Nancy, 18). If this is meant to represent a kind of Western "intellectual framework," the Russian and Japanese notions of community and space as defined by Frank and Nishida definitely represent alternatives.

Basho and *Sobornost'*:
NISHIDA Kitarō and Semën Frank

The remarkable fact is that Nishida as well as Frank steer around these undertakings. In general it can be said that when Nishida and Frank talk about *basho* or *sobornost'* they produce an intercultural philosophy from a paradoxical standpoint that is "metaphysical yet empiricist [and] that maintain[s] ties to God without departing from the actual world of fact" (Nishitani on Nishida).[34] Also, they produce a philosophy within which, according to Karsavin's formula, "the West provides the empirical components and the East provides the Absolute."[35] Nishida's focus on "emptiness" as a component of Japanese culture leads *not* to reflections on "the spiritual" as something abstract but to the consideration of "empty *space*." Henk Oosterling holds that *basho* circumscribes a *sensus communis* on an affective, 'localized' tensional field" (Oosterling 2000: 62). What appears strange to a "Western" mind is not as unusual in the Russian tradition. The Slavophiles disagreed with the Roman Catholic and Protestant Churches because they insisted that the spiritual content of religion cannot be found in the form of "pure spirituality" but takes place in rituals. In other words, the spiritual is supposed to be played *within space* in order to be a subject of interest for theology.

Let us start with Frank. One of the thoughts that are dominant in all of Frank's philosophy is that God cannot be understood through *analysis* but that absolute qualities like God should be approached through *relationships*. In principle, Frank is a Christian democrat reflecting upon the fallacies of individualism in the modern world and uses *sobornost'* to define the nature of social being and to crystallize the spiritual nature of society, a project that is both more modern and more sophisticated than a Tönniesian opposition of *Gemeinschaft* and *Gesellschaft*. Generally speaking, *sobornost'* is for Frank the "invisible," inner, and "supratemporal" part of society to which he opposes the visible *obshchestvennost* (best to be translated into English as "communality" and into German as *Gesellschaftlichkeit*).[36]

The definition of the 'I' as a social being occupied Frank for decades. Already in 1917, while still in Russia, Frank attempted, in *Man's Soul*, to define the consciousness of a person, that is "his 'I' as a special reality. This consciousness has, for the most part, the character of a sudden revelation, an unexpected empirical disclosure."[37] *Man's Soul* abounds with quotations from William James and establishes psychic life as something living and dynamic.

In 1930, eight years after his emigration to Germany, Frank published *The Spiritual Foundations of Society*,[38] in which he characterizes *sobornost'* as "the primary inner unity, a primordial *multi-unity*, [a] specific form of being" (69). In this book Frank concentrates on the 'I' in the context of the formation of a social "we," which culminates in a description of *sobornost* as "the indivisible unity of 'I' and 'thou,' growing out of the primordial unity of 'we'" (63).

In 1939, in his most mature work, *The Unknowable*[39] (which translator Boris Jakim has called "possibly the greatest work of Russian philosophy of the twentieth century," ix), Frank revisits the theme of the 'I' and the 'thou' and offers even, in a special section of the book, a very systematical treatment of the topic. Though *sobornost'* is not mentioned in this context, Frank describes the "we" as a collective in which the individuality of the 'I' is conserved: "The being of 'we' overcomes, even if it also conserves, (in the dual, Hegelian sense of *aufheben*), the very opposition between 'I am' and 'thou art,' the opposition between 'I' and 'thou'" (149).

In *Spiritual Foundations* Frank lays the ground for these thoughts by concretely linking them to *sobornost'*. Frank holds that the nature of social being "can be adequately expressed neither in purely 'subjective' categories nor in purely 'objective' categories. Social being in its nature transcends not only the 'material-psychic' antithesis but also the 'subjective-objective' antithesis. It is subjective and objective at the same time . . ." (79). It is in this sense that *sobornost'* becomes for Frank an important term when it comes to the definition of social being. The primordial multi-unity of *sobornost'* should not be mistaken for a sociological model of interaction (72).[40] Being itself is a concrete total-unity whose essence can be grasped by neither naturalism nor idealism nor positivism (100). In the same way, social being (the 'we') is more than only a subjective synthesis—that is, more than a derivative unification of many 'I's.' Frank expresses deep resentments towards organic theories of social life whose "naturalism" shares all the inconsistencies of naturalism in general (43). For Frank, "paths in forests and fields do not arise because many individuals have agreed to make them, but because individuals separately—one after the other—go into a certain direction . . ." (37).

It is in this context that parallels between Frank's and Nishida's definitions of cultural space become most explicit because the definitions of both Nishida's *basho* and Frank's *sobornost'* are linked to parallel treatments of the relationship between the 'I' and the 'thou.' In his essay "The 'I' and the 'Thou'" Nishida declares that "a mere isolated individual is nothing at all" which means that the 'I' exists only through its relationship with the 'thou.' More precisely, the 'I' exists in order to bring about and to maintain the 'Other-ness' of the 'thou' on the one hand; and in order to grant the 'I' its quality as an 'I' on the other. In this sense 'I' and 'thou' "flow out of the same environment" and are determined by a "common consciousness."[41] Any cultural environment flows out of such kind of interaction.[42]

Nishida's environment that is constituted by an interrelationship of the 'I' and the 'thou' is not an organic model of social interaction. The reason is that Nishida strongly objects to the idea of a socio-historical world as a fusion of different individual bits of consciousness. For Nishida, the 'I' and the 'thou' do not simply merge in order to create an environment, a society, or a place. On the contrary: within the environment they create, they remain 'I' and 'thou' through mutual recognition. Nishida writes about intuitive processes that apparently help to understand the other: "Intuition—of which the model is normally thought to be artistic intuition—does not mean that we are immediately united with things. It is rather that deep down inside us resides the absolute other, so that at the bottom of its self, the self has to become the 'Other'" (*I and Thou*, 390).

Also Frank is convinced that "if 'I' and the subject of knowledge coincided in the sense of complete identity, I could never encounter other beings like me" (47). There must be something like a 'thou' because . . .

> . . . another 'I' for me is not merely an *object* that I know and apprehend but also a subject who apprehends *me*. In communion, another consciousness is for me what is expressed grammatically as 'thou,' the second person pronoun. But what is 'thou' if we analyze it in terms of abstract epistemology? It is also another consciousness which I apprehend as apprehending me (48).

Only through the interaction of the 'I' and the 'thou' can society, as the experience of the 'we' that it is, create itself. The 'we' is not derivative of the 'I.' Nor is it the sum or aggregate of many 'I's but it is "rather a primordial form of being, correlative to 'I'" (51).

For Frank the unity of 'we' resides in the primordial *unity* of *multiplicity itself*. It resides "in the fact that the very multiplicity of individuals can live and act only as the self-revelation of the unity which embraces and pervades this multiplicity" (52). The unity of society exists "as the *consciousness of communality* that is as the idea of 'we' in its individual members" (45). Should these individual members really fuse into an organic community, this consciousness of communality would cease to exist. "Knowledge of another 'I' and a living meeting with this other 'I' are possible only because 'I' primordially seeks this meeting" (49).

Frank perceives a mirroring effect of the 'I' and the 'thou' when he states that "even as two mirrors facing each other give an infinite number of reflections, so the meeting of two consciousnesses—understood as mutual external apprehension—presupposes an infinite number of such apprehension" (48). Also for Nishida the 'I' and the 'thou' determine each other even *before* any reflection takes place: "'I' and the 'Other' do not become one here, but I am asked to see in myself the absolute other. This might be an unthinkable contradiction" (Nishida 1932: 390). Frank declares that "'I' ideally has a relation to 'thou' before any external meeting with a separate 'thou.' This ideal relation to 'thou,' constitutes the very essence of 'I'" (49). Nishida holds that the contact between 'I' and 'thou' creates a "self-consciousness" that is based on *social consciousness* instead of on simple perception. This means that the "place" created by the relationship between the 'I' and the Other represents a kind of "play of reflection" in which the 'I' and the 'thou' are not opposed to each other.

Both Nishida and Frank attempt to overcome what they consider a typically "Western" idea of individual 'I's as materialized "objects." Procedures like *Einfühlung* or intuition are inefficient (Frank, 48) because all they do is to transform the other, from the point of view of the 'I,' into an object.[43] Nishida writes:

> Even if we adopt an intuitive point of view that will be thought as the unity of subject and object, consciousness will not be detached from the general-conceptual; on the contrary, we attain thus the utmost of the general-conceptual. . . . If intuition means nothing more than that there is neither subject nor object, it is no more than an object. As soon as one talks about intuition, one has already distinguished the knower and the known and again reunited both (Nishida 1926: 222).[44]

Frank concludes along the same lines:

> If even 'he,' i.e., another consciousness as a pure object, turns out to be
> an impossible category for the point of view for which the world breaks
> down in 'I' and 'not-I,' then how much more impossible or unexplain-
> able must be for this point of view the concept of 'thou,' the concept of
> the member of living communion who stands opposite to me (49).

Once these objectified entities have been established, they can be
fused into organic communities. Another way to say this is to suggest
that Western sociology has scheduled "social being as belonging to the
domain of *psychic life*" (Frank, 71).[45] Through Descartes' *cogito*, Western philosophy became able to view the 'we' as a similarly individual
quantity as the 'I': "Starting with Descartes, modern Western-European
philosophy views 'I' as the bearer of personal, individual consciousness,
which cannot be compared with anything else and embraces everything
else" (Frank, 46). Against this materializing tendency Frank holds that
"social life is not material but *spiritual*" (71). There is neither *cogito* nor
knower but only "self-consciousness." This last thought represents for
Frank the ideal definition of *sobornost'*.

Also for Nishida the 'I' does not represent a firm subjective basis
into which, within the process of understanding, the 'Other' can be integrated through assimilation. Since the "fusion" of 'I's into a community
is not an empirical fusion in the sense of empathy or abstract scientific
theories, Nishida's decides to avoid such a fusion by opposing to the
cogito the idea that "I know you because you answer me, and you know
me because I answer you" (Nishida 1932: 392). Both Nishida and Frank
are convinced that humans live in society not because many individuals
have joined together. Something in man's essence determines him to be a
member of society. *Sobornost'* is constituted by, and at same time constitutive of individuals. It is concretely individual without being a *subject
of consciousness* separate from society. Nishida expresses the same paradox by saying that society develops itself out of itself as a center that is
a self-contradictory identity. This is certainly related to the subject of
Oneness or All-Unity discussed in Chapter One, which Nishida also
formulates in terms of self-identity (*jiko dōitsu*). For Nishida, as Piovesana has written, "the dialectical aspects of the self, as well as the negation of it in relation to others, evolve into a fundamental oneness, which
is also knowledge of one's self. Through this identity in the dialectic of
the absolute we come . . . to the absolute nothingness and its religious
implication" (Piovesana 1997: 115).

In both philosophies the notion of "place" is supposed to explain
what eludes scientific definition. Nishida's *basho* is not a Hegelian organic whole (a community or a nation) but a "self-determinating world"
which cannot be examined from a scientific point of view because sci-

ence views society and history as intellectual objects. *Basho* creates its own structure from the inside and thus represents an "infinite unity" in the sense of unformed matter that is still full of potentialities. For Nishida, the peak of philosophical achievement is neither the definition of the state as a *moral* substance, nor that of the community as a *cultural* substance, but the religio-aesthetic definition of a place as the perfect unity of opposites.

In an almost identical way Frank puts the act of *differentiation* at the center of the formation of the 'I' and the thou:' "'I' itself is first constituted by the act of differentiation, which transforms a certain fused primordial spiritual unity into the correlative connection of 'I' and 'thou.' But what is this primordial unity? It is nothing else but the principle that is grammatically expressed in the word 'we' (Frank, 49)." The being called 'we' is supported by no original nuclear element called 'I' nor by an all-uniting organic structure called 'we.' All there is is difference between 'I' and 'thou.'

Nishida's approach is more extreme as he uses the idea of "nothingness" as a self-expressive element flowing out of a similar process of differentiation. Certainly, all cultures, époques and states have a definitely individual character; but the place in which they create themselves is not entirely "positive," it is not the expression of fixed—Deleuze would say "biologically determinable"—elements, but it flows out of "nothingness" as a differentiation active between the elements themselves. Emptiness as an absolute absence of form permits the "place" to accommodate contradictions without resolving them. In this sense the "place" is an open ended "horizon."

Transversal Contacts between Frank and Nishida

Some of the reasons for the striking parallels between Nishida and Frank are inscribed on another level of comparative philosophy, a level that needs to be pointed out because the encounter of Nishida and Frank is far from being hypothetical and constructed. Nishida's philosophy has been continued in the area of psychology by the eminent Japanese psychologist KIMURA Bin (born 1931) who studied in Germany with Ludwig Binswanger (1881-1966). Like Binswanger, Kimura is deeply dissatisfied with the orientation of psychology towards the natural sciences. It happens that Binswanger was Frank's closest Western-European friend by whom he was supported for years whilst in emigration and in whose house he lived.

Like Frank's, Kimura's psychological writings are lengthy meditations about the status of the "I" as opposed to the empirical self. His idea is to evaluate Nishida's idea of *pure experience* in the context of psychoanalytic theory, criticizing that for Western schools of psychotherapy psychic experience represents always a verbalizable experience and "even non-verbal phenomena like dreams [and] transfers . . . can be entered into the field of psychotherapy, to the extent that they can be translated into words either by the patient himself or by the therapist."[46] Verbalization is materialization of psychic experiences. In Western psychoanalysis, Kimura concludes, the patient is obliged to make his consciousness an object in order to construct his psychic life (1991, 200). In the same way, psychology proceeds to the materialization of the 'I.' Kimura insists that the 'I' should be seen as a non-substantial entity that exists only by "reporting itself to itself"[47] and declares self-perception (*jikaku*, 自覚) the original place of human existence: it is through self-perception that humans resist all "objectification" of psychic life in order to perceive the Being of things "immediately."[48]

It is clear that this strategy fully coincides with Frank's thoughts though we have no reason to believe that Frank developed them *only* under the influence of Binswanger. Already in his pre-emigration work (*Man's Soul* from 1917) Frank writes: "Psychic life is not a mechanical mosaic consisting of psychic stones called sensations, ideas, etc . . . . but a kind of unity . . ." (17-18). He suggests the "delimitation of psychic life from objective being" as an element of experience which leads him to the accentuation of interrelational space. The exclusive existence of the "I" within an "interrelational" space concords not only with Kimura's Nishidaian ideas but also with Binswanger's for whom this space has been a topic of interest as he writes:

> . . . the curious problem that just *where* you *are*, "arises" a place (for me). Instead of ceding a position "to the other" within the predetermined spatiality of the *ratio* and the corresponding loss of my own space, what appears is the curious phenomenon of an "unlimited" increase of one's own space by *giving away* one's own space! Instead of a predetermined region as such *in* which the one would dispute "the place" or "the position" to the other, one perceives a curiously undetermined . . . depth [and] breadth in which places and positions no longer exist.[49]

Basho, Sobornost', and the Eurasianists' "New Globalism"

Through the notion of *basho* Nishida resolves the aporia of the coexistence of existence and essence. Reflecting all individuals and their mutually determining way-of-being within itself, *basho* is a place in which all living and non-living things come into being, it is a "place" of relational existence in which one perceives the idea of nothingness or emptiness. On the basis of this religious "negativity" introduced into the idea of community, both *basho* and *sobornost'* positively engage in reflections on the global world order. Nishida's theory of the *basho* is opposed to federalism as well as to imperialism but brings forward a new globalism within which each nation is supposed to develop its own culture. This theory avoids ethnic egoism as well as any harmful form of nationalism and comes close to Sergei Bulgakov's concept of a "brotherhood of peoples"[50] which Bulgakov preferred to "nationals, atomized 'citizens' or 'proletarians of all countries.'"

Nishida's later developments of *basho* are also reminiscent of the "community of nations" (*sobor narodov*) of the Eurasianists,[51] for whom the *Aufgehen* of the individual in the collectivity had been important. In general, Eurasianist, who formulated perhaps the clearest anti-Western model that has ever existed in Russia, adopted "organic" tones well known since the Slavophiles and Pan-Slavism. They also formulated a critique of Western philosophy as well as reflections on Khomiakov's idea of *sobornost'* together with impressive degrees of cultural relativism and anti-colonialism. Curiously, these rather conservative thoughts are combined with distinctly progressive ideas about the organization of a multicultural state as laid out by the liberal conservative economist Pëtr Struve (1870-1944), a friend of Frank who was, like Frank, a proponent of political realism. Though Struve certainly entertained a Slavophile "nostalgia for the precapitalist world,"[52] his ideas were clearly Western and European.

For the Eurasianists, the state organization had at its center a personal god and the "symphonic personality" of Russia-Eurasia represented a nonegoistic, communal consciousness or, as expressed by Karsavin, a collective personality (*"sobornaja lichnost'"*). For the Eurasianists, any relationship between individual and state is rooted in *sobornost'*. However, in spite of their conservative and paternalist background, it is possible to see in the Eurasianist writings an "early post-modernist strain" (Girenok) because their idea to identify Eurasia as a localized culture pushes the very opposition East-West towards theories of cultural conversion or transculturalism. Especially the democratic and decentralized "third way" that left-wing Eurasianists like Dimitry Sviatopolk-Mirskii suggested, aims at overcoming Russian nationalism and emphasizes the supra-national character of Eurasianism.[53] The Eurasianist geographer Savitzky, for example, introduced the idea of the "symposium of people" when writing: "Eurasianists understand Russia as the *sobor narodov*. They believe that political unity of this vast territory is a result not only of the efforts of just Russian people but of many peoples of Eurasia."[54]

The *sobor narodov* can be understood as an "internationalized" version of *sobornost'*. For the Eurasianists there would be a large quantity of "local patriotisms" sustained by a weak, all-Russian patriotism of the elite. "Eurasian culture" would not simply be the sum of different single cultures but these cultures would "converge" into a symphonic reunion. This is compatible with Nishida's suggestion that a "new world order" can be attained via the typically Japanese idea of "self as nothingness:" just as individual selves exist by mutual self-determination and self-negation, so do nations in global place.

Conclusion

The reading of the Russian and Japanese authors that has been provided in the present chapter helps to overcome Huntingtonesque fear of a clash of civilizations. Also Christopher Goto-Jones affirms that Nishida's "alternative model of the inter-civilizational order predates Huntington's 'new world order' by some sixty years."[55] The difference is that Nishida's civilizations manage to avoid the Hobbesian clash because they are not material entities. While it remains true that the world is an unfolding of various types of civilization (as Nishida also would affirm), each of these expressions should be recognized as an *immediate* expression that cannot be subsumed in one single Hegelian idea of "civilization." In other words, every singularity is an expression of the Absolute, and the "harmony" that Frank and the Eurasianists look for when talking about *sobornost'*, is always more than a totalizing Hegelian universalism but comes closer to a Schellingian revelation.[56] There is no dialectical synthesizing but rather the expression of a general truth.

More important than to theoretically define the limits between different types of Pan-associations (or perhaps pondering about ways to harmonize single cultures by imposing upon them some sort of holistic spirit), is to show ways how these limits *can be* and—as a matter of fact—constantly *are* overcome. It is, for example, more important to think about the relationship between the 'I' and the 'thou,' about the formation of human communities dependent on the contact with the "outer" world (or simply arising through opposition to it), than to define "civilizations" as self-sufficient and egocentric entities.

Contemporary discussions on the "new world order," at the moment they ground their arguments on "cultural" elements, on the other hand, can easily shift towards a Huntington-style cultural essentialism. In *Nation and Narration*[57] Homi Bhabha argues against this tendency to essentialize Third World countries into a homogenous identity. At the moment a world order is no longer established "artificially," i.e., with the help of valid *political* ideas, cultural components are called for in order to establish an "organic" order by creating coalitions between cultures in an almost "natural" way. Such ideas accord with historical ideas of Nishida or of Eurasianism only as long as we take a superficial look. The present chapter was supposed to show that these Japanese and Russian philosophies developed concepts of space through which cultural communities appear as more than merely organic, self-enclosed units. These philosophies constantly confront the contemporary reader with a paradoxical conceptual linking of openness and closedness, of self-awareness and awareness of the other, of reality and transcendence. Like this they manage to overcome both particularism and universalism.

Notes

1. Vasily V. Zenkovsky: *History of Russian Philosophy* Vol. 2 (London: Routledge and Kegan Paul, 1995), 872.

2. Cf. Martha Nussbaum: "Patriotism and Cosmopolitanism" in Joshua Cohen (ed.) *For Love of Country: Debating the Limits of Patriotism* (Boston: Beacon Press, 1996).

3. Homi Bhabha: *The Location of Culture* (New York: Routledge, 1994), 2.

4. See Peter K. Christoff: "Khomiakov maintained that they could have used either *vsemirnaja* or *vselenskaja* (universal) synodal, cathedral, or even social (public)." (*An Introduction to Nineteenth Century Russian Slavophilism. A Study in Ideas*, Vol. 1: A. S. Xomiakov ('S-Gravenhage: Mouton, 1961), 146.

5. The German philosophical term *Aufgehen* is translated as "absorbtion" though it differs from the idea of fusion in that it permits the autonomous existence of the merging elements as individualities.

6. Elmar Weinmayr: "Thinking in Transition: Nishida Kitaro and Martin Heidegger" in *Philosophy East and West*, 55: 2, 2005, 235.

7. See Christopher Goto-Jones: "Transcending Boundaries: Nishida Kitarō, K'ang Yu-Wei, and the Politics of Unity" in *Modern Asian Studies* 39: 4, 2005, 793-816, 795.

8. N. Berdiaev: "Духовные задачы эмиграций" *Put'* 1, 1925.

9. Thomas, G. Masaryk: 1955. *The Spirit of Russia. Studies in History, Literature, and Philosophy* (3 Vols.). London: Allen & Unwin 1955 [1919], 14.

10. Sergei Bulgakov: *The Orthodox Church* (Crestwood: St. Vladimir's Seminar Press, 1988), 74-75, quoted from Christoff, 173.

11. Cf. Nicholas V. Riasanovsky: "Asia Through Russian Eyes" in Wayne S. Vucinich (ed.): *Russia and Asia: Essays on the influence of Russia on the Asian Peoples*, 9.

12. Alexander Hilferding: *Sobranie sochinenii* Vol IV *Istoriia baltiiskikh slavian* (St. Petersburg 1874), 68-69. Quoted from Boro-Petrovich 1956, 82.

13. The Slavophile Konstantin Aksakov held that *obshchina* is a peasant commune leading to organic mutuality and social self-abnegation. This is naïve and not plausible as holds also Christoff (Christoff, 154).

14. Nicolas Riasanovsky: "Khomiakov on *sobornost'*" in E. J. Simmons (ed.) *Continuity and Change in Russian and Soviet Thought* (Cambridge, MA: Harvard University Press, 1955), 193.

15. Nicolai Berdiaev: *The Russian Idea* (New York: Macmillian, 1948), 50.

16. Riasanovsky: *Russia and the West in the Teachings of the Slavophiles: A Study of Romantic Ideology* (Cambridge, MA: Harvard University Press, 1952), 162.

17. Cf. Victor Bychkov on *sobornost'* in the Encyclopedia of Aesthetics (Ed. M. Kelly; Oxford University Press, 1998): "Sobornost' signifies the essentially extrapersonal (supra-personal) and a-temporal nature of aesthetic consciousness. This is the consciousness of a community (sobor) of people, akin in spirit, who have reached, in the process of communal liturgical life, a spiritual unity with each other and with the higher spiritual levels, ideally with God . . ." (196).

18. It remains to mention that as a political term, on the other hand, *sobornost'* became fashionable up to the point that Dostoevsky could confirm that "the idea of socialism has given way to that of *sobornost'*" (Christoff, 238). Dostoevsky was disgusted by the French bourgeoisie, which symbolized for him pettiness, false morality, materialism, and selfishness. He contrasts them with *sobornost'*: "The highest value a man can make of his individuality, of the completed development of his I, would be to destroy this I, to return it entirely to all and to each inseparably and supremely. And this is the greatest happiness. In this way the law of I merges with the law of humanity and both are one, and I and all (which appear to be two opposed extremes) are both mutually destroyed, while at the same time they attain the higher goal of their own individual development on this basis." (Notebooks entry 16. April 1864 quoted from Lossky's *History of Russian Philosophy*, New York: International University Press, 1951). Dostoevsky's statement is realistic: Herzen accepted the Russian peasant community as a model for socialism because he found that, contrary to the Asian (Indian) peasant community, the Russian forms of community were more adaptable for modern needs, being less rigid and less patriarchic (Cf. Alexander von Schelting: *Russland und Europa im russischen Geschichtsdenken*, Bern: Francke, 1948, 221): "As an organic unity that functions through mutuality and social self-abnegation, the *obshchina* is certainly to be regarded as the precursor of *sobornost'*" (see Christoff, 154). Herzen even designed a form of "revolutionary Slavophilism" (MacMaster) intended to replace Khomiakov's religiosity with a secular brand of humanism suitable for a rationalist, socialist eighteenth century (cf. Robert MacMaster. *Danilevsky: A Russian Totalitarian Philosopher*, Harvard University Press, 1967, 181).

19. On *mir* and *mura* see Rudra Sil: *Managing "Modernity": Work, Community and Authenticity in Late-Industrializing Japan and Russia* (Ann Arbor: University of Michigan Press, 2002), 129ff and 197ff. Quotation from page 278.

20. Philip Boobbyer: *S L Frank: Life And Work Of A Russian Philosopher 1877-1950* (Athens: Ohio University Press, 1995), 146.

21. Cf. Harootunian, *Overcome by Modernity: History, Culture, and Community in Interwar Japan* (Princeton University Press, 2000), 299-300. Repre-

sentatives of native ethnology are Gondō Seikei, Tachibana Kōsaburō, Inoue Nisshō, and Nakano Seigō.

22. Today *sobornost'* is also identified as a kind of precursor of Bolshevik socialism. The neo-Eurasian Igor Panarin identifies *"sobornost'* as an aggressive rejection of individual private interests, . . . [which produces] on the whole a lack of initiative, responsibility, independent activity, and high-quality professionalism. . . ." A. S. Panarin: "Return to Civilization or 'Formal Isolation'?" in *Russian Studies in Philosophy* 31: 2, 1992, 61. Panarin's communitarianism, which does not more than idealizing the social whole, does not reflect the sophistication that Frank enclosed to the concept of *sobornost'*.

23. The *kokutai* synthesizes Confucian and Shintoist ethical elements and expresses, since the late Tokugawa shogunate, political contents focusing communitarian issues. Through its partly Shintoist identity, *kokutai* is tied to the emperor as the patriarch of the national family. Curiously, it was also used in Chinese modernity (as *kuo-t'i*) by the Hung-hsien reign (See: Joseph R. Levenson: "The Suggestiveness of Vestiges: Confucianism and Monarchy in the Last" in Arthur F. Wright (ed.): *Confucianism and Chinese Civilization* (Stanford University Press, 1964, 314). The word *kokutai* comes originally from China where it had another meaning.

24. Constantinople was the Second Rome. Some Sixteenth Century Russian writers held that "both Romes" had failed the mission of leading Christianity and required that political and religious supremacy should be granted to Moscow.

25. See Mikhail Epstein, 1995b. *After the Future: The Paradoxes of Postmodernism and Contemporary Russian Culture* (Amherst: Massachusetts University Press, 1995), 281.

26. See my *Place and Dream: Japan and the Virtual* (Amsterdam, New York: Rodopi, 2003), 127ff.

27. *From the Acting to the Seeing* (*hataraku kara mono miru mono e*) NKZ IV, 6 (1927).

28. Cf. John Maraldo: "The Problem of World Culture: Towards an Appropriation of Nishida's Philosophy of Nation and Culture" in *Eastern Buddhist* 28: 2, 1995b.

29. "Une conscience . . . semble bien accompagner l'occident depuis ses débuts: à chaque moment de son histoire, il s'est déjà livré à la nostalgie d'une communauté plus archaïque, et disparue, à la déploration d'une familiarité, d'une fraternité, d'une convivialité perdues." Jean-Luc Nancy: *La Communauté désœuvrée* (Paris: Christian Bourgeois, 1986), 31.

30. Durkheim's study of the "lien social" (social link), mainly developed in *De la Division du travail social* (Paris: Presses universitaires françaises, 1893), asked how people form groups in a more and more individualized society. In traditional societies which showed only minimal differences with regard to production processes, social solidarity was mechanistic and based on geographical proximity, shared histories and values, etc. This communitarian society is replaced by a more organic form of solidarity defined mainly by interdependence. Talcott Parsons developed Durkheim's ideas on common sentiments and values for example in *The Structure of Social Action* (2 vols.), (New York: McGraw Hill, 1937), *The Social System* (New York: The Free Press, 1951).

31. Ferdinand Tönnies: *Gemeinschaft und Gesellschaft* (Leipzig: Fuess, 1886).

32. Though *sensus communis* can be translated into English as "common sense" it has nothing to do with what we generally refer to as common sense today. Cf. § 20 of Kant's *Critique of Judgment* (The Condition for the Alleged Necessity by a Judgment of Taste is the Idea of a Common Sense): "If judgments of taste had (as cognitive judgments [Erkenntnisurteile] do) a determinate objective principle, then anyone making them in accordance with that principle would claim that his judgment is unconditionally necessary. If they had no priciple at all, like judgments of the mere taste of sense [des bloßen Sinnengeschmacks], then the thought that they have a necessity would not occur to us at all. So they must have a subjective principle, which determines only by feeling rather than by concepts, though nonetheless with universal validity [allgemeingültig], what is liked or disliked. Such a principle, however, could only be regarded as common sense [Gemeinsinn]; for the latter judges not by feeling [Gefühl] but always by concepts [Begriffe], even though these concepts are usually only principles conceived obscurely." (trans. Werner Pluhar, Indianapolis: Hackett, 1987) (Orignal: p. 237-38).

33. ". . . only under the presuppositon, therefore, that there is a common sense [Gemeinsinn] . . . can judgments of taste [Geschmacksurteile] be made" (ibid).

34. NISHITANI Keij: *Nishida Kitarō* (Berkley, Los Angeles and Oxford: University of California Press, 1991), 71. It is interesting to note that Nishitani held such a standpoint to be "unthinkable in the West."

35. Lev P. Karsavin: *Vostok: Zapad i russkaja ideja* (Petrograd: Ogni 1922) quoted from Mehlich, 108.

36. See. von Schelting, 221: "The *obshchina* rested on the principle of *obshchinnost* (communality)."

37. Semën L. Frank: *Душа человека: опыт введения в философскую психологию* (1917) (republished by Nauka, in Moscow: 1995) Engl.: *Man's Soul: An Introductory Essay in Philosophical Psychology* (Athens: Ohio University Press, 1993). I quote from the English translation 14.

38. S. L. Frank: *Духовные основы общества: введение в социальную философию* (Paris: YMCA Press, 1930; republished in New York, 1988). Engl: *The Spiritual Foundations of Society: An Introduction to Social Philosophy* (Athens: Ohio University Press, 1987). I quote from the English translation. The book's section "I and We," part of the book most discussed in the present chapter, appeared as a separate article entitled "I and We" in the *Collection of Essays in Honor of P. B. Struve* (Prague) already in 1926.

39. S. L. Frank: *The Unknowable: An Ontological Introduction to the Philosophy of Religion* (Athens: Ohio University Press, 1983) originally published as *Непостижимое* in *Put'* May/Sept. Nr. 60, 1939.

40. "In other words, the spiritual unity considered here is not the simple, absolute unity of a subject, but precisely a *multi-unity*, a unity that exists and acts only in harmony and unitedness of many individual consciousnesses." (45)

41. Nishida: 私と汝 (Watashi to nanji; I and Thou) [1932]. NKZ 6: 341-427, 348ff.

42. See Chapter Four.

43. "Another consciousness as a pure object, turns out to be an impossible category for the point of view for which the world breaks down into 'I' and 'non-I,' then how much more impossible or unexplainable must be for this point of view the concept of 'thou,' the concept of the member of living communion who stands opposite me?" (Frank, 49). "This unity of 'we' is not only a unity that opposes multiplicity and separation, but it is also, primarily, the unity of multiplicity itself, the unity of all that is separate and antagonistic, the unity outside of which no human separation and multiplicity are conceivable" (51).

44. 我々が主客合一と考えられる直覚的立場に入る時でも、意識は一般概念的なるものを離れるのではない、かえって一般概念的なるものの極致に達するのである。〔・・・〕直覚というのが単に主もなく客もないということを意味するならば、それは単なる対象に過ぎない。既に直覚といえば、知るものと知られるものとが区別せられ、しかも 両者が合一するということでなければならぬ。

45. Frank, 71: "This is the absolutely insuperable limit to all social materialism, to all attempts at a biological or physical interpretation of social life."

46. KIMURA Bin: "Signification et limite dans la formation psychothérapeutique" in P. Fedida and J. Schotte (eds). *Psychiatrie et existence* (Grenoble: Millon, 1991), 191, my translation.

47. KIMURA Bin: 1982. 時間と自己 (Jikan to jiko; Time and I). (Tokyo: Iwanami, 1982), 7, my translation.

48. KIMURA Bin: *Ecrits de psychopathologie phénoménologique* (Paris: Presses Universitaires de France, 1992), 40, my translation.

49. Ludwig Binswanger: *Grundformen und Erkenntnis des menschlichen Daseins*. Zürich: Niehans, 1953), 31, my translation. A more direct contact between Nishida's philosophy and Frank does not seem to have existed. KIMURA Bin never met Frank (correspondence with the author).

50. Sergei Bulgakov: "Heroism and Asceticism (Reflections on the Religious Nature of the Russian Intelligentsia)" in M. Shatz and J. Zimmermann (eds), *Signposts - vekhi* (Irvine: Schlacks, 1986), 44.

51. For Eurasianism see "Explanation of Terms." For "sobor narodov" see Sergei Glebov: "Science, Culture, and Empire: Eurasianism as a Modern Movement" in *Slavic & East European Information Resources* 4: 4, 16.

52. Richard Pipes: *Struve. Liberal on the Left, 1870-1905* (Cambridge, MA: Harvard University Press, 1980), 78.

53. See Igor Torbakov's "From the Other Shore: Some Reflections of Russian Émigré Thinkers on Soviet Nationality Policies 1920s-1930s" in *Slavic & East European Information Resources* 2003, 4: 4 (copublished with Jared S. Ingersoll (ed), *Russian and East European Books and Manuscripts in the United States: Proceedings of a Conference in Honor of the Fiftieth Anniversary of the Bakhmeteff Archive of Russia*. Torbakov quotes Sviatopolk-Mirskii from "National'nosti SSSR" in *Evrazija* (Paris) 22, 1929 (44).

54. Pëtr Savitzky: *Kontinent Evrasia* (Moscow: Agraf, 1995), 424, quoted from Torbakov, 44.

55. Goto-Jones: "If not a Clash then What? Huntington, Nishida Kitarō, and the Politics of Civilizations" in *International Relations of the Asia Pacific* 2, 2002, 223-243, 224.

56. Schelling's philosophy of revelation ("Philosophie der Offenbarung," a lecture held in 1854) defines philosophy as a science transcending mere rational

knowledge. Whatever philosophy creates can be perceived only through experience and revelation. Three forms of revelation of the absolute are: art, religion, and philosophy.

57. Homi K. Bhabha: *Nation and Narration* (New York: Routledge & Kegan Paul, 1990).

Chapter Four

Space and Aesthetics:
A Dialogue between NISHIDA Kitarō
and Mikhail Bakhtin

Introduction

In the preceding chapter I have crystallized Japanese and Russian common ideas about the 'I' and the 'thou' as paradoxical notions of
self-perception as well as of the perception of the Other and as models
leading to particular conceptions of space and community. It will now be
interesting to develop the idea of inter-subjectivity and self-reflection in
the more aesthetic context of *stylistic* unity. In Chapter One as well as
elsewhere it has been suggested that space is also an aesthetic phenomenon to the extent that it can represent not only a political unity but also
religio-aesthetic consciousness. However, while the preceding thoughts
remained in the realm of an "aesthetic sensibility" enabling the formulation of something that is "common" to a group of people, what remains
to be done is to explore the same phenomenon within the domain of a
more formal kind of aesthetics.

The Russian literary critic Mikhail M. Bakhtin (1895-1975) serves as
an interesting example because, unlike Frank's, Bakhtin's theories extend
into contemporary (postmodern) thought, dealing with style not only as a
suggestive communal phenomenon but as a basis for a theory of civilization. At the same time, his thoughts on inter-subjectivity and
self-reflection can be examined as phenomena of consciousness that are
presented in a way that overlap on several points with Nishida's.[1]

It is clear that this dissimilarity produces at the same time the need
for justifications: while Nishida's and Frank's thoughts developed on the
common ground of religious philosophy, Nishida's and Bakhtin's intentions and identities do not reveal any immediate common denominator.
Both authors come from different hemispheres and different traditions,
apparently linked only through having shared some decades of the same
century. While Nishida and Frank are contemporaries, Bakhtin is eigh-
teen years younger than Frank and and twenty-five years younger than
Nishida and clearly belongs to another generation. Going by the intellectual biographies of Nishida and Bakhtin, one can easily doubt that these
two authors are really comparable: Bakhtin (who never emigrated) grew
up in the milieu of Russian modernism, authored books on Rabelais and
Dostoevsky, and a great number of works on literary aesthetics. His critical attitude towards his Russian Formalist contemporaries made him
interesting, and his interest in language made him popular in Russia in
the Sixties and Seventies, and later also in the West.

Nishida developed a Western style philosophy out of early Zen experiences, and during his lifetime manifested a constant interest in Zen
Buddhism as well as in philosophical questions concerning religious experience.

All this establishes, of course, a considerable distance. Added to this
comes a "formal" problem within studies of comparative *philosophy*.
Bakhtin was "officially" not a philosopher but a literary critic who built
an aesthetic theory mainly around the novels of Dostoevsky. Nishida re-
lied mainly on Eastern and Western *philosophical* sources and tried to
design a Japanese *philosophy* compatible with Western standards.

On the other hand, Bakhtin has dealt, like Frank, with the subject of
the 'I' and the 'thou' in principal parts of a well known article and comes
to conclusions whose proximity with Frank is surprising. It is also obvious that for both, reflections on the 'I' and the 'thou' represented a major theme with regard to both Nishida's and Bakhtin's development of
the entire body of their thought.

A further parallel occurs, providing a hint that Nishida's and Bakhtin's treatment of the 'I' and the 'thou' might not only work in parallel
with regard to the topic itself, but also take place in a similar philosophical context. A decisive addition occurs when considering that both authors were, when treating the subject of the 'I' and the 'thou,' concerned

with the phenomenon of *space*. Both Bakhtin and Nishida were constantly working against *abstract* concepts of space, replacing them with more "cultural" and concrete ones.

Nishida's work presents itself "officially" as a philosophy of space. His notion of *basho* is generally translated as *place* and has been considered, together with the notion of *ma* (developed by KIMURA Bin, see Chapter Three), as a East Asian contribution to theories of space in philosophy, architecture, and urbanism as well as a philosophical source of attempts to wrench the modern treatment of space from its Cartesian background.[2] I will refer to Nishida's idea of space from here on as "place" and for convenience's sake, I will do so also with regard to Bakhtin. Bakhtin's contribution to the philosophy of place is less well known and more difficult to recognize. In spite of the overwhelming amount of Bakhtin criticism, the general tendency is to treat Bakhtin's ideas of dialogism, *heteroglossia*, (or even of place-related topics like the "chronotope") in the context of society, literature, and language, and not of urbanism or architecture. Still, it remains a fact that what has later been called Bakhtin's "anti-idealism" rested on his conviction that any reality should not be transposed in an "extra-social" as well as in a "внепространственный" (extra-spatial) and "вневременный" (extra-temporal) realm (Medvedev 1928: 25/14). For reasons that will hopefully become obvious in this chapter, I believe that Bakhtin's theoretical suggestions concerning polyphony, carnival, and other cultural phenomena, should not be seen *only* as social, institutional, artistic, or language-related devices, but as making concrete suggestions about cultural *space* and the life taking place within it.

Bakhtin insists throughout all of his philosophy that time and space are not physical but that time is historical and space is social. On this point he is indeed comparable with the later Nishida for whom, as has been shown in Chapter Three, the *basho* is a place in which things do not simply "exist" but in which they are "local," i.e., in which they "are" in a concrete way. On a first level, Bakhtin's and Nishida's definitions of "place" or "locality" are outspokenly "organicist"; both of them can be put into the group of those people who attempt to think place as more than as a Newtonian extension of space. NAKAMURA Yūjirō has said in regard to Nishida, that from Aristotle's *chôra* to modern speculations about a Big Bang, the idea of "organicity" has represented a constant challenge. There is a link between Bakhtin's concern in spatio-temporal "chronotopes" (a term Bakhtin derived from Einstein but which he never defined rigidly) that should constantly be reflected against the "unity of the world," and Nishida's philosophy of "place" that deal with very similar questions. Seen like this, both philosophies occupy respective positions within the same twentieth century current of organicist philosophy particularly interested in the definition of place (Nakamura 2000: 369 and 375).

However, the parallel concerning "place" is twofold, which makes the entire subject even more stimulating. Within their analyses of the relationship between 'I' and 'thou,' both Bakhtin and Nishida force us to see not only the 'I' and the 'thou' within place but also to see *place itself as being constituted* by a relationship between the 'I' and the 'thou.' This means that both thinkers needed, at a certain moment of their reflections on the non-abstract character of place, to refer to the relationship between humans and were interested, when it came to the topic of "human space," not just in "subjective humans" and their way of perceiving space. Neither was interested in the relationship between humans as long as it was a relationship between the 'I' and the 'He' or the 'He' and the 'He.' For both authors, the most interesting aspect of human, cultural place could be revealed through an examination of the relationship between the 'I' and the 'thou.'

Most generally speaking, Nishida and Bakhtin aim to define "cultural place" as something non-scientific and "human," as opposed to abstract and objective definitions of space. At the same time, however, both are not giving in to, but rather combating subjectivist theories by putting forward the *individualist* side of culture as well as of place (or language and literature in the case of Bakhtin). Bakhtin would never give in to unidimensional definitions of a "milieu" (среды), soil (почвы), or earth (земли) (Bakhtin 1979: 35). A priori, this affirmation of non-objective values combined with the rejection of subjective concreteness, is a paradox and the choice of the 'I' and the 'thou' as a common topic can, finally, only be explained by insisting on this paradox. The only way to get "out" of the paradox was not to talk further about abstract, "everybody's" space, nor about individualist, subjective space, but about that space which exists—in a "dialogical" way—*between* humans whose interconnection is neither abstract nor concrete. This is the place marked off by a "strange" relationship, the relationship between the 'I' and the 'thou.'

Until here, Frank's attempts to delimit psychic life from objective being are identical with Nishida's and Bakhtin's. However, while Frank joined Nishida's philosophy of space almost completely by basing his main argument on *sobornost*, the comparison of Bakhtin and Nishida shows what comparative studies can perhaps show only in the most lucky cases: that the one needed what the other had, and vice versa. Nishida needed the existence of the 'thou' in order to remain close to "concrete" social reality—and he became aware of it very late (only after 1934 when he began transforming *basho* into a place of socio-historical determination). This represents a problem for interpretations of Nishida, and the particular religious, Buddhist connotations of *basho* do not make things easier. And this is the more true since it is especially because of these connotations that his philosophy of place tends, by some people, to be received exclusively as a *religious philosophy* trying to *negatively* overcome rationalist separations of the subjective self and the objective world, or of *noesis* and *noema*. In any case, I want to show in this chapter that Nishida needed a *dialogical challenge* and that we recognize this challenge best when comparing him with Bakhtin.

While for Nishida the 'thou' was a relatively late discovery, Bakhtin was aware of it from his youth; but *he* needed something else. What it is that he needed is actually difficult to spell out, but let me make some suggestions why this could be called "non-Western."[3] My point is that the contradictions between the theoretical positions announced Bakhtin's texts can be resolved, at least to some extent, within a theory of cultural place that is not based on something "positive" but on "nothingness." In other words, instead of looking, for example, for the "positive" side of Dostoevsky's artistic forms, one can approach Bakhtin also by concentrating, from the beginning, on his "negative" side, analogous to the method that has been considered the only appropriate one for the treatment of a "metaphysical" theory of place developed by Nishida.[4]

"Contradictions" are not only present in Bakhtin's arguments themselves, but flow also, as is well known, out of comparisons of his works with each other, even those which chronologically belong close together. I believe that this fact becomes particularly interesting in the context I am trying to create in the present chapter. Already in textbooks one can read that "Dialogic Imagination" contradicts "Dostoevsky's Poetics."[5] I want to emphasize this contradictoriness, because I believe that an approach to Bakhtin's dialogical place of 'I' and 'thou' through Nishida's religio-cultural place of 'I' and 'thou' can indeed produce a new and useful perspective on Bakhtin.

The contradictoriness becomes manifest through a comparison of three of Bakhtin's earlier texts, "Author and Hero," "Discourse in the Novel" (the latter now contained in *Dialogic Imagination*) and "Problems of Dostoevsky's Poetics," works which are, intellectually and historically, immediately related to Bakhtin's reflections on 'I' and 'thou.'[6] In the present chapter I concentrate mainly on these three works. The ultimate incompatibility of the positions announced in these three texts from the 1920s or just after can be summarized thus: The "modernity" presented in the latest text, "Discourse in the Novel," leaves un-centralized "chaos" as the last possibility of the development of human culture, spelling out nothing "positive" in regard to a perspective that can easily appear as pessimistic. Bakhtin speaks out against the "great centralizing tendencies of European verbal-ideological life [that] have sought first and foremost for *unity* in *diversity*," (1975b: 87/274) and criticizes the exclusive "orientation toward unity" (установка на единство) relying on "mono-semic" (односмысленных) and phonetic evidence. However, *where* finally a "real ideologically saturated 'language consciousness'" (ibid.) should be found, he never says.

It is difficult to bring this attitude together with the "authorial discourse" argument of the earliest of the three texts, "Author and Hero" (1924-27). It is equally difficult to assume the compatibility of both ideas with the stylistic theory brought forward in the middle text, "Dostoevsky's Poetics," in which an organic, though "supra-personal" and "transcendental" (Bakhtin 1979: 20), *style* seems to be the final offering of a self-sufficient aesthetic theory of civilization.

This constellation of facts, especially within this comparative analysis of Nishida, raises serious doubts as to whether Bakhtin can really be apprehended as a "social philosopher." When I say that Bakhtin needed a "non-Western logic" I mean, in fact, that his philosophy of dialogue needs a metaphysical foundation that cannot be reduced to a "socio-aesthetic theory," shifting between the insistence on the structurally binding character of laws and institutions on the one hand, and the reduction of Bakhtin's arguments to "aesthetics" on the other. Nor does his philosophy require a kind of neo-mysticism conjuring the otherworldly, unifying powers of "dialogue." It must be said that, at the point where Bakhtin criticism presently stands, there seem to be relatively few alternatives between these two options, the first one presented, roughly speaking, by an American-liberal ("aesthetic") and British "anti-capitalist" coalition, and the second one by a new Russian theological-philosophical movement apparently still searching for its intellectual identity.[7] In both camps, however, nobody has ever thought that Bakhtin's "dialogism" could be based on something like a "metaphysics of nothingness."

When we say thus that our comparison is supposed to push Bakhtin towards a "philosophy of place," we mean that Bakhtin's ambition, particularly visible in the essay "Discourse in the Novel," is to do research into dialogue itself, and not only into the positive or "relevant" components of dialogue. The *"absence* of the author" announced (and at the same time not announced) by Bakhtin in this essay, comes close to our supposition of a *negative* place replacing positive dialogical structures. The same can be said of Bakhtin's avoidance of any positive definition of a *chronotope* as an "idyllic" place of time-place interaction, as well as about other typically Bakhtinian "un-finalized" concepts.

This perspective also permits one to see a coherence between texts that would otherwise be difficult to link to each other. Attempts to establish a *"negative place"* occur not only in the later text but announce themselves, albeit modestly, earlier as well. In "Dostoevsky's Poetics" Bakhtin without hesitation calls the discovered "multiplicity of styles" also the "absence of style" (Bakhtin 1979: 20).

From a comparative perspective, the interpretative struggle between the "disintegration" and the "progressiveness" of Bakhtin's dialogical literary work (and the modern world it symbolizes) may well turn out to be irrelevant. While Nishida is known and appreciated for his use of philosophical paradoxes, any paradoxical input traced in Bakhtin's philosophy—be it only a certain "open-endedness" of a structural framework—runs the risk of being perceived as a drawback. In his book on Bakhtin and democracy, Ken Hirschkop asks: "Does democracy need help from even a reconstructed stylistics, though? Isn't it a matter of institutions and political structures first, and language, if ever, afterwards?" (Hirschkop: 1999: 26) The "problem" with Bakhtin is that the obvious "lack" of "author-ity" in his purely stylistic world leaves nothing but a vague (aesthetic) inter-subjectivity, and this lets him too easily appear to be living "beyond this world." Hirschkop writes with rhetorical irony: "So enthralled is he with the vivid intercourse of socio-ideological languages and the stylistic acrobatics of the novel that he hardly pauses to consider what the point of the style is or how he will justify a world so dominated" (Hirschkop 1999: 77). I want to show here that Bakhtin's, as well as Nishida's, cure for the modern world is neither naïve aestheticism nor a positive theory of communication. Their philosophies should rather be seen as opposing both positive science describing the self in terms of a purely socio-historical environment *and also* aestheticising descriptions of the world.[8]

Einfühlung and Answerability

The gist of Bakhtin's and Nishida's common point about the 'I' and the 'thou' is that both insist on the paradoxical nature of the perception of the Other. Both Bakhtin and Nishida are more outspoken than Frank about the idea of "fusion," from which arises a striking parallelism. On the one hand, one could presuppose that a fusion of the 'I' with the 'thou' could be nothing but beneficial to the 'I' at the moment it wants to understand the 'thou.' One could think that the 'thou' is well *understood* at the very moment a real assimilation of the 'I' to the 'thou' has taken place. However, in that case the 'I' will no longer be the 'I,' and the 'Thou' will no longer be the 'thou.' The aim must rather be to understand the 'Thou' as a 'thou' by maintaining the status of the 'I.' Only if a clear-cut *distinction* between both is maintained is the perception of the 'I' by the 'thou' possible. For Bakhtin, these thoughts, which he pursued with an almost fanatical perseverance, are linked to his lifelong combat against an aesthetics and epistemology of empathy. Bakhtin develops these thoughts in his youthful text "Автор и герой в эстетической деятельности" ("Author and Hero in Aesthetic Action"),[9] an essay on aesthetics heavily indebted to phenomenology and Neo-Kantianism. The young Bakhtin's approach towards the problem of perception consists of pointing again and again to the impossibility of an understanding of the 'Other' as long as this understanding implies a theorization of any kind. Such a theorization or objectification already takes place at the very moment the 'I' attempts to understand the other in the same way in which it understands itself. Bakhtin discovers the essential paradox that the willful negation of differences between the 'I' and the 'thou' through an act of abstraction (as it is represented for example by intuition or *Einfühlung*) does not lead at all to a "concrete" understanding of the other but rather to its antithesis. Intuition, empathy, or any approach substantially implying, as Bakhtin sees it, the idea of a "merging" with the other, will only understand the Other *as the 'I.'* In a dramatic passage in *Art and Answerability* Bakhtin claims:

> Пусть он останется вне меня, ибо в этом своем положении он может видеть и знать, что я со своего места не вижу и не знаю, и может существенно обогатить событие моей жизни. *Только сливаясь с жизнью другого, я только углубляю ее безысходность и только нумерически ее удваиваю.*
> Let him rather remain outside of me, for in that position he can see and know what I myself do not see and do not know from my own place, and he can essentially enrich the event of my own life. If *all* I do is merge with the other's life, I only intensify the want of any issue from within itself that characterizes my own life, and I only duplicate his life numerically (Bakhtin 1994a: 157 /87).

In Bakhtin's view, to understand the 'Other' is rather an act of cultural creation and the idea of a simple "merging" with the other contradicts the concept of an "active" understanding. Bakhtin intends to establish the "Otherness" of the 'thou' as an important component of the 'I''s understanding of the 'thou' *as the 'thou.'* Expressing it in terms that were current in Russia at the time of formalism, one could say that the negation of an essential strangeness clinging to every 'thou' as soon as it is perceived by an 'I' will simply turn the 'thou' into an abstract idea. A concrete 'thou' cannot be understood through its assimilation to an 'I' but only through an act of *reaction* guarantying the autonomous existence of the 'thou' as something "strange." In this way Bakhtin writes:

> Мы не должны ни воспроизводить—сопереживать, подражать, - не художественно воспринимать, а реагировать ответным поступком.
> I must neither reproduce it—imitate or co-experience it—nor apprehend it artistically, but react to it with an answering act (Bakhtin 1994a: 207/148).

The conclusion is that, by *reacting* to the 'thou,' the 'I' understands the 'thou' better than through an act of self-conscious abstraction from itself, even if this abstraction is meant to provide a "neutral" perception of the other.

We should remember now that Nishida's thoughts about the 'I' and the 'thou,' though they occupy such a special position within the development of his philosophy, appear at first sight incompatible with some of his earlier thoughts. If we consider his early definitions of *pure experience* in *Zen no kenkyū*, we recognize *pure experience* as a kind of individual consciousness that is supposed to constitute a "sole reality." Strictly speaking, nothing seems to contradict here the compatibility of Nishida's philosophy with the "idealism" combated by Bakhtin. Nishida insists on a difference between immediate experience and conceptualizing approaches because conceptual universals fail to embrace "individuals," and his alternative to conceptualism remains linked to attempts to grasp the individual "as such" (Nishida 1926: 218; cf. Abe 1988: 363).

Later, in the text "Basho" from 1925, one sees Nishida designing a theory of "place" in which intuition is still guaranteed through a reflection of the self (*jiko*) in the self. In spite of obvious attempts to grasp the process of intuition contained in *pure experience* with the help of a geographical metaphor, the "place" is not thought of in the sense of a socio-historical reality containing a 'thou' or an Other. It seems rather that the individual, subjective consciousness has become "interiorized" to the utmost degree by thinking of the subject as being subsumed in the "predicative thing" called *basho*. This is still *pure experience*, though a certain reflective moment has been installed within the act of intuition. It is not a reflection of the 'I' against a 'thou' but rather of an 'I' within an 'I.' However, even if the Other does not play a role here in "Basho," it is also true that "intuition" stands for more than simply the fusion of a subject with its objective world. Even if the alternative to the "general" is still the "individual," this individual is not thought of as a subsumption of general aspects within one individuality. Let me quote once again this decisive passage:

我々が主客合一と考えられる直覚的立場に入る時でも、意識は一般概念的なるものを離れるのではない、かえって一般概念的なるものの極致に達するのである。〔・・・〕直覚というのが単に主もなく客もないということを意味するならば、それは単なる対象に過ぎない。既に直覚といえば、知るものと知られるものとが区別せられ、しかも　両者が合一するということでなければならぬ。

Even if we adopt an intuitive point of view that will be thought as the unity of subject and object, consciousness will not be detached from the general-conceptual; on the contrary, we attain thus the utmost of the

general-conceptual . . . . If intuition means nothing more than that there
is neither subject nor object, it is no more than an object. As soon as
one talks about intuition, one has already distinguished the knower and
the known and again reunited both (Nishida 1926: 222).

I want to explain this thought by comparing the *basho* to the notion
of play. The individual of *pure experience,* like the individual of the *basho,* is an "individual in action" which does not exist as a substance but
which "comes into play." For Nishida, the *basho* is a place where a certain game determines itself "all alone," without referring to subjective or
objective foundations, because for the game there is nothing but the place
itself. In this place singularities, like "selves" form themselves. A "self"
formed in a place is not formed by following rules borrowed from a
sphere outside the game but the self shapes itself by simply "playing"
what is the game of the place.

This idea, which suggests a strongly paradoxical structure, becomes
understandable when one considers that the game is no "substantial force"
either. A game is not "something" that one can see or measure. A game
is only an action creating its sense all alone while acting. The game's
sense exists—a game is not an arbitrary action—but it exists only inside
a place that is created by the game itself.[10]

Within this framework, the existence of the 'thou' and the dialogical
character of human existence represented a new challenge for Nishida
from the early 1930s. It permitted him to depict *basho,* including the 'I'
and the 'thou,' as dialogically determined. This did not topple his already
existing ideas about *basho* as an activity linked to self-perception (the
integration of the 'thou' into *basho* must probably be seen as an unsolved
problem). On the other hand it helped put things differently. In the texts
immediately following *I and Thou* (*The World of Action,* 1933 and *The
Dialectical World,* 1934, both contained in Nishida 1933-34), the self is
no longer conceived of individualistically: On the contrary, the fact of
seeing the 'thou' as completely detached from the existence of the 'I'
gives rise to criticism of contemporary Marxist worldviews (Dilworth
1978: 250). As a consequence, in Nishida's later texts, we can read
statements like: "a mere isolated individual is nothing at all" (Nishida
1944: 114). *Basho* appears now like a place in which all living and
non-living things come into being: it reflects all individuals and their
mutually determining way-of-being within itself (cf. Abe 1988: 371).
This means that the place still subsumes individuals, but this time "all"
individuals seem to be concerned.

What was it that brought about this change in *I and Thou?* Here Nishida postulates for example, that the 'I' and the 'thou,' because of their
inter-determination, must "flow out of the same environment" (同じ環境
から生れ) (348), and that the 'I' must always be seen as being deter-

mined by a "common consciousness." But what is in question is not at all the fusion of different individual bits of consciousness. A mere "fusion" would not represent a real socio-historical world. Nishida insists that any idea of "merging" would neglect an essential component of human understanding. The act of intuition must incorporate the knowledge of the 'thou' *as the 'thou'* by the 'I' as it is expressed in this central passage from *I and Thou*:

> Intuition—whose model is normally thought as artistic intuition—does not mean that we are immediately united with things. It is rather that at the bottom of ourselves resides the absolute other, so that at the bottom of its self, the self has to become the 'Other.' 'I' and the 'Other' do not become one here, but I am asked to see in myself the absolute other. This might be an unthinkable contradiction (Nishida 1932: 390).

The "ground" of intuition is not a subjective interiority contained in the 'I' but it is the relationship between the 'I' and the Other through which the Other becomes a 'thou.' The idea of *place* becomes here a type of intuition that will never become "numerical" or abstract. It will never run out of concrete content as long as the 'I' sees itself in the 'thou.' One can say that the "place" creates a kind of "play of reflection" in which the 'I' and the 'thou' are not really opposed to each other, but are, even *before* any reflection takes place, determining each other.

In Nishida therefore, the 'I' does not represent a firm subjective basis into which, within the process of understanding, the 'Other' could or should be integrated through assimilation. If the 'I' and the 'thou' approach each other, then they do so not in order to merge until the 'thou' becomes the 'I,' but rather in order to discover the 'Other-ness' not only of the 'thou' but also of the 'I.' I would argue that, for Nishida from the time he wrote the text 'I' and 'thou,' "self-consciousness," even in regard to its profoundest psychological layers, is not based on self-perception but on a *social consciousness*.[11]

Would it now be wrong to say that what Nishida characterized in the passage quoted above from "Basho" as an empty generality whose claim to be "objective" might be justified, but which fails to provide any "knowledge" about the "objective" world that the subject intends to perceive, comes close to Bakhtin's notion of an empty and "numerical" "duplication" of the other? Nishida criticizes the idea of a "merging" of subject and object as a type of intuition that will lead to abstraction and objectification. We have seen that Bakhtin criticizes the same idea because it will lead to the establishment of a "numerical reality." Also for Bakhtin, this numerical reality can be avoided the moment we respect the paradoxical relationship between the 'I' and the 'thou.' Nishida's ideas not only fully correspond to Bakhtin's concerning the "social character" of psychic life, language, art, and society, but they imply a certain logic of "answerability," i.e., a logic of human understanding that attributes more importance to active *reaction*, than to passive *intellectualization*. David Dilworth has said that in Nishida's later thought "personal action," presupposes "the concrete fusion of the individual and environment, particular and universal, and subject and object in the dialectical field of the social historical world" (Dilworth 1978: 250). This means that "social and historical components of the real world are illustrated in every instance of personal action" (ibid.). This "fusion" is not an empirical fusion in the sense of empathy or of even more abstract scientific theories. The idea of action actually prevents it from becoming such a fusion. "I act therefore I am" is Nishida's way of avoiding the Cartesian *cogito*. In regard to the consciousness of the 'I,' one could paraphrase Nishida's sentence as "I *re-act* therefore I am." It is most efficiently expressed in the phrase: "I know you because you answer me, and you know me because I answer you" (私は汝が私に応答することによって汝を知り、汝は私が汝に応答することによって私を知るのである) (Nishida 1932: 392).

The idea, as it stands here, is certainly more than merely reminiscent of Bakhtin. In Nishida's *I and Thou*, the act of "answering each other" or the "echo-like encounter of those who are opposed" (ibid.) is presented as the basis of human existence and contrasts with all concepts of "unification." Even artistic activity is based on this kind of "answerability between persons" (人格と人格との応) (394), because art also exists in the realm of reality in the sense of "actuality"; and such an actuality takes place only within an encounter of 'I' and 'thou.'

For Bakhtin, in carnival, as he shows in his Dostoevsky book as well as in his revised thesis on Rabelais (Bakhtin 1965: 98/88), the individual person manages to exist, at least for a while, in an "in-between," i.e., in a place "between" persons, and negates in this way its biological body in order to become one with the "people," with mankind, and with the entire cosmos. Here, the body is no longer biological but *historical*. In this sense, also Bakhtin's idea of playacting as a unity of imagination and creation overlaps (as is best shown by his concept of carnival) with a kind of place that is half real and half playacted; and here one finds an obvious element indicating a certain "negativity" in his idea of consciousness.

It is true that Nishida would most probably not have been willing to push the playful fusion of the 'I' with the 'thou' as far as that. His philosophy of the 'I' and the 'thou' is developed within the limited framework of *metaphysics* concerned with the unification of opposites. Still, Nishida would agree that for example history could be seen not only as something "*real*" but also as a realization of the "*unreal*" (cf. Schinzinger 1958: 60). Do such statements really need to be read as quasi-religious affirmations or can they not also be understood as being concerned with "real" human relationships? Any detection of parallel developments and differences with Bakhtin is here supportive of an understanding of Nishida's thought.

As for Bakhtin, he liked, in his juvenile fervor, to present the world as a stage in which all action is playacting. However, even while conjuring the most extreme forms of confusion about human identities (for example in carnival), Bakhtin always seems to be ready to concede that carnival needs to be seen as a ". . . modus of interrelationship of man with man" (Bakhtin 1979: 141/123; cf. Medvedev 1928: 91/64ff). It would certainly require much more research than could be presented within the limits of this chapter, but perhaps specialists of consciousness studies will some day find similarities between Bakhtin's "dialogical consciousness" and Nishida's concept of consciousness as a manifestation of *basho*. Several points could support such a hypothesis: Bakhtin opposes not only laughter to seriousness, dialogue to monologue, coincidence to necessity, but also dream to *logos*. Logos is not only "logic" but also language. One needs now to be aware that, in Western philosophy, *logos* is seen as residing "above the contradictions of spatial and temporal existence" (Dilworth 1978: 260). This is exactly the point that Nishida also criticizes. Bakhtin prefers non-materialized psychic life that is not yet molded in language to linguistic expression.[12]

Stylistic Unity and Nothingness

Bakhtin's dynamic unity of style, which appears, especially in "Discourse in the Novel," as "self-negating," i.e., simultaneously present and absent, suggests conclusions concerning a parallel development of Bakhtin's and Nishida's "place" defined through an ontology of play. Can the idea of the "organic" be seen, at least when it comes to art (but perhaps even elsewhere), as a *stylistic* unity? To this interesting question Bakhtin and Nishida give similar answers. Bakhtin somehow "borrowed" the concept of style to describe the interdependence of language and ethics. Because he wanted to avoid any Kantian formalism, his ideas on cultural dialogicity are based on the rejection of *any stylistic unity* (be it formal, empirical or even spiritual). Still, the idea of a cultural unity is introduced by recognizing the existence of a "place of play" in which the signs provided by social and historical reality interact. In this way, stylistic unity exists, but it must be "played" so it can be shaped after the ontological conditions provided by a concrete place. Nishida claims that art styles would represent a contradictory "self-identity of subject and environment" when he writes:

芸術的様式は主体と環境との矛盾的自己同一として、民族とその
環境とによって 異ならなければならない (. . . art styles, as con-
tradictory self-identity of subject and environment, are, according to the
respective people and environment, distinct from each other.) (Nishida
1941: 238).

There is a paradox clinging to style, which incited Bakhtin to develop a methodology (of dialogue) intending to show the insufficiencies of
the quasi-structuralist approaches of Wölfflin when it comes to the novels of Dostoevsky. Nishida has a similar idea in mind when writing:

ウェルフリンの様式範疇の如きものの中に、東洋芸術の様式をは
め込めてよいであろうか。私は疑なきを得ない (If Eastern Art
could ever be forced into something like Wölfflin's Categories of Style?
I very much doubt so.) (Nishida 1941: 241).

Nishida is aware that the price to pay for abstract definitions of
"styles" is the transformation of spatial extension into something abstract.
There is, in Nishida's philosophy, an essential relationship between style
and place. Style appears like a *basho*; it has no geographical extension
but is a matter of mirroring self-reflection.

From here we are led to a consideration of Nishida's idea of "mirroring" (*utsusu* 映す), a difficult term essential for the 'I'-'thou' relationship as well as for all issues related to it, and we are led to a comparison of this notion with corresponding thoughts of the Bakhtin Circle. At
the root of the idea of Nishida's mirroring is the Buddhist insight that
being can best appear "as it is" in the "Mirror of Emptiness." *Basho* does
not simply contain an 'I' "in" itself as if it were a subject surrounded by
an objective environment. Nishida uses the Buddhist metaphor of mirroring to *elude* such a directional relatedness between subject and object,
as well as the separation of subject and object itself. Nishida's "mirroring"
is not a simple "reflection"—rather it needs a certain "negative" surplus
since it is supposed to produce an inter-subjective *consciousness*. The
above-quoted passage from "Artistic Creation as a Formative Act" continues with a sentence attempting to specify in which way Worringer's
"limitation of space" could nevertheless lead to the creation of a *basho*.
What would be needed is an "artistic" input that will be based on the effect of mirroring:

… それが芸術的立場であるかぎり、同時に物において自己を映
す、物において自己 を見るということが含まれていなければな
らない (. . . as far as this [limitation of space] produces itself artisti-

cally, it immediately turns things into a mirror, and simultaneously implies that the Self is seen in things (Nishida 1941: 238).

As a matter of fact, the described complex relationship between 'I' and "things" represented such a "mirroring" because the 'I' sees itself in "things" and vice versa. The terms of the Russian formalists, "alienation" and "self-alienation," are suggestive here: would not a "simple," narcissist reflection of the 'I' in the 'I,' produce an "alienation" or even a "self-alienation" of the subject? What is necessary is a more "open" mirroring which includes in itself an entire environment that is produced through this act of mirroring.

In principle, such a philosophical model of open, or "negative," "mirroring" in the context of reflections on the formation of consciousness is not limited to the Buddhist sphere but can be found also in the West. One can quote Richard Rorty, who has discussed the problem of consciousness within cognitive processes by using as a methodological guideline the metaphor of the mirror. His main argument, developed in *Philosophy and the Mirror of Nature*, suggests that

> . . . it is as if man's Glassy Essence, the Mirror of Nature, only became visible to itself when slightly clouded. A neutral system can't have clouds but a mind can. So minds, we conclude, cannot be neutral systems (Rorty 1980: 86).

As a matter of fact, what Rorty calls "clouds" could also be called "distortion" or "refraction," which is not just a mirroring but which contains a certain negative surplus. In any case, it is during a creative mirroring process that a "place" is produced that involves both the object and the self-conscious subject. The "cloudy" reflection that Rorty speaks of can never be pure.

For Bakhtin, in "Discourse in the Novel," the process of refraction (*prelomlenie*) as a producer of style represents a central topic. For the Bakhtin Circle in general, the opposition of refraction and reflection represents one of its main theoretical tools when it comes to statements about the formation of consciousness. Voloshinov insists, in an essay that also appeared in the early 1920s (thus at a time when his relationship with Bakhtin was close) that human existence "отраженное в знаке, не просто отражено, но преломлено" (". . . reflected in sign is not merely reflected but *refracted*," Voloshinov 1929: 31/23).[13] This is, of course, because "таким образом, конститутивным моментом для языковой формы, как для знака, является вовсе не ее сигнальная себетождественность, а ее специфическая изменчивость" (". . . the constituent factor for the linguistic form, as for the sign, is not at all its self-identity as signal but its specific variability," Voloshinov 1929:

82/69). "Variability" means here that we have to do with a refraction of the individual through its social environment that is seen as a process of *stylization* through which the individual as well as the environment create a "stylistic existence." For Bakhtin all essential devices of dialogism and polyphony are embedded within such a "refracting" act of stylization. This process of refraction is polyphonic, which is also the reason why no conventional *stylistics* has ever been able to grapple with this problem. The environment within which the refraction takes place must be *open* because the world itself is a dialogue involving many opposing elements constantly refracting each other. The result of this polyphonic refraction can never be "*one* style" or "one consciousness," but it will be an open field of consciousness appearing like a polyphonic stylistic event.

For Bakhtin, this refraction is directly opposed to the idea of *Einfühlung* as it has been presented at the beginning of this chapter. Any "пассивом отображения удвоения переживания другого человека во мне" ("passive mirroring or duplication of another's experience within myself," Voloshinov 1929: 170/102), on the other hand, which does not include the active, stylizing act of answering necessary for real understanding, must be likened to positivism or the impressionist aesthetic of an empty play (161/92). Bakhtin's "theory of culture" is based on this concept of mirroring, as he writes in "Discourse in the Novel":

> Languages of heteroglossia (разноречия), like mirrors that face each other, each of which in its own way reflects (остражает) a little piece, a tiny corner of the world, force us to guess at and grasp behind their inter-reflecting aspects for a world that is broader, more multi-leveled and multi-horizoned than would be available to one language, one mirror (225-26/414-15).[14]

Because a cultural environment can come about only through the dialectical refraction of the self with itself as well as with its environment, the mirroring effect of the *basho* must be active. Only in this way can feelings and will produce themselves within the "self-reflecting mirror" (自己自身を照らす鏡, Nishida 1926: 213).[15]

Further Perspectives

Bakhtin, Zen, and Laughter

In spite of obvious parallels between Bakhtin and Nishida, some people might still have doubts whether Bakhtin, with his adoration of laughter, carnival, and the grotesque, will not always remain a far cry from Nishida. His carnivalistic tendency lets him appear close to Nietzsche but certainly not to a Nishida who is as un-dionysian a philosopher as can be. However, Nishida's philosophy is directly determined by personal Zen experience; and the subject of laughter, especially when it is given, as in Bakhtin's philosophy, a religious quality, is not so far removed from Zen culture. Both Bakhtin and Zen use "laughter" as a means of opposing moral abstractions. Bakhtin wanted to challenge the rigid morality of Russian Orthodox religion (for which laughter is impermissible) but also, or even more, the Western rational spirit "controlling" laughter by submitting it to a hierarchy of civilizational values. Neither Bakhtin nor Zen set out to design an alternative abstract ethics. In both, laughter or carnival are supposed to establish a certain "affective feeling" that is supposed to make rational reflections more "earth-bound." Both Bakhtin and Zen pursue the idea of an "un-materialized" as well as "un-formalized" kind of laughter. Modernity, as Bakhtin explains in his Rabelais book, "formalizes the heritage of carnival themes and symbols" (Bakhtin 1965: 55/47). Finally, "the bourgeois nineteenth century respected only satirical laughter, which was actually not laughter but rhetoric" (59/51). This means also that Bakhtin's interest in the grotesque and in laughter as typical manifestations of Medieval and early Renaissance cultures is directed towards the *pre-linguistic* expression of these phenomena. In general, Bakhtin preaches the necessary "loss of a feeling for language as myth, that is, as an absolute form of thought" (1975b: 178-79/367). "Truth" is for him "non-linguistic." It does, as he says in "Discourse in the Novel," "not seek words; she is afraid to entangle herself (запутаться) in the word, to soil herself in verbal pathos" (1975b: 123/309). The parallel with Zen Buddhism's and, in particular, Nishida's ideas of pre-linguistic or non-linguistic experience is obvious.

The "Body of People"

Even more interesting is the fact that, linked to these thoughts on the non-materialized perception of the world, Bakhtin manages to establish a certain concept of the *body* that appears particularly non-Western and non-modern. Bakhtin insists that the "exaggeration" of the grotesque is supposed to be understood "as such," that is as the original experience it represented to the people who experienced and produced it and not as an act of *Verfremdung*. In no case should it be molded into abstract concepts depending on moral categories (designing it as a *caricature*) (Bakhtin 1965: 71/62), or psychology (designing it as the *id* or as an expression of *power*) (56/49). It is out of these considerations for the importance of laughter in premodern Western culture, so closely linked to the bodily grotesque, that Bakhtin develops a concept of the *body* whose resemblance with Nishida's cocept of the body cannot be escaped. In which other Western author could we read that in pre-Renaissance culture the body was no individual entity but prolonged in the form of a "body of the people" (народный тело)? Only since the Renaissance, Bakhtin writes, "the individual body was presented apart from its relation to the ancestral body of the people" (35/29). Bakhtin is convinced that in premodern Europe

> the bodily element is deeply positive. It is presented not in private, egoistic form, severed from the other spheres of life, but as something universal, representing all the people. As such it is opposed to severance from the material and bodily roots of all the people. As such it is opposed to severance from the material bodily roots of the world. . . . We repeat: the body and bodily life have here a cosmic and at the same time an all-people's character; this is not the body and its physiology in the modern sense of the words, because it is not individualized. The material bodily principle is contained not in the biological individual, not in the bourgeois ego, but in the people, a people who are continually growing and renewed. This is why all that is bodily becomes grandiose, exaggerated, immeasurable (Bakhtin 1965: 24/19).

Rabelais is certainly Western, but Bakhtin is among the few critics who insist that in regard to this writer, modern Western concepts of culture and the body need to be annulled if his ideas are really to be understood. It is remarkable that one of the results of this approach is not only, as mentioned above, a rather Japanese-sounding concept of the human as an "in-between," but also a non-individualist conception of the "body of people" that remains strangely reminiscent of Nishida's "historical body" (歴史的身体, see Nishida 1937 and 1938: 91ff), a notion Nishida developed later in his life. The "body of people" is not the biological body but the body seen as a *function* (機能) existing within a certain place. "Bodily existence can be thought of by extending its function all the way to language," writes Nishida (Nishida 1937: 277). The body is not an object used by individual consciousness but always actively involved in the world.

Conclusion

Like Nishida, Bakhtin does not provide a comprehensive theory of communication, but notions like inter-subjectivity, self-reflection, or multi-linguality are supposed to be accepted as autonomous phenomena of consciousness. There is no elucidation of a technique or formalist device that would make obvious how this consciousness would come about. On the contrary, consciousness is a device itself—and the only one—producing itself autonomously. Like Nishida, Bakhtin does not believe that the potential world (of consciousness, of art, or of culture) would preexist and wait to be uncovered.

In Nishida's later philosophy the 'I'-'thou' relation has been extended to a relation between the 'I' and the World: The immediate, "irrational" experience of the Other through action or an "answering act" leads, for Nishida, to self-realization through action within a dialogically organized stylistic place. Only when this dialogical "place" is philosophically established are we able to also see the world as a world of mutually determining individuals.

I hope to have shown that the particular Buddhist connotations of the *basho* which negates all distinctions between *noesis* and *noema*, do not make Nishida's philosophy "metaphysical" *in an exclusive way.*[16]

The early American philosopher Ernest Hocking has said that religion "speaks not primarily to the man-within-the-nation but to the man-within-the-world" (Hocking 1956: 47). However, strictly speaking, there is no reason to say that history and sociology would *not* be part of a "World" but only of a "Nation." On the contrary, it is precisely within the historical and social world that reality is so much mixed with imagination that an analysis in terms of "institutions" will probably be unable to grasp the essence of any dialogical-ideological environment. What both Nishida and Bakhtin have in common is that their "dialogical consciousness" includes some of the kind of negativity that neither the "positive" social sciences *or* traditional Western aesthetics have been able to attain.

Notes

1. There are, of course, deeper *historical* reasons for the parallels between Bakhtin and East Asian thought in general that run along the lines of those facts that have been mentioned in the previous chapters of this book. Bakhtin's insistence that the "unity of *being* in idealism is turned into the principle of unity of

consciousness" (Bakhtin 1979: 76), is certainly reminiscent not only of East Asian sources but also of Bakhtin's own, more "mystically-minded" predecessors, the pre-revolutionary, "organicist" thinkers Vladimir Solov'ëv (1853-1900) and Lev Lopatin (1855-1922) and, finally, Semën Frank.

2. Cf. Berque and Nys 1997; Berque 2000; and Sauzet and Berque 1999.

3. In general, allusions in critical literature to Bakhtin's possible links with East Asian theories remain suggestive, if not to say mystifying, typically like the brief footnote in an article by Hwa Yol Jung containing the information that "Bakhtin's dialogics is most close to the Chinese transformative logic of *yin* and *yang*" (Hwa Yol Jung 1998: note 7). Another example would be a statement by the eminent Bakhtin scholar Viacheslav V. Ivanov who points, when pondering possible parallel developments to a Bakhtinian 'I'-'thou' line of thought in the history of philosophy, to a tract by a Buddhist logician entitled "Obosnovanie chuzhoi odushevlennosti" (roughly translatable as: "The Substantiation of the Presence of Soul in the Other") which had been translated into Russian by Fedor Shtcherbatskoi, the famous author of *Buddhist Logic*. Ivanov indicates neither the author of the "tract" nor where it has been published, but insists that it had been translated in the early 1920s, the time when Bakhtin developed his thoughts on the 'I' and the 'thou' (Ivanov 1993: 5). It should be noted how amazingly close the title of this Buddhist tract comes to topics treated by Russian philosophers at the end of the nineteenth century, for example the Neo-Kantian Alexander Vvedensky.

4. There is enough reason to believe that Bakhtin's refusal of any "either/or," obvious in his philosophy since at least "Discourse in the Novel" (1934-35), is indeed part of a search for a more outspoken "non-Western logic." This becomes clear even through very general considerations. First, Bakhtin is working against the oppositions of subjective-objective, individual-general, and all those binary oppositions that Western metaphysics usually takes for granted. He refuses *both* the linguistics of an "abstract objectivism" represented by Saussure, *and* "individualistic subjectivism" represented by the tradition of Humboldt and Vossler. Furthermore, in texts preceding "Discourse in the Novel," his appreciation of Dostoevsky's non-linear and non-historical way of presenting events within a novel is incompatible with Western metaphysical, scientific, linear, concepts of time. From Dostoevsky's works Bakhtin derived his ideas of ambivalence and polyphony which are essentially subversive in their ambition to make impossible the establishment of a "global" truth, by giving preference to different "local" truths existing next to each other within a single discourse. Also, his related idea of dialogue does not follow the progressive structure of Hegelian dialectics but becomes, as an eternal "dialogicity," an "end in itself" (как самоцель) (Bakhtin 1979: 252 and 338). Finally, this lets dialogue appear as something like a *consciousness*, but not a conceptualized, graspable consciousness designed by Western psychoanalysis, but rather the consciousness of an author whose intentionality is "deep-seated" though not absent (Bakhtin 1975a: 129-30). This is where one can find, once again, the refusal of an either/or. In spite of the "chaotic" character of the Dostoevskian consciousness that Bakhtin seems to adopt as something "positive," he never announces the dissolution of sense in literature whatsoever, thus never giving way to pure avant-garde devices or even "postmodernism" of any sort. Bakhtin continues to believe that "in spite of it all" the "consciousness of the author," determined by an "artistic thinking"

(художественный мыслеие, 360) remains a reliable source of meaning. The poetical character of the work is, and remains, "organic" and "coherent" (9).

5. This is all the more so remarkable because "Dostoevsy's Poetics" is not represented here by the book of 1929 but by the entirely overhauled version from 1963.

6. Ken Hirschkop has crystallized the incompatibility of the three different positions announced in the three texts from the 1920s very well (Hirschkop 1999: 73ff).

7. For the opposition of these two tendencies see Hirschkop 1999: 6-7; and Bazhanov 1999.

8. The German heritage that both authors share needs to be mentioned. Both Nishida and Bakhtin can appear as typical representatives of *scholars* imbued with German hermeneutic and Neo-Kantian philosophy of their time, and were heavily influenced by Dilthey and Rickert. Their German-biased education often becomes obvious even in regard to the bibliographical angle they choose when it comes to art theory. Both philosophers can be expected to quote, for example, Semper, Riegl, Wölfflin, and Worringer as art theorists whose works merit discussion. Another immediate parallel is that Bakhtin's research on the relationship between the 'I' and the 'thou' was inspired by Martin Buber's book *Ich und Du*. Cf. also the short essay "Zur Geschichte des dialogischen Prinzips," same volume). However, though it is known that Nishida also read this book, it is uncertain whether his own work with the same title was already influenced by it or not. As Ryōsuke Ohashi has pointed out, Nishida mentions Buber's book for the first time in his diary on August 20th 1934, thus two years after the appearance of his own study (cf. R. Ohashi 2000: 342). See also James Heisig who claims in his article on Nishida and Buber that Nishida "had not read Buber's book but did know of it indirectly through the writings of the dialectical theologian, Friedrich Gogarten" (Heisig 2000). In *Ich und Du*, Buber attempts to redefine the value of a personal 'thou' as an alternative to an alienated, modern environment in which the "Other" is mainly experienced as a numerical accumulation of information. Buber's theory of the 'I' and the 'thou,' which was so essential for Bakhtin, has had considerable influence on alternative formulations of the idea of *place* as opposed to modern concepts of *space* as a geometrical extension in the twentieth century. The authentic experience of "place-like phenomena" dear to Western philosophers of space has been successfully related to Buber's 'I-thou' experience. Cf. Relph 1976: "An unselfconscious experience of space as an authentic sense of place is rather like the type of relationship characterized by Martin Buber as 'I-thou,' in which the subject and object, person and place, divisions are wholly replaced by the relationship itself" (65). And: "An 'I-thou' experience of place is a total and unselfconscious involvement in which person and place are indissociable" (78). See also Hase 1998 on the matter.

9. Bakhtin 1994. Fragments or, as Clark and Holquist also say, different unfinished attempts to write the same book, from a period between 1918 and 1924. Another essay contained in the same volume is "Art and Answerability," a piece from 1919 and his first published work. English translations of these essays are contained in Liapunov & Holquist: *Art and Answerability: Early Essays* ed. by M. Holquist & V. Liapunov (Austin: University of Texas Press 1990).

10. Ryōsuke Ohashi has shown in his study of the *basho* and the idea of "play" that Nishida's theory of the place has affinities with existing theories of play/game. When drawing links with Neumann and Morgenstern's game theory, Ohashi is eager to show that any theory of play/game should not reduce social and mental phenomena to *mathematical* phenomena by redescribing the world as a "numerical reality" (Ohashi 2000: 339ff). In Ohashi's view, Nishida's theory could consciously avoid this because the *basho* is designed as a quantity bearing an essentially "negative" character.

11. Nishida's reflection of the 'I' against the 'thou' produces even a certain conception of sociological time: The historical world as a single, eternal presence, is determined by a dialectics of time based on an answering play of 'I' and 'thou': "今日の私は 昨日の私を汝と見ることによって、 昨日の私は今日 の私 を汝と見る ことによって、私個人的自己の自覚というものが成立 するのである、非連続の連続として我々の個人的自覚というものが成立 するのである" (Today's 'I' sees yesterday's 'I' as a 'thou,' and yesterday's 'I' sees today's 'I' as a 'thou.' In this way arises self-consciousness as a discontinuous continuity, Nishida 1932: 415). The 'I' is neither general nor natural but *historical*, and the ideas put forth by the Bakhtin Circle about "time as events of social intercourse" (Medvedev 1928: 160/102ff) seem to also apply to this conception of time.

12. An early statement deploring the strategies of "material aesthetics" seems to contain the whole program of the Bakhtin Circle's anti-Freudian campaign against "materialized," isolated bits of psyche: "Any feeling, deprived of the object that gives it meaning, reduces to a bare factual (голо-фактического) state of the psyche, and extra-cultural state" (Bakhtin 1975a: 14/264). In another early text, in his Dostoevsky study, Bakhtin says: "When we look at each other, two different worlds are reflected in the pupils of our eyes" (Bakhtin 1979: 168). This idea clearly establishes a self-determining world within which the subject is not opposed to a material world, but in which the true consideration of a socio-historical reality manages to overcome subjective rationalism. In the same book Bakhtin says about Dostoevsky: "It is not the multiplicity of fates and lives in a single objective world as seen by a single authorial consciousness that develops in his work, but precisely *the multiplicity of equal consciousnesses with their worlds* which is combined here, preserving their own integrity in the unity of a certain event" (Bakhtin 1979: 140).

13. The notion of refraction becomes important for the establishment of the human, inter-individual, *sign* in opposition to the "animal" *signal*. Cf. Voloshinov 1929: 81/68. In Voloshinov's work, the word "reflection" almost never appears alone, but is usually accompanied by the term "refraction" in order to show that what is in question is not a simple reflection of signs but their refraction in society. Cf. Voloshinov 1930: 5. The idea is developed by Bakhtin, especially in "Discourse in the Novel," but can be seen even in his latest texts.

14. Interestingly, Bakhtin's previously mentioned idea of "duplication" has also been translated by Emerson and Holquist as "mirroring." Cf. "Discourse in the Novel: "But even a more concrete *passive* understanding of the meaning of the utterance, an understanding of the speaker's intention insofar as that understanding remains purely passive, purely receptive, contributes nothing new to the word under consideration, only mirroring (дублирует) it, seeking, at its most

ambitious, merely the full reproduction of that which is already given in the world" (1975b: 94/281).

15. The synthesis flowing out of this is that Nishida's mirror effect is not linked to *naturalism* but rather it is grounded on a *cultural stylistics* for which the moment of the refraction of the world is more important than its mere mirroring. We are reminded here of the fact that Nishida's self-reflecting mirror is not a cliché-like pan-Asian quietism, which, on principle, makes no effort to actively refract nature, but accepts the world as it is in order to merely reproduce it. Nobuyuki Yuasa says about the production of *haiku* poems in the foreword to his translation of Issa's *Oraga Haru*, that *haiku* aesthetics of "objectivism" which claims to "learn about the bamboo only from the bamboo," would be no "incitement to simple naturalism but rather for true symbolic expression. The intention of the *haiku* poet is not simply to set the mirror up to nature . . . but to find identity in nature" (Issa 1960: 18). Similarly, when Nishida insists on the *basho*'s function as a self-reflecting play, he does not have in mind an organic environment perfectly reproducing nature, but rather, to use an expression which repeatedly occurs in *Art and Morality*, a "style [that] is self-awareness in action" (Nishida 1921-23: 32).

16. NAKAMURA Yūjirō is convinced that Nishida's philosophy would, being purely religious and concerned with "transcendental problems," remain incompatible with concrete questions concerning a socio-historical environment. Nishida's "religious metaphysics" would, on principle, be inappropriate for an examination of history and society. These would need to be examined, as Nakamura says, in terms of institutions (Nakamura 2000: 375).

Chapter Five

From Community to Time-Space Development: N. S. Trubetzkoy, NISHIDA Kitarō, and WATSUJI Tetsurō

Community and Society

As mentioned in Chapter Three, Emmanuel Kant defines in Section 20 of the *Critique of Judgment*[1] the "community sense" (*Gemeinsinn*) as the human ability to judge according to the same "feeling" (*Gefühl*). While common sense (*sensus communis*) communicates common forms of cognition, the human attitude towards community is not based on reason and understanding. The *Gemeinsinn*—and thus community itself—is a matter of subjectivity that transcends the feeling of the single person in order to become *common*. For Kant, community is not a matter of common *reasoning* but of common judgments about taste and ethical matters.[2] The reflection of the Kantian model against non-Western models permits us, in the present chapter, to examine a supplementary aspect of the community. The Japanese and Russian philosophers find a way of defining the nation *spiritually* without ending up in political totalitarianism. Even more, they incorporate a moment of convergence into their theories that represents a model of cultural cooperation.

Japanese society might by definition represent the ideal example of a Kantian community united through common judgments about taste. As mentioned in Chapter Three, Roy Andrew Miller has written that in the seventeenth century, Japan, "in spite of civil unrest, was still united in what may be thought of as a fixed axis of basic taste."[3] Miller wrote this in a book on Japanese ceramics and his sentence has no further political implications. *Philosophers* who come from such an "aesthetically united" country and who decide to philosophize about "culture," on the other hand, *will* have to face questions about their attitude towards particularism.

The two preceding chapters defined Japanese and Russian conceptions of space and community as being due to common ideas about the 'I' and the 'thou' as well as to particular models of inter-subjectivity and self-reflection. In the present chapter I want to compare, once again, Russian and Japanese notions of community and space, but this time by crystallizing their internal dynamics that leads them to combined uses of *space* and *time* and a common notion of time-space development.

The point of departure is, once again, the *sensus communis*. Some characteristic strains of thought that exist in both Russia and Japan had similar starting points, overcame similar problems and arrived at similar results. In general, in Japan and Russia, the nostalgia for the *community* has been strong because one felt that in *society* through modernization something of the *particularity* of one's culture had been lost.[4] As a consequence, both in Japan and in Russia allusions to the German sociologist Ferdinand Tönnies' book *Gemeinschaft und Gesellschaft*[5] (Community and Society) are frequent (see Chapter Three). At the same time, the expressed nostalgia not always simply suggested to replace modern *society* with a more archaic *community*. While society has frequently been seen as a degradation or loss of community, "community" can also signify the loss of society. The advancement of "community" can signify the degradation of the free citizen who enjoys all the privileges a sovereign society can offer. In this chapter I first want to show how NISHIDA Kitarō, WATSUJI Tetsurō and Nicolas S. Trubetzkoy fundamentally rethought the meaning of national self-determination. I will then show that all three philosophers suggest the existence of a non-linear movement of convergence as a model for cultural cooperation. In the end I associate the Japanese as well as the Russian ideas with neo-Darwinian versions of the theme of evolution as it has been developed by Henri Bergson, Gilles Deleuze, and Felix Guattari.

Ferdinand Tönnies distinguished between community (*Gemeinschaft*) that is determined by natural will (*Wesenswille*) and society (*Gesellschaft*) dependent on rational will (*Kürwille*). References to Tönnies are frequent in Watsuji and Nishida.[6] Apart from that, also MIKI Kiyoshi and RŌYAMA Masamichi were working, in their Shōwa Research Association, on a *Gemeinschaft*-like, typically "Oriental," brand of community called *kyōdōtai*.[7] For Japan as an emerging agrarian community, Tönnies' organic community could appear as an alternative to modern models of society. A *minzoku* (community) could be seen as a natural community that had not yet been mediated by the state, unlike the *kokumin* (society).

In Nineteenth Century Russia the Slavophiles[8] accused rationalistic models of social organization based on Roman law of corroding the community (Kireevsky) and of undermining organic social totalities. In particular, the Slavophiles reevaluated the notion of *sobornost'*, an old notion that represented already for the Orthodox Church an "organic synthesis of multiplicity and unity."[9] For the orthodox tradition *sobornost'* is a *spiritual* unity of supra-personal and atemporal nature that comes close to a religio-aesthetic consciousness than to a political unity.[10]

Though Tönnies belongs to the next generation of social thinkers, his organic understanding of the community that cannot be grasped by rationalism comes very close to that of the Slavophiles. The "supplement" the Slavophiles provide is that they present society as a derivative of the Roman "state" and see "community" as an all-unifying totality. Tönnies' themes, enriched by Slavophile-like anti-Western (anti-Roman/American) motives, recur in Japanese discussions of the early Twentieth Century. Tönnies himself was influenced by conservative German philosophers like Justus Möser and Adam Müller who agitated against French rationalism around 1800.[11] This brings him indeed temporally close to the Slavophiles[12] which shows that the problem of Japan's transformation from a people to a nation reached the Japanese consciousness relatively late (Naoki SAKAI even holds that only Maruyama's *Studies of Tokugawa Japan* brought up this problem). The curious time gap persists in other contexts. Totalitarian spatial metaphors like Watsuji's *fūdo* resemble the Slavophile's *sobornost'* or Nicolai Y. Danilevsky's cultural space to the extent that all of them are said to develop out of a close relationship between nature and history.[13] It appears extremely strange that a concept like *fūdo* could be developed in the 1920s.

What *fūdo*, the Slavophiles' *sobornost'* as much as Tönnies' *Gemeinschaft* are all lacking is a certain "negativity." These three models are static spaces within which contradictions between the conscious and the unconscious, the conflict between past and present, as well as the possibility of overlapping of totalities cannot and will not be considered. They are spaces in which authenticity has been achieved through a simple and idealizing identification of time *with* space. In the writings of the botanist and historian Danilevsky (who was important for the develop-

ment of Eurasianist thought), the Slavophiles, and Watsuji, we are
haunted by specters of such totalitarian spaces because any cohabitation
of individuals is seen here in an almost one-dimensional way, excluding
the possibility of a dynamic time-space development that was dear to
Nishida or the Eurasianists.[14] Watsuji and the Slavophiles see community
as a unity in society and culture (Bellah about Watsuji), or as a Durk-
heimian "harmony of collective representations" (Walicki about the
Slavophiles)[15] in which man as a subject is simply owned by the totality
(Sakai on Watsuji).[16] In other words, Watsuji's *fūdo*, like the Slavophiles' *sobornost'*, ignore an essential moment of difference and dislocation within space and within culture and remain unable to see community
though a certain time-space development that constantly delocalizes
fixed spatial or temporal positions. Though Watsuji's main aim was to
redefine space, and not just imprison the individual in an inherited conception of space, the metaphysical notion of self-negation, linked to the
theory of pure experience rooted in Buddhist philosophy, has not been
incorporated in these ideas about the formation of the state through *Gemeinschaft*.

While all this has frequently been stated, it seems that something
important has been overlooked. Let me contrast two main critics of
Watsuji, Robert Bellah and Naoki SAKAI who each approach Watsuji
from a different angle.

While Bellah finds fault with Watsuji for not defining social existence in terms of democracy (Bellah 589), Sakai chides Watsuji that he
never attempts to construct and define social existence through individual authenticity (Sakai 94ff). While Bellah suggests overcoming communalism through the more scientific system of democracy, Sakai criticizes the lack of negativity in communalism because this community is,
somehow, too empirical and too scientific. Certainly, the two critiques
differ considerably. Still, if we suppose that Bellah's idea of democracy
is one of a political system that helps people to attain the highest degree
of individual authenticity, we can say that both Bellah and Sakai, in spite
of the apparent discrepancy, are motivated by a similar desire: they wish
to establish individual authenticity in society.

I suggest examining other social models against this background,
starting with the Slavophiles. In defense of the Slavophiles it must be
said that for them the *state* represented from the beginning a *spiritual*
(and not social) authenticity of the individual within the community. For
the Slavophiles, *sobornost'* was an invisible Church (Khomiakov). As a
consequence, just like Watsuji, the Slavophiles were criticized for their
inability to distinguish between the essence of social life and the essence
of spiritual (Church) life.[17] The Slavophiles insisted that there is a spiritual quantity that is *immanent* in community, a quantity that is not imposed by the Church as an authority but preexisting.

Sakai would certainly criticize this immanentism because he would only see in it just another concept of totality "serv[ing] to guarantee that the fixity of a subjective position is immanent in the person anterior to his or her conscious recognition of it (85)" (this is Sakai's criticism of Watsuji).

There are, however, ways of *spiritually* defining the nation that do not equal immanentism with all-dissolving totalitarianism. There is a concept of "spirit" that the German philosopher Joseph Piper speaks of which "is a capacity for relations of such all-embracing power that its field of relations *transcends the frontiers* of all and any environment. To talk of 'environment' where spirit is concerned, is a misunderstanding. . ."[18] This kind of spirit cannot be obtained in isolation but "to have spirit," means rather to exist facing the entire universe.

As noted in Chapter Three, Jean-Luc Nancy holds that the community, since it is no absolute subject (self, will, spirit), is by its nature not inscribed in any logic of metaphysics.[19] This idea completely contradicts philosophical ambitions that attempt to highlight the spiritual nature of society as one of the foundations of social being. Nishida insisted on "the religious value of culture."[20] It is obvious that in this philosophy, "spirit" receives a sense of openness that makes it incompatible with models of totalitarian enclosure. For Nishida the "real state must be religious at its roots"[21] because the religious value of culture is linked to the particular Buddhist idea of "self as nothingness." Nishida writes: "Only when every state and every people develops itself and at the same time transcends itself in order to create a world of worlds, every single culture creates, following its regional tradition, a special world. The particular worlds that have formed itself on this historical foundation unite so that the whole world represents a worldly world."[22] Intercultural space is here created through self-negation.[23]

Here we come across a line of thought developed by the Russian Eurasianists, in particular by its main representative, the linguist Nicolas S. Trubetzkoy. The Eurasianist suggestion represents an unexpected step in the line of Russian civilization: throughout the nineteenth century Russians considered their country as *European*.[24] The fact that persons, who do not seem to have any reason to consider themselves as Asians, identify themselves in an outspoken way with Scythians and Mongols makes the Eurasianist case unique. It is preceded perhaps only by Okakura's vision of Asian's cultural identity that would include, apart from Japan, China, and India also "Arab chivalry [and] Persian Poetry," leading to the characterization of Islam as "Confucianism on horseback, sword in hand."[25]

Eurasianism cannot be reduced to one or the other idea of ideocracy or dictatorship. True, at first sight, Eurasianism looks like a step backward in the direction of the first Slavophiles (whom they praised) and who decided to define Russia as separate from Europe. The main difference remains, however, that the Eurasianist motive for Russia's separation from Europe was not nationalism but the insistence on cultural affinities between Russians and Asians. It is here that Eurasianism comes curiously close to Japanese Pan-Asianism. In the end, both insist on the Unity of Asia.

Like Nishida, Trubetzkoy holds that once a "spiritual identity" is achieved, the nation will instantaneously transcend itself. Trubetzkoy is aware that "every international is by its very nature atheistic"[26] and looks for moral and spiritual factors that bind human communities. However, the cultural spirit (even when backed by geographical distinction) does not encourage enclosure: "National self-determination" is never an egoistic act of establishing one's own nation but a necessary condition for a people's self-awareness of their position within the world. Trubetzkoy suggests that "the first duty of every non-Romano-Germanic nation is to overcome every trace of ego-centricity in itself"[27] and to subsequently "combine the nationalism of every individual people of Eurasia . . . with Pan-Eurasian nationalism, or Eurasianism."[28]

Formal internationalism or socialism do not grant such an opening since they are no more than the prolongation of egocentric nationalism towards the international: "Actually there is nothing 'national' and no 'self-determination' whatever in this set of attitudes, and this is why national liberation movements often incorporate socialism, which always contains elements of cosmopolitanism and internationalism" (Trubetzkoy, 75).[29] Nishida's ideas of Asia that "must awaken to her own world-historical mission as East Asian peoples" all of whom "must all transcend themselves and construct their own distinct world"[30] are identical to Trubetzkoy's. Also Nishida makes certain not to "confuse nationalism with mere racism" (76). Since "all nations and peoples have their own historical life, . . . each nation and its people [should] transcend themselves while remaining true to themselves and construct a single multi-world" (74). Japanese spirit is not simply the expression of nationalism.

From a historical point of view the parallels between the Eurasianists and Nishida (who was, at times fascinated by the idea of "Pan-Asia")[31] are not surprising since in the 1920s, both Japan and Russia find themselves in a paradoxical situation: Both countries are simultaneously colonizers and quasi colonized. Being aware of the worldwide rise of colonial peoples and the possible decline of imperialism, Eurasianists as well as NISHIDA Kitarō, WATSUJI Tetsurō, and others, try to organize a cultural stronghold able to serve as an orientation mark to "second rate" nations that would otherwise be lost in a sea of individual civilizations and fall victim to European imperialism. What H. Harootunian and NAJITA Tetsuo call an "anti-imperialist imperialism," dependent on the curious geographical position of Japan,[32] is formulated in philosophical terms in the Japanese culturalism (*bunkashugi*)[33] of the 1920s as well as in Russian Eurasianist writings of the same period.[34] In both countries, philosophers proceeded to the rare combination of *time* and *space* in order to develop relatively complex models of a "cultural place." Such a combination is highly unusual in philosophy in the 1920s. The result is a time-spatial model that could serve as the theoretical basis for the coordination of different peoples within larger systems, granting each people its cultural autonomy.

Towards a Theory of Convergence

All aforementioned authors are in search of ways of *spiritually* defining the nation that do not equal immanentism with all-dissolving totalitarianism. Laurent Muraviec's recent book *The Spirit of Nations*[35] talks about the "spirit" of nation as if this spirit were not a socio-moral totality into which the individuals are imprisoned, but a kind of "cultural DNA" full of possibilities. We find an echo of this in the works of Watsuji and Trubetzkoy. Both Watsuji and Trubetzkoy reject cosmopolitanism because they identify it with chauvinism. They deny the superiority of European culture ("Anglo-American" for Watsuji and "Romano-Germanic" for Trubetzkoy) and reveal the hypocritical nature of "universalism, humanism, civilization, progress as well as the 'depersonalized character' of 'democracy in general'" (Watsuji).[36] However, instead of lazily recurring to general principles like "capitalism" or "socialism," they attempt to fundamentally rethink the meaning of national self-determination. Also the "solutions" they suggest are similar: both develop a spatio-temporal approach that transgresses the limits of "national character studies" in the sense of a *Kulturtypenlehre* ("theory of cultural typology"); furthermore they avoid cultural essentialism in the form of a celebration of the "natural culture."

On the preceding pages, Watsuji's philosophy has been described as "totalitarian." I would now like to draw a more nuanced picture of him that considers the potential and the possibilities contained in his earlier thoughts. As a matter of fact, Watsuji did more than just considering "aesthetic works, and literature in particular" (Sakai, 109) in order to formulate a straightforward particularistic "culturalism." As a young scholar he was tempted by an open form of culturalism that refrains from substantialization of national culture. This form of culturalism is a necessary consequence of "Silk Route Cosmopolitanism" and, to the extent that it is based on a certain non-linear model of cultural convergence, it has also a philosophical extension. As William LaFleur has shown,

Watsuji's early fascination with Nara's Silk Route Cosmopolitanism let him perceive Nara as a multiple world, as a Pan-Asian mixture of east and west entirely opposed to Japan's later culture of isolation.[37] Recognizing cultural influences that go back as far as the Mediterranean on the one hand, and emphasizing the well known implication of Indian and Chinese elements in Japanese culture on the other, Watsuji defines Japan as a country that possesses an exceptionally well-developed capacity to unite antagonistic cultures through an act of convergence.

Creating a slightly forced parallel, Watsuji describes ancient Greece and ancient Japan as similar cultures because, he argues, both excelled in the creation of icons. As a matter of fact, Watsuji could have compared the Silk Route Cosmopolitanism of Japan with that of Russia, because in both spheres *cultural convergence* has a prominent position. He could have equated the temples of Nara with the churches of Kiev. In general, the cultures of both Russia and Japan developed in the periphery of larger cultural areas: in the case of Japan it was China, in the case of Russia it was Byzantium. Both Japan and Russia incorporated elements from that larger cultural sphere into their own culture up to the point that it became an expression of their own national identity."[38] E. V. Barabanov affirms that Russia did "not put forth any fundamental ideas of its own that are independent of the Greco-Roman, Byzantine, or modern Europe philosophical legacy."[39] The same can be said about the introduction of Buddhism to Japan. However, it is "only through the Christian doctrine that [Russia] receives also the pagan civilization of the ancient world" (Kireevsky).[40] A second wave of Chinese and Byzantine culture reached both countries in the Fifteenth and Seventeenth Centuries respectively. Paradoxically, in Japan the introduction of Neo-Confucianism by Zen-Buddhist monks made Japanese culture more independent from Chinese culture. The parallel with Russia and the consequences of the fall of Constantinople to the Turks in 1453 is obvious. Now Byzantine influence was strengthened in Russia to the point that at some later time Moscow could be considered a third Rome.

In both Russia and Japan, *convergence* is of paramount importance. No wonder that the idea of Eurasianism has a starting point that is very similar to that of the young Watsuji. While for the Slavophiles Hegel's idea of history as a dialectical development of one Absolute Idea is still binding, already for Danilevsky, the nineteenth century predecessor of the Eurasianists, the Hegelian system of history as a unilinear development made no sense. A professional botanist, Danilevsky derived his theories of the development of history from most recent trends in the science of classification. At his time, unilinear classifications of plants and animals came to be abandoned and were replaced by "natural classification," that divides plants and animals into a number of different types of organisms.

Danilevsky applied this system to cultural anthropology. The natural system does not classify according to arbitrarily selected criteria, but considers the entire sphere of a phenomenon by trying to understand how this sphere is divided up into parts.[41] In reality, for Danilevsky even this "natural" system was not natural enough because it remained unable to "comprise the entire multitude of those appearances and therefore necessarily leads, just like botanics, to an artificial system of scientific structures (88)." Danilevsky found that it is wrong to force nature into an artificial hierarchy leading towards perfection because each organism develops according to its own plan, each of which is perfect in itself.

The same goes for culture. As a consequence, for Danilevsky, "no civilization can pride itself in having attained the point of civilization that is highest compared to predecessors and contemporaries—and this in all domains of development" (83).

Out of Danilevsky's multilinear conception of world history flows a system that is at least on some points reminiscent of anti-Darwinian theories of convergence. Greek civilization has been sparked off through the reception of Persian influences; greco-Roman civilization has been spread by Byzantine emigrants; overseas discoveries initiated the main advances of modern European civilization (85). Here culture is seen as a mixture and, very often, a mixture of east and west. In this way, Danilevsky thoroughly challenges traditional concepts of "western" as much as of "eastern" culture.

In the end, Danilevsky pronounces no real cultural theory of convergence through contiguity in a way in which it has been developed by Eurasianism later. Darwinist as he remained, his theories are clearly inscribed in a Pan-Slavist line.[42] Above that, for Danilevsky war with the West remains unavoidable (237)[43] which led MacMaster to classify him as a "totalitarian philosopher." Eurasianism on the other hand, used some of Danilevsky's insights in order to interpret Eurasian culture as a converging and unified flow of different cultures. Certainly, parallels between Danilevsky's *Russia and Europe* and Trubetzkoy's *Europe and Mankind* are limited to some thoughts on a *Kulturtypenlehre*; but Trubetzkoy's new claims concerning convergence are indirectly linked to some of Danilevsky's potential.

In principle, Trubetzkoy tries to find an alternative able to replace both "zoological nationalism"[44] and European cultural universalism. Once he has identified a hypocritical European form of "Cosmopolitanism" as the last derivative of linear conceptions of history, he presents Eurasian culture as a prototype of a new nonlinear cosmopolitanism. In the domain of linguistics Trubetzkoy proves that similarities between languages cannot always be traced back to a common ("natural") origin, but that lasting mutual influence leads neighboring languages towards convergence. With this, Eurasianism bases the development of culture on an anti-Darwinian system of convergence.

Savitzky applied Danilevsky's natural system to geography. Already Trubetzkoy held that culture *migrates*, that its centers constantly change in geographical space. Like Danilevsky, Savitzky refuses to divide the world into clearly defined continents because that would be a "natural classification" following the natural lines of oceans, mountains, etc. Instead Savitzky suggests the term "geographical worlds" in which characteristics can overlap.[45] The unity of Eurasia, for example, is not "natural" but based on a model of convergence: "The influence of South, East, and West constantly alternated and consecutively dominated the world of Russian culture."[46] Cultures are no "undifferential entities" (*nedifferenzirovannij sovokupnosti*) (ibid, 13): without Tartars there would be no Russia[47] and Russia itself is a combination of sedentariness and steppe elements (ibid).[48] Unilinear and progressive evolutive systems become impossible: "When the line of evolution extends itself into different branches, there can be neither an ascending movement nor gradual and constant self-accomplishment. This or that cultural milieu or series [of milieus] is an accomplishment from one point of view but looks like a decline from another point of view" ("Evrasijstvo," 13).

Savitzky introduces the term *mestorazvitie* (space-development), a theoretical notion through which socio-historical components can be seen as integral parts of geographical conditions. The individual, not unlike the personality, is supposed to appear as a "geographical individual."[49] Interestingly, the notion of *mestorazvitie* as a "natural milieu" avoids determinism because there is no "predestination."[50]

Later, the Eurasianist historian George Vernadsky (1887-1973) gave historical flesh to Savitzky's geographical theories by stressing "the decisive significance of the relation between steppe and the forest societies on the enormous Eurasian plain, the ethnic and cultural complexity of Russia, and the major organic contribution of Eastern peoples, especially the Mongols, to Russian history."[51]

Some of Savitzky's thoughts are reminiscent of Watsuji's (which is not amazing since both Watsuji[52] and the Eurasianists use German geographical theories[53] to define the particular position of Asia). A climatic determinism is preponderant already in Danilevsky who writes on the first pages of *Russia and Europe* that "our climate is different from that of the West (58)." Watsuji (as well as a number of Japanese writers like Tanizaki who discovered the relationship between geography and cultural style) define civilization as determined by climatic and geographical factors; they come amazingly close to Savitzky who identified "cultural centers" whose developments were linked to climate.

The drawback becomes crucial when determinism adopts a "totalitarian" scope. If the description of "climate" and "geographical environment" serves no other purpose than locking the human into a certain "space" supposed to be appropriate for "her culture," then the *Lebensraum* becomes a subjective realm sealed by spontaneity and abstract intuition. Of course, the temptation towards geographical particularism, reinforced by "natural" components like climate, is as strong in Japan as in Russia (still Roman Jakobson insisted that "Russia is a special geographical world"). The more so is it important to break down these temptations by a consistent application of theories of convergence.

When reading *Fūdo* one cannot help but conclude that Watsuji's main problem is that he decided to oppose "Pastoral Europe" to "Monsoon Asia." Certainly, as with everything concerning the parallelism between Nara and ancient Greece that he wanted to establish, *this* must have been the issue that occupied him most. Watsuji was personally obsessed with themes that could potentially explain the difference between Europe and Asia. However, as long as he talks of the "desert as a human way of being" or of "green mountains as a climatological expression of a way of life" (39-40) he really creates the Japanese national narrative that Naoki SAKAI finds so unbearable. A look at the Eurasian continent could have awakened a theoretical potential inspired by ideas of convergence, a potential that *is* unquestionably present in the book. In principle, any theory about the spatiality of the human being, that is, the *combination of space and time*, is a theory of convergence *par excellence*, simply because history is not *past*, but "here and there," in space. In other words, history is always present through fusion and through human creativity.

Paradoxically, connections with more profound Nishidian concepts like *aidagara* as an immediate quality that exists prior to subject-object distinction are here not helpful at all to advance a more culturological[54] interpretation of Watsuji that would reveal underlying patterns of convergence. It would have been more useful to explore the fact that *aidagara*, the being-in-between, does not take place within a fixed community but within an environment that constantly transcends itself in order to converge.[55]

Nishida's own ideas, that "nations transcend themselves while remaining true to themselves and construct a single multi-world," and that in East-Asia all nations should eventually "transcend themselves and construct their own distinct world"[56] looks much more like a culturological means of overcoming of cultural egocentricity. It comes amazingly close to Trubetzkoy's ideas. Nishida's plea, made in the article "The Historical Body," to see formative life not only as a dialectically temporal development, but more like a spatial environment cannot be understood except as the suggestion of a culturological system of convergence.[57] The same goes for statements like the following: "Each self-determining individual harbors a focal point of the world and stands in opposition to others and interdetermines with these others along this pivotal axis, i.e., in historical, worldly time."[58]

Trubetzkoy opposed a concept of "true nationalism" to "egocentric nationalism" which he links to a national self-determination of "petty conceit." "True nationalism" on the other hand, is attained through "self-awareness" as "the single, highest goal in this life for any human being" ("On True and False Nationalism" in *The Legacy*. . . 67). [Only] "self-awareness will show a person his place in the world" (66) and "in pursuing self-awareness, every individual comes to know himself as a member of a nation" (70). These passages are not by Nishida but by Trubetzkoy though they run entirely in parallel with Nishida's statement that "true nationalism must reflect this concept of global formationalism."[59]

Some critics of Eurasianism take a stance that is similar to Sakai's. Girenok holds that any combination of space and time leads to totalitarianism because at the moment we link time to space (or vice versa), we cannot help but identify historically with the space around us. When we really see space through time and time through space, we can no longer be creative.[60]

I think that this is a misunderstanding of the Eurasianist ideas. If the Eurasianists had really been eager to "identify" with something, they would have very quickly adopted either a Euro-centrist or an Asia-centrist position. Still, the Eurasianist position remains decentered by definition, which is a proof for its openness and potential creativity.

Evolution and Convergence

I would urge critics to associate Eurasianist ideas with neo-Darwinian versions of the theme of evolution as it has been developed by Henri Bergson, Gilles Deleuze and Felix Guattari. In 1945, George Vernadsky's father, the scientist Vladimir Vernadsky (1863-1945), coined the term "noosphere" (from Greek *noos*, mind). Vernadsky believed that man had become such an important geological agent that what he had earlier called the biosphere had now been replaced by the noosphere.[61] In his earlier work on the biosphere[62] Vernadsky tried to break with the romantic vision of earth sciences relevant since the time of Humboldt. By formulating the principles of the noosphere ("sphere of reason"), Vernadsky tried to go one step further. He wanted to create a kind of anti-ecology able to conceive of even biological givens as man-made. In a way of speaking, in Vernadsky's theory, man is not a part of the ecosystem; rather the ecosystem is a part of man. Vladimir Vernadsky's "cosmism" had an immediate impact on the Eurasianists.[63]

Though there are no direct links, it has been asserted that Vernadsky is indebted to Bergson for his anti-Darwinian concepts of biosphere and noosphere.[64] Contemporary bio-philosophers like Keith Ansell Pearson insist on similarities between Vernadsky's noosphere and contemporary biological theories of convergence. Bergson insisted that evolution goes through time (duration) and that it is therefore always creative. Deleuze and Guattari took up some of Bergson's points and combined them with those made by French Darwinian thinkers such as Jacques Monod and François Jacob. One of the main arguments of Deleuze's biophilosophy is that "germination" never takes place at a fixed moment and at a fixed place of origin. What counts more than the thing itself (the egg, the germ) and its fixed position in time and space is the *tendency* that pushes it towards invention, innovation, evolution, and, finally, convergence. Bergson called this tendency "vital energy." More important than entities like cells, are the ways in which molecules interact in time and in space.[65] Deleuze and Guattari depict creative evolution as a "thinking of difference and repetition" that they oppose, as an absolutely open system called "plane of immanence," to Darwinian closed systems (*Mille Plateaux,* cf. Ansell Pearson, *Germinal Life,* 8). An egg "is an egg of germinal intensity that does not simply denote a fixed moment of birth or a determinate place of origin" (cf. Ansell Pearson, 9).

It is not difficult to see here also parallels not only with the Eurasianists but also with Nishida whose paradoxical combination of metaphysics and empiricism joins Bergson's biophilosophy. In the *kokutai* article, for example, Nishida explains: "Of course, life phenomena may always be explained chemically and physically. However, these types of explanations, too, are grounded in the facts of direct existential intuition. Without the active intuition of life itself there is no biology, chemistry, or physics."[66] Active intuition leads to convergence; the *basho* is a field in which the Self and the Other unfold their identity and at the same time their difference. This absolutely self-determinating present enjoys a freedom that is flawed neither by a subjective 'I' nor by an environment.

Nishida clearly moves one step away from the celebration of the "natural culture" (Sakai) of Japan towards which Watsuji had been so inclined, and works towards more scientific systems of convergence coming closer to Deleuze's adaptation of Bergson's "creative evolution." Evolution is "a ceaseless play between limited inventions of complex living systems, such as organisms and species, and the desire of the impulse of life or ever renewed vitality" (*Mille Plateaux,* 49). For Deleuze and Guattari "the embryo does not testify to an absolute form pre-established in a closed milieu; rather, the phylogenesis of populations has at its disposal an open milieu, an entire range of relative forms to select from, none of which is pre-established (68)." These are ways of philosophically defining places, in which evolution creates itself out of itself, determining itself through acts of differentiation.

Eurasia as a Trubetzkian-Savitzkian combination of spatial-temporal "undifferential entities" as well as Nishida's vision of Asia as a *basho* can be seen as structureless *plateaus* or *rhizomes*[67] in which acts of territorialization and deterritorialization, of organization, and rupture, form what Deleuze and Guattari call a "demonic" or chôraic place that is stratified but without precise limits.[68] Also for Savitzky, Russia is a combination of sedentariness and nomadic steppe elements. It is an ideal model for a Deleuzian geographical rhizome made of lines without being shaped by profound, metaphysical structures. One could also call this "geography of interaction" since for Marie-Laure Ryan rhizomatic organization represents a typical example of interactivity (Ryan 2001: 8).

Deleuze and Guattari manage, through the formulation of their particular geophilosophy, to explain the phenomenon of "imitation" in a way that overlaps exactly with what some people have stated about cultural imitation in Russia and Japan (see more on this in the section on "The Myth of Uniqueness" in Chapter One). Trubetzkoy claimed that it is impossible "for any nation to assimilate *in toto* a culture created by another nation . . . so that the creator of the culture and its borrower merge into a single cultural entity."[69] He concluded that materializing sociology pursues a false course when trying to crystallize static cultural entities and Lotman made the same point some forty years later by using methods of semiotics: "[In Russia] the tendency develops to find within the imported world-view a higher content which can be separated from the actual national culture of the imported texts. The idea takes hold that 'over there' these ideas were realized in an 'untrue,' confused or distorted, form and that 'here,' in the heart of the receiving culture they will find their true, 'natural' heartland."[70] A similar pattern of "creative imitation" can be observed in Japan. Nativist stances like SUZUKI Daisetsu's who holds that Buddhism received in Japan the most exquisite outfit and is thus more "real" than Buddhism as it existed in its homeland, are widespread in Japanese literature reaching from *nihonjinron* writings to serious philosophy.[71]

Deleuze and Guattari hold that "to imitate" does not mean to adopt concrete characteristics or abstract forms of the phenomenon one desires to imitate but it means to produce, within the new territory, the "imitated" phenomenon on a "molecular basis."[72] Nothing could be further removed from Watsuji's determinism. The above-described "vitality" is virtual in the sense that it cannot causally be linked to anything concrete.

Spaces like the Eurasianist Eurasia or Nishida's Asia are not determined by evolutionary linearity, hierarchy or geometrical orientations, but are made of infinite processes of variation and expansion. Like (Deleuzian) rhizomes, they have no beginning and no end but they begin in the middle and rely neither on transcendental laws (roots) nor on abstract models of unity.[73] In these spaces culture can produce itself by developing its own internal dynamics.

Conclusion

Contrary to the earlier Pan-Asianism of KITA Ikki or ŌKAWA Shūmei and to Pan-Slavism or Slavophilism, Eurasianism as well the philosophy of Nishida must be considered as post-World War I, post-Revolutionary ideologies shaped by bitter memories of the past. No matter if Asians were asked to gather under a "Japanese roof" (Nishida) or under an "Orthodox dome" (Suvchinsky), the ambitions were not "imperialist" and all political messages these thinkers convey remain profoundly "anti-messianic." Both are rather struggling between determinism and freedom of the spirit, finding no politically fundable way out of the conundrum. Be it the Eurasianist concept of a "symphonic unity of peoples" or Nishida's "Principle of a New World Order"—both remain painful attempts to come to terms with unsolvable intellectual paradoxes and are a far cry from colonial strategies. The only "solutions" that these thinkers develop are "conversionist" theories of culture.

Notes

1. See Kant's quotation in Chapter Three, note 32.

2. See Chapter 3, note 33.

3. Roy Andrew Miller: *Japanese Ceramics* (New York: Crown, 1961), "Foreword," no page numbers.

4. It should be noted that also in China between 1890 and 1920, KANG Youwei, LIANG Qichao, YAN Fu and others discussed the concepts of community and society in order to arrive at an appropriate definition of "civil society" for the Chinese people (cf. Bastid 1989). Liang saw *Qun* (群, community) as a bridge between the Confucian idea of a moral community and the incipient idea of a nation (see Hao CHANG 1972 and Peter Zarrow: "Liang Qichao and the Notion of Civil Society in Republican China" in J. Fogel and P. Zarrow (eds) *Imagining the People: Chinese Intellectuals and the Concept of Citizenship 1890-1920* (Armonk, NY: M. E. Sharpe, 1997).

5. Ferdinand Tönnies: *Gemeinschaft und Gesellschaft* (Leipzig: Fuess, 1886).

6. In his *Rinrigaku*, Watsuji defined cultural, existential space as determined by a *Gemeinschaft* when writing: "As Tönnies has said, family bonds are realized in the home, neighborly unions in the matrices of historical tradition, and

110 *Chapter Five*

in turn they create new historical traditions day by day" (Watsuji 1937: quoted from Dilworth's trans. 1998: 276). Nishida also uses Tönnies as a reference in his *kokutai* article: "A historical society that actually exists does not arise in the manner of 'from many to one.' It develops in the form of transition from communal society to profit society. To use Tönnies's word, it arises from an essential will, *Wesenswille*. And an actual existing society is always comprised of both *Gemeinschaft* and *Gesellschaft* dimensions. It begins as a center that is a contradictory identity" (Nishida 1944c: Appendix 2, 425).

7. Cf. Miles Fletcher: "Intellectuals and Fascism in Early Showa Japan" in *Journal of Asian Studies* 39: 1, 1979, 52.

8. The Slavophiles were a group of Russian intellectuals who defined the values of Russian civilization as independent from Western-European culture. See "Explanation of terms."

9. Nicolas Riasanovsky: 1952. *Russia and the West in the Teachings of the Slavophiles: A Study of Romantic Ideology* (Cambridge, MA: Harvard University Press, 1952).

10. For Victor Bychkov's definition of *sobornost'* in the Encyclopedia of Aesthetics see Chapter Three, note 17.

12. See Klaus Epstein: *Die Ursprünge des Konservatismus in Deutschland* (Berlin: Ullstein 1973).

13. Khomiakov drew very much on the German catholic thinker J. A. Mohler who formulated his thoughts at the same time. Mohler's main book is: *Die Einheit der Kirche oder das Prinzip des Katholizismus* (1825).

14. According to MacMaster Also Herzen, Dostoevsky and Lenin believed in a direct relationship between history and nature. They believed in a "huge, dialectical, spiritual-material medium operating to immanent or relatively immanent laws of its own." Robert MacMaster, 305.

15. On Eurasianism see the chapter "Explanation of terms."

16. Andrej Walicki: *The Slavophile Controversy: History of a Conservative Utopia in Nineteenth-Century Russian Thought* (Oxford: Clarendon Press, 1975), 199.

17. Naoki SAKAI: *Translation and Subjectivity. On Japan and Cultural Nationalism* (Minneapolis: University of Minnesota Press, 1997), 92.

18. Peter K. Christoff: *An Introduction to Nineteenth Century Russian Slavophilism. A Study in Ideas*, Vol. 1: A. S. Xomiakov ('S-Gravenhage: Mouton, 1961), 154.

19. Josef Piper: *Leisure: The Basis of Culture* (London: Faber & Faber, 1947), 114, my italics.

20. Jean-Luc Nancy: *La Communauté désœvrée* (Paris: Christian Bourgeois, 1986), 18.

21. ("On the National Polity," *Sourcebook. . .* 79) 1944c. '哲学論文集第四補遺' (Tetsugaku ronbun shū dai yon hoi; Fourth supplement to the philosophical article) in NKZ 12: 397-425. Engl. transl.: 'On the National Polity' in D. A. Dilworth, V. H. Viglielmo and Augustin Jacinto Zavala (eds) *Sourcebook for Modern Japanese Philosophy*. Westport, CT: Greenwood, 1998: 78-95.

22. Nishida: 場所的論理と宗教的世界観 (Bashoteki ronri to shūkyōteki sekaikan [1944]) in NKZ 11: 371-464. Engl. transl.: 'The Logic of *Topos* and the Religious Worldview. Part 1 in Eastern Buddhist 1986, 19(2) 1986: 1-29;

Part 2 in *Eastern Buddhist* 1987, 20(1): 81-119, quotation from the English translation, 19.

23. ("Fundamental Principles of a New World Order," NKZ 12, 429). 1933-34. 哲学の根本問題 (Tetsugaku no konpon mondai; Fundamental problems of philosophy) in NKZ 7: 3-173. Engl. transl: *Fundamental Problems of Philosophy: The World of Action and the Dialectical World.* Tokyo: Sophia University Press, 1970.

24. Cf. John Maraldo: "The Problem of World Culture: Towards an Appropriation of Nishida's Philosophy of Nation and Culture" in *Eastern Buddhist* 28: 2, 1995.

25. Russians considered themselves to be Europeans especially after 1700. Cf. Riasanovsky: "Yet once Uvarov and Pogodin turned to Asia, they immediately and consistently, and without exception proceeded to consider themselves and their country as a part of the single body of Europe and European culture. Eurasianist doctrines belonged to a later age." "Russia and Asia: Two Eighteenth Century Russian Views" in *California Slavic Studies* 1, 1960.

26. OKAKURA Kakuzō. 1905. *Ideals of the East.* New York: Dutton, 3.

27. Nicolai S. Trubetzkoy: "The Tower of Babel and the Confusion of Tongues" in *The Legacy of Gengis Khan and Other Essays on Russian Identity* (Ann Arbor: Michigan Slavic Publication, 1991), 151.

28. "On True and False Nationalism" in *The Legacy. . .*, 66.

29. "Pan-Eurasian Nationalism" in *The Legacy. . .*, 241. Vladimir Solov'ëv's views are here identical as he preaches to overcome national egoism in politics: "The moral law requires of a people first of all that it renounces to national egoism and that it overcome its natural limitations and steps outside its isolation." Preface to the second edition of *The National Question of Russia* in *Collected Works* 6, i-iv.

30. Cf. here Heidegger who makes the same point: "Every nationalism is metaphysically an anthropologism, and as such subjectivism. Nationalism is not overcome by mere internationalism; it is rather expanded and elevated thereby into a system." *Basic Writings* (New York: Harper & Row, 1977), 177.

31. Nishida: "世界新秩序の原理" [1943] (Sekai shinchitsujo no genri) in NKZ 12: 426-34. Engl. trans.: "Fundamental Principle of a New World Order" in D. A. Dilworth, V. H. Viglielmo and Augustin Jacinto Zavala (eds). *Sourcebook for Modern Japanese Philosophy.* Westport, CT: Greenwood, 1998, 75.

32. The idea of "Pan-Asianism" developed out of contacts between Okakura and Tagore. See "Explanation of terms."

33. Harry Harootunian and NAJITA Tetsuo: "Japanese Revolt Against the West: Political and Cultural Criticism in the Twentieth Century" in Peter Duus (ed.) *The Cambridge History of Japan* (New York & Cambridge: Cambridge University Press, 1988), 711-774, cf 734.

34. Thinkers in the 1920s-30s expressed themselves in a complex manner through the movement of culturalism (*bunkashugi* also called *kyōyō-shugi* 教養主義). Philosophers and writers like NISHIDA Kitarō, WATSUJI Tetsurō, KUKI Shūzō, TANIZAKI Jun'ichirō, YANAGITA Kunio, and YOKOMITSU Riichi are representatives of culturalism. They were not linked by a programme but by a search for spiritual values and critique of (Western) culture. On *bunkashugi* see Tessa Morris-Suzuki: "The Invention and Reinvention of Japanese Culture" in *The Journal of Asian Studies* 54: 3, 1995.

35. I consciously avoid the term "geopolitical" but use "geographical." Though I believe, as I explain in Chapter Three, that, contrary to what is held by Susi Frank, Eurasianists acquired a "global" perspective and limited their thought *not* to the locality, I think that their thoughts remain in the domain of philosophy. See Susi Frank: "Eurasianismus: Projekt eines 'Dritten Weges' und heute." Internet source from the University of Konstanz, 213ff.

36. Laurent Muraviec: *L'Esprit des nations: culture et géopolitique*. Paris: O. Jacob, 2002.

37. William LaFleur, 256: "[Watsuji] drew explicit parallels between Imperialist Rome and both the Imperialism and cultural style of Anglo-Saxon peoples, Americans in particular [in a *Shisō* article from 1921]." Trubetzkoy writes in "Europe and Mankind" that "cosmopolitan" means nothing other than that "the culture that ought to dominate the world . . . turns out to be the culture of the very same ethnographic-anthropological group whose supremacy is the lodestar of the chauvinist's dreams" (5).

38. Watsuji: "Pilgrimage" in WTZ 17-353. See LaFleur 1990, 249: "Watsuji read in 1919 *Koji Junrei* [A pilgrimage to old temples] 古寺巡礼. Thus he went to Nara on an intellectual pilgrimage to see art as the physical embodiment of ideas. "What this author recovered he also promoted, and the point about Nara that interested Watsuji was that it was a thoroughly international culture. It thrived on cultural and intellectual exchange between Japan and the rest of Asia, and as such Nara served as the idea of a Japan completely open and receptive to all cultures within its reach. Nara, so Watsuji, was a Japan transcending its own insularity; the Japan of that period was, above all, the Japan of the Shōsōin, the imperial storehouse holding treasures from the whole Silk Road."

39. Another parallel is represented by the fact that both countries are centuries old emperorships in which the emperor had a divine function. Cf. here Cyril Black et. al. *The Modernization of Japan and Russia: A Comparative* Study. New York: The Free Press, 1975.

40. Barabanov, E. V. 1992. "Russian Philosophy and the Crisis of Identity" in *Russian Studies in Philosophy* 31: 2, 24-51, 24.

41. Kireevsky, Ivan. 1966. *Russischer Intellekt in Europäischer Krise* (Köln, Graz: Böhlau), 107.

42. Danilvesky 1867, 65-66. Danilevsky, Nicolai. 1867. *Россия и Европа* [Russia and Europe].

43. Pan-Slavism represents a mixture of nationalist and supra-nationalist elements developed by non-Russian Slavs who felt the need for cooperation. See "Explanation of Terms."

44. Here Danilevsky's theories divert from those of the Eurasianists and remain clearly inscribed in a Pan-Slavist line (*Russia and Europe* is called the "bible of the Pan-Slavists).

45. "On the Idea of Governing the Ideocratic State" in *The Legacy. . .*, 274. Trubetzkoy gives the following examples of cultural zones in Asia: Muslim, Hindu, Chinese, Steppe-Pacific, and Arctic. With the exception of the Muslim zone, with its religious foundation, the others are based on geographic criteria. It was important to prove that Russia had always belonged with the steppe nomads rather than with West Europeans.

46. Savitzky, *Geograficeskij obzor* 27, 1927. See also Stefan Wiederkehr "Der Eurasianismus als Erbe N. Ja. Danilevskijs? Bemerkungen zu einem Topos

der Forschung" in *Studies in East European Thought* 52, 2000, 135. Danilevsky suggests similar things. See Danilevsky, 17.

47. "Evrasijstvo" in *Evrazijskij vremennik*. Bd 4 Berlin 1925, 8.

48. 'Степь и оседлость' [Steppe and sedentariness, 1922] in Novirkovka & Sisemskaja: *Россиа между Европой и Азией: Евразийский соблазн. Антология* (Moscow: Nauka 1993), 123.

49. The only purely "geographical" definition of Eurasia that Savitzky admits is actually rather climatic than geographical. It represents the continental block where "the normal succession of climatic zones from North to South is least disturbed by the non-latitudinal factors, such as the sea or the mountains." Boris Ishbolin: "The Eurasian Movement" in *Russian Revue* 5: 2, 1946, 64-73.

50. Savitzky: *Rossija—osobyj geograficheskij mir* [Russia—a particular geographical world] (Prag 1927), 30, 31.

51. See Vladimir Weidlé on the anti-deterministic character of *mestorazvitie* in 'Russia and the West [1956]' in A. Schmemann (ed.), *Ultimate Questions: An Anthology of Modern Russian Religious Thought.* (Crestwood: St. Vladimir's Seminar Press, 1976), 16.

52. Riasanovsky in "Russia and Asia" in Wayne S. Vucinich (ed.): *Essays on the Influence of Russia on the Asian Peoples* 'Stanford University Press, 1972), 23.

53. Quotation from the German translation 181.

54. Heinrich Rückert: *Lehrbuch der Weltgeschichte in organischer Darstellung* (Leipzig: Weigel, 1857) was important for Danilevsky. Among the most important geographical theories were those of Ferdinand von Richthofen (1833-1905) who worked also on Asia and on climatic aspects.

55. I am using this term not necessarily in the Russian sense as an identity-oriented humanistic research but in the German or American sense of Kulturwissenschaften or cultural turn coined in the 1960s. (In Russia culturology is often a compulsory part of university courses that largely replaces the teaching of dialectical materialism).

56. Cf. Sakai, Chapter Three note 14: "However, in spite of the identity of the term *mu*, Nishida and Watsuji employ this philosopheme in very different contexts, and the essentializing or substantializing tendency of Watsuji is very obvious in this case too . . . despite his etymological examination of the Chinese and Japanese words for 'being,' Watsuji's anthropology could never dislodge itself from the ontology of subjectivity or what Nishida called *ronri-teki shugo-hogi* (logical subjectivism)."

57. Nishida: 哲学の根本問題 (Tetsugaku no konpon mondai; Fundamental problems of philosophy) [1933-34]. in NKZ 7: 3-173. Engl. transl: *Fundamental Problems of Philosophy: The World of Action and the Dialectical World.* Tokyo: Sophia University Press, 1970, 74.

58. Cf. Nishida in "The Historical Body:" "But the thinkers who have thought of life down to the present time have not included the concept of environment in their thinking. Even if they speak of life as formative, because they think of it as only making various things in immanently temporal dimension, they do not adequately thematize the concept of environment." '歴史的身体' (Rekishiteki shintai) in NKZ 14: 264-291 [1937]. Engl. transl.: 'The Historical Body' in D. A. Dilworth, V. H. Viglielmo (eds). *Sourcebook for Modern Japanese Philosophy.* Westport, CT: Greenwood, 1998. 37-53, quotation from p. 44.

114 *Chapter Five*

59. 場所的論理と宗教的世界観 (Bashoteki ronri to shūkyōteki sekaikan) in NKZ 11: 371-464 [1944] Engl. transl.: "The Logic of *Topos* and the Religious Worldview. Part 1" in *The Eastern Buddhist* 1986, 19(2) 1986: 1-29. Quotation from p. 10 of translation. See also his statement from Fundamental Problems 100: "Life, however, is not the mere determination of the environment. A mere determination of the environment would only be nature, and life cannot appear from mere nature." Man is not a biological but a social and historical entity."

60. "On the National Polity," Engl. 82.

61. Girenok quoted by Alexander Antoshchenko, "On Eurasia and the Eurasians: Studies on Eurasianism in Current Russian Historiography" http://www.karelia.ru/psu/ chairs/PreRev/bibleng.rtf 2000.

62. Vladimir Vernadsky: "The Biosphere and the Noosphere," *Scientific American* 33 (1), 1945, 1-12. Cf. Eugene Odum: *Fundamentals of Ecology* (Philadelphia: Saunders, 1971), 34ff. The term "noosphere" was suggested by Eduourd Le Roy (1870-1954), in collaboration with Pierre Teilhard de Chardin (1881-1955). The Russian biologist Theosodius Dobzhansky separated Teilhard's ideas from theology in the 1960s. Teilhard also developed the concept of noosphere. See Gregory Stock *Metaman: The Merging of Humans and Machines into a Global Superorganism* (New York: Simon & Schuster, 1993), 14 and 252 note 8 and Vadim Borisov, Felix F. Perchenok, Arsenii B. Roginsky: "Community as a source of Vernadsky's Concept of Noosphere" in *Configurations*: 3, 1993, 415-438.

63. Vladimir Vernadsky: *The Biosphere* (New York: Copernicus, 1998). It is interesting to note this parallelism because Vernadsky's system of the biosphere suggests further parallels with Chinese cosmology, as "in the Chinese mind there is no real distinction between the world of the supernatural, the world of nature, and the world of man" (Derk Bodde: *Essays of Chinese Civilization*, Princeton University Press, 1981, 138). Vernadsky strove to see the earth and the universe as a unified biological system. Also the Chinese insisted on "an intimate parallelism between the mathematically expressible regimes of the heavens and the biologically determined rhythms of life on earth." Quoted from Li Xiaodong: "The Aesthetic of the Absent: The Chinese Conception of Space" in *The Journal of Architecture*, Vol. 7 Spring 2002. Vernadsky's concepts of biosphere and noosphere continue to fascinate theorists in the field of posthuman studies who examine the merging of humans and machines into superorganisms. For the use of biosphere see also James Lovelock: *The Ages of Gaia: A Biography of Our Living Earth* (London: Norton, 1988) and Moisseiev et al.: "Biosphere Models" in R. Kates et al. (eds): *Climate Impact Assessment* (London: John Wiley & Sons, 1985).

64. See Sergei Glebov, 2003, 16.

65. Keith Ansell Pearson: *Germinal Life: The Difference and Repetition of Deleuze* (New York: Routledge 1999) He speaks of Bergson's influence on "Vernadsky's now widely recognized classic study of biosphere. Although not explicitly referenced Bergson is one of the most important influences on Vernadsky."

66. Cf. Gilles Deleuze et Félix Guattari: *Mille Plateaux: Capitalisme et schizophrénie 2* (Paris: Minuit, 1980). See Keith Ansell Pearson "Viroid Life: On Machines, Technics and Evolution" in: Ansell Pearson (ed.) *Deleuze and Philosophy* (Routledge 1997).

67. In Dilworth & Viglielmo: *Sourcebook for Modern Japanese Philosophy* (Westport, CT: Greenwood, 1998), 89.

68. Cf. *Mille Plateaux*, 16: "Tout rhizome comprend des signes de segmentarité d'après lesquelles il est stratifié, territorialisé, organisé, signifié, attribué, etc. mais aussi des lignes de déterritorialisation par lesquelles il fuit sans cesse. Il y a rupture dans le rhizome chaque fois que des lignes segmentaires explosent dans une ligne de fuite, mais la ligne de fuite fait partie du rhizome." [Every rhizome contains signs of segmentarity according to which it can be stratified, territorialized, organized, attributed, etc., but also lines of deterritorialization through which it incessantly escapes. There is a rupture in the rhizome every time the segmentary lines explode in a *ligne de fuite*, but the *ligne de fuite* is part of the rhizome.]

69. Cf. Manola Antonioli: *Géophilosophie de Deleuze et Guattari* (Paris: Harmattan, 2003), 26.

70. Trubetzkoy: "Europe and Mankind" in *The Legacy. . .*, 36. Homi Bhabha notes similar patterns of "flexible mimickry" in a postcolonial context in his "Of Mimicry and Man: The Ambivalence of Colonial Discourse" in *October 28*, Spring 1984, 125-133.

71. Yuri Lotman: *Universe of the Mind* (London & New York: Tauris & Co, 1970), 147. See also Lotman in "The Poetics of Everyday Behaviour in Eighteenth Century Russian Culture" in Nakhimovsky, A. D. & A. S. (eds.): *The Semiotics of Russian Cultural History* (Ithaca: Cornell University Press, 1985), 70: "The image of European life was reduplicated in a ritualized playacting of European life. Everyday behavior became a set of signs for everyday behavior. The semiotization of everyday life, the degree to which it was consciously perceived as a sign, increased sharply. Daily life acquired the characteristics of a theatre." Above that, "copying" has a long tradition in Japan. YASUDA Yojūrō (1910-81), a member of the *rōman-ha* Japan Romantic School, claimed that since Emperor Gotoba's reign (1183-1198) "Japanese culture has slowly decayed to the point where, in modern Japan, its only unique characteristic is a propensity for copying." While Yasuda interprets this deterioration in a nationalistic way as a logical consequence of the separation of culture from its divine origin (the emperor), his diagnosis that "culture itself has been reduced to merely an attempt to incorporate and mobilize various foreign elements" remains interesting. YASUDA Yojūrō quoted from Kevin M. Doak: *Dream of Difference: The Japan Romantic School and the Crisis of Modernity* (University of California Press, 1994), 22. HAZEGAWA Nyozekan points to a similar phenomenon when explaining that the "tendency on the part of the common people to follow the dictates of the upper classes" has finally "blocked individuality and independence of thought." He continues saying that "since the Meiji Era this attitude has assumed the form of the widespread adulation paid to superior imported Western culture..." "The Lost Japan and the New Japan" in R. Tsumoda & Th. De Bary, *Sources of Japanese Tradition* (New York: Columbia University Press, 1964), 386.

72. See Suzuki's early writings *Japanese Spirituality* and *Zen and Japanese Culture*. Even Nishida interpreted the notion of no-mind (*mushin*) as a pure manifestation of Japanese spirit. See Bernard Faure's article "The Kyoto School and Reverse Orientalism" in Steven Heine & Charles Wei-hsun Fu (eds): *Japan*

in *Traditional and Postmodern Perspectives* (Albany, NY: SUNY Press, 1995), 254ff.

73. This is what Deleuze and Guattari say about the "becoming woman" of a man: "Nous voulons seulement dire que ces aspects inséparables du devenir-femme doivent d'abord se comprendre en fonction d'autre chose: ni imiter ni prendre la forme féminine, mais émettre des particules qui entrent dans le rapport du mouvement et de repos, ou dans la zone de voisinage d'une micro-féminité, c'est-à-dire produire en nous-mêmes une femme moléculaire, créer la femme moléculaire. Nous ne voulons pas dire qu'une telle création soit l'apanage de l'homme, mais, au contraire, que la femme comme entité molaire *a* à *devenir-femme,* pour que l'homme aussi devienne ou puisse le devenir" (ibid., 338). [We only want to say that these aspects that are inseparable from the becoming-woman must first of all be understood in the context of something else: they neither imitate nor do they adopt the shape of the woman, but send out particles that enter the relationship of movement and stillness, or enter the zone of the neighborhood of a micro-feminity, that is they produce in us a molecular woman, they create the molecular woman. We do not want to say that such a creation is the heritage of man but on the contrary, that the woman as molar a entity has a *becoming-woman* in order to enable man to become a woman.]

Conclusion

The purpose of the present book is to show that in Russian and Japanese philosophical traditions, the notion of space is formulated in a unique way. To fulfill this purpose, the reader has been forced through several intellectual domains, some of which appeared to have no natural link at first sight. Still the link has been provided by space and by nothing else. The aesthetic *presentation* in Noh-plays and icons, for example, develops a quality of space that strives to establish a realm outside the physical framework of space-time and of matter. By "losing their dimensions," Noh-plays and icons create realities that include their own ontological bases. The concepts of community like *sobornost'* or *basho* have been reflected against this background. The particularity of space in these traditions has been explained by referring again and again to the relationship between the 'I' and the 'thou,' a relationship, which could even be expanded into an inter-civilizational notion that is important for conceptualizations of the contemporary world order. Bakhtin, with his reflections on inter-subjectivity, self-reflection, and multi-linguality helped to define space as a dialogical place related to Nishida's *basho*. At the end of the book it had become possible to describe these Russian and Japanese philosophers as producers of "conversionist" theories of culture.

It should have become clear that non-Western concepts of community like *sobornost'* or *basho* differ from an idea of "community" that could arguably be called "Kantian." On the one hand, Kant's ambiguous presentation of *sensus communis* as a "universal subjectivity" appeared interesting because—as everybody will agree—communities cannot be dependent on *subjectivity* only. On the other hand, it appears as strange just because it remains difficult to interpret such a hybrid term in a

117

Western metaphysical context, let alone in a postmodern one: What is universal? What is local?

The "non-Western" alternatives that have been presented throughout this book should be considered as useful additions to our contemporary political discourses. *Basho* and *sobornost'* fracture metaphysical items like "self," "will," or "spirit." Former Czech president Vaclav Havel explained only recently that "I merely reject the kind of political notions that attempt, in the name of nationality, to suppress other aspects of the human home, other aspects of humanity and human rights."[1] The dichotomy of reasoning against feeling, of the rational against the familiar, of the modern against the archaic persists in our thinking. The Russian and Japanese authors dealt with in the preceding study reject such dichotomies and try to think of the community within the principles of convergence in which the relationship between the 'I' and the 'thou' is no longer inscribed in these schemes.

Note

1. Vaclav Havel: "On Home" in *New York Review of Books* 5.12.1991 quoted from Griffin 1998.

Postface

Resistance and Slave Nations

Takeuchi and the Master-Slave Syndrome

The Japanese cultural critic and sinologist TAKEUCHI Yoshimi held that the two countries that have made the greatest efforts to resist modernity are China and India.[1] Even into the 1970s Takeuchi saw Chinese mass protest against foreign domination as a desirable model for Japanese society.[2] Contrary to Japan (which Takeuchi preferred to compare with Turkey), Takeuchi found that in China modernization adopted from the beginning a more "internally generated" character, producing, for example, a socially concerned literature that stays close to daily life. The reason, as Takeuchi sees it, is that in China modernization emerged from the country's own demands. True, Japan, as she so quickly managed to eliminate feudalism and create a modern nation state, has been more flexible and particularly able to adapt to modern requirements; from a Japanese point of view, China must therefore look backward. However, the surplus that Chinese modernization offers in Takeuchi's view is that here modernization was "received on an ethnic-national basis and transformed into a subjective force . . ." (Takeuchi, 99). Furthermore Takeuchi points out that nations like Japan and Turkey are "slave nations," a concept that he borrows from the Chinese writer LU Xun. Slave nations imitate their masters very successfully without noticing that their success—since it is based *only* on imitation—is in reality a failure.

119

China, Japan, Russia

Some might indeed oppose that China should be integrated in the present comparative study. It is true that also in China intellectuals attempted to reform the country: in the 1890s, KANG Youwei recommended that the Emperor forcefully tell the whole country, as had been done by Peter the Great in Russia and in the Meiji Restoration in Japan.[3] It is also true that in China intellectuals formulated a cultural critique partly guided by Pan-Asian considerations. Even leading Qing dynasty officials developed *tong-zhong* (same kind/same race) ideologies and called for a Japanese-Chinese alliance against Russian expansionism in order to revive Asia (*yazhou*).[4] At the turn of the century, the late Qing scholar LIANG Qichao (1873-1929) (who around 1903 briefly cooperated with Sun Yat-sen's revolutionary movement) emerged as an original reformer and historical thinker and called for a merging of cultural systems and a modern synthesis of Buddhism and science.[5] And like in Japan, the interest in Asian cultural geography led Chinese intellectuals to an awareness of global space that they had to put in relation with the historical space of China.

However, neither Liang nor other thinkers of his kind would mold these or other ideas in a metaphysical philosophy in the way Nishida or Watsuji would do only two decades later.[6] We are therefore unable to confirm that the Chinese produced something that could be compared to the attempt of "recenter[ing] the ontological ground of reality away from bureaucratic hierarchies toward a spiritual largely individual world of consciousness and activity," as has said Victor Koschmann about NISHIDA Kitarō.[7] In China, the intellectual debate remained rather limited to political theory. It reappeared as such in the 1930s in the form of a confrontation of Eastern spirituality and Western materialism that remains very reminiscent of Japanese Meiji thinkers like FUKUZAWA Yukichi (1835-1901) or Westernizers like TOKUTOMI Sohō (1863-1957).[8] The striving for an integration of the problem of the "absolute" in thoughts about history or culture which is so present in Japanese philosophers like Nishida, Tanabe, and Miki, on the other hand, is absent in China. It appears rather that in the 1910s and 1920s, the world of Chinese reformers was still, as Peter Harris has said, an "uneasy mixture of the Chinese and the Western, [of] particularism and universalism."[9]

With regard to Japan, in principle, Takeuchi repeats what Fukuzawa had said seventy years earlier about Japan when declaring that "even if they did imitate the West, [what Japanese modernization achieved] could not be called civilization" since "the mere existence of 'Western styles' is no proof of civilization."[10] However, Takeuchi seems to overlook the writers, ethnologists and philosophers of early Shōwa and late Taishō culturalism who moved away from Meiji ideals of civilization and enlightenment (*bunmei kaika*). He refuses to acknowledge TANIZAKI Jun'ichirō's writings of the early 1930s, which demonstrate a clear resistance towards modernization and announce a "return to Japan" (though without being sufficiently committed to expressions of "protest" that Takeuchi favored). Tanizaki developed an ironical method of "celebrating" the ideals of Japanese aesthetics by resisting not only Westernization but also Japanese essentialism or a purely nativist vision of Japanese culture.[11]

Japan and Russia emerge as two similar countries in which modernization has been carried out quickly and efficiently. In both countries "resistance" was stifled to some extent but it *did* exist. In Russia criticism towards Western civilization never appeared with simply anti-modern attitudes since here a single thinker can hardly be accredited with an unmitigated "pro-Eastern" or "anti-Western" attitude. Straightforward attitudes might have existed on the side of governments, but as soon as ideologies became more sophisticated, positions tended to be ambiguous. In Russia, most "Modernizers" were also Russian patriots in the largest sense: "Westernization" rarely ever meant to simply replace Russian culture by Western culture, which led Dostoevsky to his famous claim that "Slavophilism and Westernizers is a great . . . misunderstanding."[12] Of course, there are themes that are typically "Westernizing" like the 1860s political radicalism, post-Hegelian materialism, French enlightenment, or science worship. Still, most of the so-called "Westernizers" (like Herzen's, Chernyshevsky, Pisarev, Bakunin) were also sensitive to a particularly "Russian" approach towards civilization, modernization, and socialism.[13]

What the works of these Japanese intellectuals in the 1920s-30s and those of Russian thinkers linked to Eurasianism have in common is that they transcend the most basic ideas of both modernism and of national salvation. At the same time it is true that both are confronted, while involved in these projects, with a common danger. Both were constantly tempted to transpose a large part of their discontentment with "Western" civilization, "Western" philosophy, etc. on an "ethnic" level or, even there where the level is not outspokenly ethnic, to give in to antagonizing schemes that insist on a confrontation of "East" and "West." Still, in general, criticism of modernization in Japan and Russia, instead of questioning the idea of modernization as such, tends to deal with the *quality* of modernization.

The Contemporary Situation

In the conclusion of the last chapter of this book it has been said that Nishida's and the Eurasianists' ambitions were "anti-messianic" and not "imperialist" and that they tended towards "conversionist" theories of culture. It remains to ask what is actually left of these attempts in the contemporary "Asian" world. At the moment, Japan and Russia attract a lot of attention because, as has said Gilbert Rozman, both are "great powers with an unbalanced standing in the world order."[14] Apart from that, an entirely new factor has added supplementary complications to the picture as the present rise of China forces us to reconsider the position of Asia within the world order.

Many signs indicate that a new self-consciousness of the Asian continent will be closely linked to the formation of a new regionalism, a regionalism that will most probably be interpreted as a post-Cold War compromise between nationalism and globalism.[15] Two questions arise: will regionalism make use of Pan-Asian conceptions? And will these conceptions include a conversionist potential or not? The political scientist WANG Hui has recently affirmed that "Asia" represents an idea of civilization that can be contrasted to that of Europe.[16] However, at least on some levels, in China and Korea, "Pan-Asianism" is seen as an unworthy alternative because here Japan "is preparing to establish the capability to project power in Asia."[17]

It looks very much as if Nishida's thoughts are needed more than ever. Though in both China and Korea, East-Asian discourse had once awakened intellectuals from "an exile from the traditions of East Asia caused by a blind admiration of the West (HAN Kee-hyung),"[18] today one associates Japanese Pan-Asianism in these countries exclusively with an "expansionist strategy." Ironically, one of the hindrances to a faster development of "regionalism" in China is that here larger visions are expressed in terms of "greater China." Peter Duus' observation that "the idea [of Pan-Asia] lies beneath the surface of popular consciousness like unexploded bombs"[19] illustrates that ideas of "regionalism" or Pan-Asianism have not developed beyond the stage in which nationalists have left them in the 1920s. First, Duus' choice of metaphor indicates that he is afraid that the Pan-Asianism will be more militarist than spiritual. More detailed observations however, show that the new Pan-Asianism will be neither militarist nor spiritual but simply economic. Fu-ko LIU and Philippe Régnier have aptly noted that, though there are dramatic moves in Asia towards regional integration, these efforts, prophesized since the 1980, have "more to do with economic aspiration that with political calculation."[20] When reading academic articles on Asian Regionalism, one has the impression that references to Tagore, the

Pan-Asian tradition—often including Nishida in an ambiguous way—
and Asian cultural identity are somehow grafted on the top of the article
merely as a matter of decoration. The essential part of the story of Asian
regionalism has shifted to economic cooperation and it is difficult to
confirm that encouragements like those of KOO Jong-suh, that "the
Pan-Asian movement should take a fresh approach"[21] are really heartfelt.
While some intellectuals might still defend ISHIWARA Kanji's "beautiful dream" of Asian unity, combining history, religion, and science
(Peattie 1975: 362) the more generally accepted formula is "open regionalism against Pan-Asianism." In any case it seems that cooperation is
founded on merely abstract principles that do not emphasize the dialectical components of a typically Pan-Asian system within which identity
comes about through interaction. Instead of being on a spatialized realization of cultures, the focus is again on Eighteenth Century liberalist notions like equality and liberty.

Eurasianism, on the other hand, continues to fascinate theorists. The
reason might be that "Eurasia" represents an interesting object for various kinds of people. The American policy-maker Brzezinski claims that
even today "Eurasia is . . . the chessboard on which the struggle for
global primacy continues to be played."[22] When looking at "Eurasia"
from a geopolitical point of view, totalitarian schedules might come to
mind very quickly (Brzezinski reminds us that Stalin and Hitler also saw
Eurasia as the center of the world, Brzezinski, xiv). As a consequence,
critics like Mikhail Epstein or Anssi Kullberg see only the
neo-imperialist component in the most recent developments of Russian
Neo-Eurasianism.[23]

It comes as a rather poor coincidence that Eurasianism has recently
been revalued by the nationalist geopolitician Alexandr Dugin who re-
founded the Eurasian Movement in 2000.[24] Dugin's journal *Elementy*
agitates against globalization, the Islamic threat, and democracy (because
here the people do *not* govern) and praises national-bolshevism. The
journal's tendency is highly anti-enlightenment, spartanic, pessimistic,
and populist.[25] We are reminded that in Soviet times, Eurasianism was
especially popular among the KGB, the Red Army, and Alpha troops
(Kullberg 2001: 4) who defined Eurasianism as purely imperialist and
expansionist (Dugin himself is the son of a KGB officer).[26] Dugin uses
climatic-geographical components like the synthesis of the Forest and the
Steppe in order to pin down the cultural narrowness of the Western civilization (the Forest) and its inability to understand the Eastern Steppe
culture. The recurrence to "sacred sciences" like alchemy, astrology, and
sacred geography do not make his arguments more convincing. Ironically,
these far-right ideologies sharply collide with that of the Eastern European New Right, which continues to praise "the notion that the end of

Soviet rule is to be seen as the process of reattachment to Europe after years of being 'almost swallowed by Eurasia.'"[27]

More sophisticated is Lev Gumilev's (1912-1990) Neo-Eurasianism. In extensive historical investigations Gumilev establishes Slavic and Turkish elements as the foundations of Eurasian identity, making of Russia a synthetic civilization.[28] Kullberg points to the fact that Gumilev supported during the Cold War Greater Russian imperialism and integrates influences from fascism (Kullberg, 3). Still Gumilev recognizes himself as a follower of Trubetzkoy and Savitzky.

Russian Neo-Slavophilism seems to have understood the dangers of inappropriate combinations of philosophy and politics better. For Zinaida Smirnova "Slavophilism [must be] regarded as an integrated system of national and religious-philosophical doctrines"[29] while Serge Khoruzhy focuses on the Slavophile organic concept of communality named *sobornost'*. For Khoruzhy, Slavophilism is a religious doctrine above all, and its theoretical pronouncements are really theological rather than philosophical (Scanlan 1994, 25).[30]

I hope that the present work on space in Russia and Japan has added new ideas to *these* discussions as they seem to develop on a somehow circular basis.

Notes

1. TAKEUCHI, Yoshimi: *What is Modernity? Writings of Takeuchi Yoshimi* (trans. by Richard Calichman), (Columbia University Press, 2005), 156ff.

2. Lawrence Olson: "Takeuchi Yukichi and the Vision of a Protest Society in Japan" in *Journal of Japanese Studies* 7: 2, 1981, 320.

3. WONG Young-tsu: "Revisionism Reconsidered: Kang Yuwei and the Reform Movement of 1890" in *Journal of Asian Studies* 51: 3, 1992. This led to the so-called Hundred Days' Reform which was annulled by Empress Cixi.

4. Cf. Rebecca E. Karl: "Creating Asia: China in the World at the Beginning of the Twentieth Century" in *American Historical Review* 103: 4, 1998, 1104.

5. Liang formulated theories about a multi-ethnic (*guojiazhuyi*) state and insisted on the negative implications of the model of a Han Chinese state (*minzhuzhuyi*). See Hao CHANG: *Liang Ch'i-ch'ao and Intellectual Transition in China 1890-1907* (Cambridge, MA: Harvard University Press, 1971), 261. Liang also developed the idea of a "broad nationalism (*da minzhu zhuyi*) as a kind of corporate national identity as opposed to an ethnic "narrow nationalism (*xiao minzu zhuyi*). Cf. John Fitzgerald: "The Nationless State: The Search for a Nation in Modern Chinese Nationalism" in *Australian Journal of Chinese Affairs* 33, 1995, 87ff.

6. Liang did not espouse the religious Confucian ideas of his teacher KANG Youwei Cf. Hiroko Willock: "Japanese Modernization and the Emergence of

New Fiction in Early Twentieth Century China: A Study of Liang Qichao" in *Modern Asian Studies* 29: 4, 1995, 819. The modernizer KANG Youwei (1858-1927) tried to make Confucianism the national religion, to which Liang was opposed.

7. Victor Koschmann: "The Debate on Subjectivity in Postwar Japan: Foundations of Modernism as a Political Critique" in *Pacific Affairs* 54: 4, 1982-83, 614. It is true that many Chinese thinkers (including KANG Youwei and LIANG Qichao) went beyond the rationalism of Confucianism and dealt also with Buddhism, for example YEN Fu. Cf. Benjamin Schwartz: *In Search of Wealth and Power: Yen Fu and the West* (Cambridge, MA: The Belknap Press of Harvard University Press, 1964). However, Marriane Bastid has asked: "Even if by their traditional training most scholars and officials of the time could grasp KANG Youwei's or Zhang Binglin's moral-spiritual concerns and did share a universalistic outlook, was it not primarily the political pronouncements of these thinkers that attracted the literate audience?" Review of Hao CHANG's *Chinese Intellectuals in Crisis: Search for Order and Meaning* in *Pacific Affairs* 62: 1, 1989, 99.

8. Liang was particularly influenced by Fukuzawa's *jitsugaku* (*shixue*, practical learning) thought. Cf. Willock.

9. Peter Harris: "Chinese Nationalism: The State of the Nation" in *The China Journal* 38, 1997, 129.

10. FUKUZAWA Yukichi: *An Outline of a Theory of Civilization* (trans. by D. Dilworth and G. C. Hurst), (Tokyo, Sophia University Press, 1973), 16. Already quoted in Chapter 1.

11. Cf. Gregory L. Galley: "The Art of Subversion and the Subversion of Art" in *Journal of Japanese Studies* 21: 2, 1995, 367 and 391.

12. Dostoevsky: "Pushkin," *Diary of a writer* Vol. 2, 979-980.

13. Some of these Modernizers even passed their ideas to the Slavophile (especially the radical social thinker Vissarion Belinsky (1811-1848) who identified the cleavage between the Westernized Russian society and non-Westernized folk at a very early stage. Or they were openly sympathetic towards Pan-Slavism (Bakunin). For Belinsky, "the distinction between *narod* (people) and *natsiye* (nation), *narod'nost* and *national'nost* became the cornerstones of his interpretation of Russian history." (Andrei Walicki: *The Slavophil Controversy: History of a Conservative Utopia in Nineteenth-Century Russian Thought*. Oxford: Clarendon Press, 1975, 399) For Herzen, "the Westernerizers were increasingly aware of the need to master the themes and issues put into circulation by the Slavophiles" (Walicki: 394). Herzen took a veritable "anti-European turn" when interpreting Danilevsky and establishing Constantinople as the capital of the Russian empire. See Alexander von Schelting: *Russland und Europa im russischen Geschichtsdenken* (Bern: Francke 1948), 238-40. Also the pro-Slav philosophers (and even the conservative Slavophiles) were not simply anti-modern, but sought to lead Russia into modernization.

14. Gilbert Rozman: "Japan and Russia: Great Power Ambitions and Domestic Capacities" in G. Rozman (ed.): *Japan and Russia: The Tortuous Path to Normalization, 1949–1999* (New York: St. Martin's Press, 2000), 357.

15. AHN Byung-joon: "Regionalism in the Asia-Pacific: Asian or Pacific Community?" in *Korea Focus* 4: 4, 1996, 5.

16. WANG Hui: "Les Asiatiques réinventent l'Asie" in *Le Monde diplomatique* Février 2005.

17. RHEE Sang-woo: "Japan's Role in New Asian Order" in *Korea Focus* 4: 3, 1996, 27.

18. Cf. HAN Kee-hyung, "Sin Chaeho and Nationalist Discourses in East Asia" in *Sungkyun Journal of East Asian Studies* 2: 2, 2006 (no page numbers).

19. Peter Duus: "Remembering the Empire: Postwar Interpretations of the Greater East Asia Co-Prosperity Sphere," Occasional Paper Nr. 54, The Woodrow Wilson Center, Asia program, 18 March 1993. Quoted from Baogang He.

20. Fu-Kuo LIN: "The Renewal of Regionalism and an East Asian New Order" in Fu-Kuo LIN & Philippe Régnier (eds), *Regionalism in East Asia. Paradigm Shifting?* (New York: Routledge, 2003), 221. "There are inter-governmental forums like the ASEAN free trade area or the ASEAN Regional Forum (ARF), as well as non-governmental organizations who promote political, economic, and cultural cooperation."

21. KOO Jong-suh: "Pan-Asianism: For Primacy of East Asia" in *Korea Focus* 3: 2, 1995, 38.

22. Zbigniev Brzezinsky. *The Grand Chessboard—American Primacy and its Geostrategic Imperatives.* (New York: Basic Books, 1997), 31.

24. Anssi Kullberg, *May 2001* "From Neo-Eurasianism to National Paranoia: Renaissance of Geopolitics in Russia" in *The Eurasian Politician* 4, August 2001. Mikhail Epstein: "Response: 'Post-' and Beyond" in *Slavic and East European Journal* 39: 3, 1995a. See especially Epstein 2006, which offers one of the best English summaries of the Dugin's and Gumilev's thoughts currently available in English. Dugin calls his movement also "radical traditionalism." Some of Dugin's most important texts as well as the programme of the neo-Eurasian Movement is contained in the journals and magazines *Milyi Angel, Elementy* and the newspaper, *Den'* (since 1993 *Zavtra*). Dugin's main books are: *Mysteries of Eurasia* (1991), *Hyperborean Theory* (1992), *Conspirology* (1992).

25. Leonid Luks: "Der 'dritte Weg' der 'Neo-Eurasischen' Zeitschrift 'Elementy'—zurück ins Dritte Reich?" in *Studies in East European Thought* 52: 1-2, 2000, 49-71.

26. The conclusions to be drawn from the theory of passionarity are according to Dugin that Russians are a fresh and young ethnos, which has the potential to consolidate the super-ethnos of Russia-Eurasia. Galya Andreyeva Krasteva: "The Criticism towards the West and the Future of Russia-Eurasia" in *The Eurasian Politician*, July 2003, 4.

27. Roger Griffin: "Europe for the Europeans: Fascist Myths of the New World Order" 1922-1992 on www.alphalink.com.au.

28. Gumilev's books are: *Drevniaia Rus' i Velikaia Step'* [Old Russia and the Vast Steppe] (Moscow: Mysl' 1989); *Etnogenez i biosfera Zemli* [Ethnogenesis and the Biosphere of the Earth] (Leningrad: Gidrometeoizdat. 1990); "Gumanitarnye i estestvennonauchnye aspekty istoricheskoi geografii" [Humanistic and Scientific Aspects of Historical Geography] in *Noosfera i khudozhestvennoe tvorchestvo* (Moscow: Nauka, 1991). See here again Epstein 2006.

29. Scanlan 1994, Introduction, 24.

30. Other representatives of Neo-Slavophilism are Pavel Tulaev and Evgeny Troitsky. See Tulaev's article "Sobor and sobornost" in *Russian Studies in Philosophy* 31: 4, 1993, 25-53.

Explanation of Terms

Certain historical terms, mostly older Russian or Asian geopolitical terms meant to cope with space, recur constantly in the present book. They must be explained because not every reader will be equally versed in the Japanese and the Russian histories of ideas. A proper introduction to Slavophilism, Pan-Slavism, Eurasianism, and Pan-Asianism is supposed to establish a solid historical background for the philosophical discussion.

Slavophilism

'Slavophilism' has two meanings, depending on if it is used in Russia or in Slav countries outside Russia. In Slav countries outside Russia, 'Slavophilism' is a generic term for all pro-Slav movements, including Pan-Slavism. In Russia, Slavophilism is restricted to certain thinkers. I will talk here about Slavophilism in the "Russian" way. The main representatives of the Slavophiles are Ivan Kireevsky (1806-1856), Alexei Khomiakov (1804-1860), Ivan Aksakov (1817-1860), Konstantin Aksakov (1817-1860), and Iurii Samarin (1817-1886). The Slavophiles were a group of Russian intellectuals who defined the values of Russian civilization as independent from Western-European culture. Russian Pan-Slavism adopted certain themes of the Russian Slavophiles though it did not consciously overtake Slavophile ideals.[1] Still, Slavophilism can be seen as the precursor of Pan-Slavism, because it is the first movement coming to terms with questions of Slav cultural identity. The problem is rather that the Russian Slavophiles manifested, in general, no solidarity with the Western Slavs (apart from the period of the Crimean War) and developed their themes into a kind of imperial "Pan-Russianism." This is especially true for the period following the war against Turkey (mid 1870s) where ideologies became racist.

Slavophilism is connected with Schelling's *Naturphilosophie* that was in the air at the beginning of the nineteenth century. For Schelling nature was spiritual, an idea that could be played out against Kant's, Hegel's, and Luther's rationalism. Romantic theories of organicism were popular in the nineteenth century and Khomiakov's definition of the church as an organic unity is a logical derivation of these ideas.

A main contribution of the Slavophiles to the history of philosophy is the division of mankind into cultures. In this they precede Oswald Spengler (1880-1936) and Arnold Toynbee (1889-1975).[2] On the basis of their considerations an outline of principles of an original, independent, and self-contained Slavic culture became possible. The "authentic character" (*samobytnost'*) and "own consciousness" (*samosoznanie*) not only of Russian, but of any culture were put forward as most important principles for the consideration of world culture.

The particularism generated by the Slavophiles probably made a later Pan-Slavist unification impossible. The Slavophiles' image as "provincial gentry," their emphasis on traditions of the Russian peasantry as well as on Orthodox themes was unacceptable for non-Russian Pan-Slavs. Their reputation for being romantic, nationalist, and reactionary is certainly not unfounded. On the other hand, it is impossible to deny them some originality that exceeds a purely nationalist agenda. It is through the Slavophiles that Russia could emerge as the first non-Western nation to challenge Eurocentric models in history and philosophy.

Pan-Slavism

Two Slovak students, Jan Kollar and Pavel Josef Safarik, transformed, in the 1820s, German Romantic nationalism into Slav nationalism.[3] Pan-Slavism represents a mixture of nationalist and supra-nationalist elements developed by non-Russian Slavs who felt the need for cooperation. It had no link whatsoever with Great Russian aspirations. Characteristically, in the Western-Slav countries, it remained the work of poets and intellectuals to give ideological shape to the nations. However, unlike Pan-Asianism in Japan, Russian Pan-Slavism never represented a political force. Shifting back and forth certain themes of German romanticism, it could not develop into a proper philosophy either.

Around 1860, Pan-Slavism became also a subject of interest in Russia. The older Russian Slavophiles (just like the "first Russian philosopher," Petr Chaadaev [1794-1856]) conceived Russia still as separated from Europe. Now, as the tendency developed towards Russian integration, reflections on the "spiritual" or "historical" destiny supposed to link together all Slav nations become more central.

Non-Russian Pan-Slavism insists on the European character of the Slav nations that require recognition as European nations. In principle, Russian Pan-Slavism was sympathetic to these intentions. Official government policy, however, adopted imperialist traits, vaguely insisting that the union of Germans should be encountered with a "Union of Slavs." This was contrary to the intentions of the Pan-Slav thinkers.

Eurasianism

Eurasianism emerged in 1921 and was based on the observations of a "dying West" and a "rising East." Its representatives are the linguist Nicolas S. Trubetzkoy, the geographer Petr Nikolaevitch Savitzky, the theologian Georgy V. Florovsky, the musicologist Pëtr P. Suvchinsky, and—most often forgotten—the legal scholar Nicolai N. Alekseev. Savitzky used the word *azijskij* ("asisch" in German) in order to form the word "*evrazijskij*" (eurasian).[4] There exists today in Russia a kind of Great-Russianism claiming to be "Eurasian." True scholarly Eurasianism, however, in spite of its conviction that Russia should lead her "Asiatic sisters," has never produced a chauvinist, imperialist branch. Therefore, Eurasianism can be considered as a truly intellectual development of Pan-Slavism and Slavophilism, purging the latter two of imperialist connotations.

Eurasianism impresses through its intellectual variety. A creation of émigré intellectuals, Eurasianists interpret the Revolution of 1917 as the point where Russia left the European world. Being critical of Marx's reduction of history to class struggle, they focus on questions concerning society or the formation of the state. Their work embraces three main fields: Geography-economics, jurisprudence and state theory, and spiritual-cultural matters. Their general tendency is to emphasize religious and metaphysical questions, which enables them to establish Russia (like Byzantium) as an amalgam of European and Asian elements, and to see the existence of "Slavic culture" as a myth. Their theories adopt "organic" tones well known since the Slavophiles and Pan-Slavism, a critique of Western philosophy (reminiscent of Kireevsky) as well as reflections on Khomiakov's idea of *sobornost'*. Curiously, these rather conservative thoughts are combined with distinctly progressive ideas about the organization of a multicultural state as laid out by Petr Struve,[5] as well as with impressive degrees of cultural relativism and anti-colonialism. At some point, Eurasianism, which had, for the longest time of its existence been living beyond the distinctions between 'left' and 'right,'[6] split up into a (Prague based) "rightwing" and a (Paris based) leftwing group. The "rightwing" branch (especially Trubetzkoy) strove to unite all non-European civilizations; the "leftwing" branch worked towards a "universal culture" covering *all* national cultures. Like Spengler and Toynbee, like the Kyoto School and Japanese culturalists, the Eurasianists excelled in oppositions of East vs. West. This makes them somehow old-fashioned. They appear even more old-fashioned when one considers the proximity that their writings manifest with the analyses of Sir Halford John Mackinder, a British geographer who wrote in 1904 an essay entitled "The Geographical Pivot of History." Mackinder suggests that the control of Eastern Europe is vital to anyone who wants to control the world. He bases his hypothesis on reflections that have become classical since: "Who rules East Europe commands the Heartland. Who rules the Heartland commands the World-Island. Who rules the World-Island commands the world."[7] According to Mackinder, the Eurasian heartland is a supercontinent contained by the Volga and Yangtze rivers, the Arctic, and the Himalayas.

Trubetzkoy's writings have an eminently culturological aspect.[8] The paradoxical combination of East-West antagonisms and a Eurasian sphere based on cultural convergence shows best perhaps that "Eurasianism is a new quality rather than merely a new configuration of well-known ideas" (Slavomir Mazurek).[9] Many ideas are well known, but they acquire a new quality in the way they are presented. Here Eurasianism comes closest to Pan-Asianism which was, as stated Vladimir Tikhinov, "rather an 'ideological tool' for advancing different sets of ideas than an independent ideology per se."[10]

Pan-Asianism

Pan-Asianism represented a movement of Asian cooperation asking for the liberation of all occupied parts of Asia. Though Japan and China represented during longer phases the main axis of Pan-Asianism, it involved also other Asian countries like Thailand, Vietnam, and India. The Bengal poet and Nobel laureate for literature in 1913, Rabindranath Tagore (1861-1941), played an important role during the formative phase of Pan-Asianism. The word *ajiashugi*, signifying "Asianism," appeared as early as in February 1852 in the journal *Ajia* (edited by *Seikyōsha*) where it was written with Chinese characters.[11] There are two words in Japanese for "Pan-Asianism": *Han Ajia Shugi* and *Dai Ajia Shugi* (Greater-Asianism). Already before 1945, *Dai Ajia Shugi* was used more frequently[12] and it is the term that one can find most often in journals.

The real sense contained in the word "Pan-Asianism" is dependent on the extent to which "cooperation" means partnership or leadership. It is certain that the "New World Order" or the "Greater East-Asian Co-prosperity Sphere (*dai tōa kyōei-ken*)[13] propagated by the Japanese government during WWII can, because of its insistence on leadership, not be understood as Pan-Asianism, just as various Russian policies for the Balkans cannot be understood as Pan-Slavist.

Pan-Slavism attempted to reflect the philosophical tradition of Herder who insisted in his *Ideen zur Geschichte der Menschheit* that *peoples* and not political movements are central participants in the creation of world history. This attitude was important for all other Pan-movements including Pan-Africanism. The Romantic stance included in these projects cannot be found in the political branch of Pan-Asianism though it is certainly present in philosophical writings of *Rōman-ha* (Japanese Romantic School) and Japanese culturalists, especially in Watsuji who used Herder's same book (though sixty years later) for his climatology.[14]

The expression "Pan-Asianism" has most probably been coined in order to indicate parallels with Pan-Slavism or Pan-Germanism. However, judging merely by formal-political criteria, Pan-Asianism can, if at all, only be compared with Pan-Germanism and Pan-Europeanism.[15] Pan-Slavism, Pan-Turkism and Pan-Scandinavianism reacted on other Pan-movements that threatened the existence of their culture (Pan-Slavism reacted against Pan-Germanism, Pan-Turkism against Pan-Slavism, and Pan-Scandinavianism against both Pan-Germanism and germinating Pan-Slavism). If we decide to see Pan-Germanism as an exceptional case (since a large number of German-speaking minorities were scattered over several countries), Pan-Asianism appears to be the most ambitious Pan-movement ever.[16] Together with Pan-Europeanism, it is the only Pan-Movement that aims at the unification of an entire continent that contains diverse languages and is linked *only* by race and a vague cultural resemblance. Leaving the 'race' aside, this represents a first clue that indicates that Pan-Asianism can be more accurately compared with Eurasianism than with any other supra-national ideology.

It is possible that TOYOTOMI Hideyoshi (1536-1598) was the first person in history to suggest an idea of Pan-Asia when he wrote to his wife: "All military leaders who shall render successful vanguard service in the coming campaign in China will be liberally rewarded with grants of extensive states near India, with the privilege of conquering India and extending their domains in the vast empire."[17] In spite of its militarist pre-history, the initial impetuous for Twentieth Century Pan-Asianism came from the Japanese art historian and specialist of Indian art, OKAKURA Kakuzō, who noted in his *Ideals of the East* that the Asiatic races should "form a single web" (*Ideals of the East*, 3). Japanese as well as all other Asians should recognize their own cultural values and "weather the storm under which so much of the Oriental world went down" (241). While Japanese particularism focusing on the emperor system began to crystallize from about 1890 (thus at the same time as the Slavophiles developed their theories of Russian uniqueness) an intellectual, anti-particularistic movement made considerable advances.

The idea of "Pan-Asianism" developed out of contacts between Okakura and Tagore.[18] Another Asian thinker striving to lead the continent towards a spiritual renaissance was NOGUCHI Yonejirō who published books that display the same attitude as Okakura's.[19] At the same time, in India, Gandhi, Aurobindo, and Radhakrishnan attempted to revitalize Hinduism while in China, Tagore's thoughts were studied by writers such as GUO Moruo, XU Zhimo, and XIE Binxin. TAKEUCHI Yoshimi states that "a special issue on Tagore's work was published by China's most influential literary journal. Suffering under the same kind of oppression, many Chinese writers identified with Tagore's opposition of resistance from their own position as fellow colonized" (Takeuchi: 158).[20]

Okakura visited India in 1901-02 and met India's cultural leaders.[21] When copies of *Ideals of the East* reached India in 1903, the Pan-Asian revival they suggested met with unexpected enthusiasm among the English-speaking Indian intelligentsia.[22] Tagore came to Japan in 1916 and tried to refuel the idea of a cultural unification of all Asian countries. However, in spite of the considerable public interest in his visit, Tagore was disappointed by the emerging Japanese militarist and nationalist attitudes and left the country in anger.

The reasons for Tagore's miscarriage in Japan cannot be attributed uniquely to Japanese militarism. The equation of an India oppressed by the British, and a Japan oppressed by America could be accepted perhaps in 1901 when Okakura and Tagore met for the first time. Fifteen years later (meanwhile Okakura had died), Japan had rushed into a phase of such intense development that the achieved level of modernization had become incomparable with that of India. In this situation it was difficult to gain support in any Japanese camp whatsoever for an idealized image of Asia reunited by its own vernacular kind of spirituality. At worst, Tagore's invocation of "spiritual values" was perceived with pity as being typical for a country unable to obtain material values. Tagore's "culturalism," as it still solemnly predicted the doom of Western civilization, was incompatible with Japan's pragmatic attitude towards modernization.

On his visits to China, Tagore met with similar reactions, as Chinese leaders found that all warnings "against material civilizations" should be rejected (cf. Hay, 191). Contrary to LIANG Qichao, who had returned from a trip to Europe greatly disillusioned because he had become aware of the West's obsession with science and materialism, China's May

Fourth generation was not ready to put "spirituality" on the top if its agenda. This generation took interest neither in Tagore's messages of anti-materialism nor in Gandhi's non-violence.[23] In 1924 Tagore was invited by Sun Yat-sen to meet in Hong Kong but declined the invitation.

In spite of the negative Japanese and Chinese receptions of Tagore's attempts to conserve Okakura's and Noguchi's spiritual values, it would certainly be wrong to say that Asians would have been generally deaf to such ideas. In 1919, a "New Asianism" (*shin-asiashugi* or *xin yaxiaya zhuyi*) was propagated by the Chinese Marxist thinker LI Dazhao (1889-1927, Ri Taishō in Japanese) who opposed to Japanese imperialist Asianism a real solidarity of Asian peoples.[24]

In Japan, revolutionaries like ŌKAWA Shūmei and KITA Ikki accepted ideas like the intuitive and introspective character of Asian culture.[25] Ōkawa emphasized the Japanese moral tradition based on Buddhism and Confucianism, as well as the community that forms a cultural unity. Kita's Pan-Asianism, formulated in 1919 in *A Plan for the Reorganization of Japan*, is not simply an example of "expansionism" but concedes that every nation (especially China) should develop its approaches towards modernization on the basis of its own tradition.[26]

While early Pan-Asianism, just like Pan-Slavism, was a vague concept inspired by Romanticism and widely settled "outside the pragmatic corridors of government,"[27] the quickly developing political front adopted other tones. A sense of opposition to any form of Western intrusion soon fostered an aggressive kind of nationalism. One seemed to restage the same development that European nations had gone through in the eighteenth century. The fact that the internationalist potential would soon be transformed into what Europeans classed as right-wing nationalism was not at all predictable. In 1904, Lenin had welcomed "the awakening of Asia and the beginning of the struggle for power by the advanced proletariat of Asia" (at times he imagined a Pan-Asian movement with Russian leadership);[28] and in 1913 the revolutionary leader Sun Yat-sen had been deeply impressed with the anti-colonial Pan-Asian theme expounded to him by Japanese prime minister KATSURA Tarō.[29]

As a matter of fact, in Japan, Pan-Asian ideas were adopted for multiple purposes. A new group identity (combined with traditional conceptions of "Japan as miniature China"[30]) soon got transfigured through its fusion with revolutionary nationalism. A Pan-Asian dimension was obtained by establishing links with Chinese revolutionary nationalism, thus producing a curious amalgam of revolutionary idealism and imperialist pragmatism. The Ultra-nationalist founder of the *Genyōsha* society, TŌYAMA Mitsuru (1855-1949),[31] received Chinese visitors, some of whom plotted to overthrow the Manchu dynasty in Peking. While the choice between diplomatic approaches and simple annexation remained a subject of discussion, liberalism gradually gave way to ultra-nationalism in almost all spheres. Most important was economic success and recognition in the international community.

In 1916, KODERA Kenkichi (1878-1949), in his book *Dai Ajiashugi Ron* (1916), points to the danger of the White Peril that should be confronted with racial unity.[32] Since that date, the intellectual or pseudo-intellectual approaches justifying this enterprise do not lack in variety. SATŌ Nobuhiro and ŌKAWA Shūmei take up the ancient concept of *hakkō ichiu*[33] (eight corners of the world under one roof) (Miwa, 134; Kennedy 1968 142) in order to design a geographical structure for a Japanese-led Pan-Asia. MATSURA Takeshiho conceives of an international order starting from the genuine love of the Ainu (Miwa, ibid.), while SHIMONAKA Yasaburo attempts to base the state upon the historical intellectual heritage of an indigenous village community (Miwa, 138).[34]

Rightwing activists like UCHIDA Ryōhei develop a "China is not a state but a civilization" theory in order to justify Japan's annexation, while[35] ISHIWARA Kanji (1889-1949)[36] suggests a system roughly comparable to that of the British monarch and a Commonwealth of Nations,[37] which he morally justifies through Nichiren's view of Japan as "the Holy sea for a moral world order."[38]

Among these approaches only the more liberal Shōwa Research Association (to which belonged also the philosopher MIKI Kiyoshi) stands out through its more scientific and modern vision of Asia.[39] From 1933 onward, the policy scientist RŌYAMA Masamichi reformulates the concept of "Greater East-Asian Regionalism" with the help of German geopolitical thought, especially that of Karl Haushofer (1869-1946) (Miwa 137). Rōyama insists that the Japanese should reproduce neither Western imperialism nor Chinese nationalism (which, he believed, was supported by the West) and struggles to establish a new model for Asian regionalism that would transcend both Western and Chinese "modern" movements.[40] Through the Shōwa Research Association, a politico-geographical perspective becomes integrated into approaches that had so far been limited to juridical questions and treaties (Miwa 147). Behind this change is not only the worldwide popularity of Haushofer's works, but also the appearance of regional trade "blocs" common in the West since the 1920s (Peattie 333). Correspondingly, to propagate Pan-Asianism in the 1930s means to propagate a "national policy" that is no longer culturally idealistic but inscribed in a larger international political spectrum in which a pragmatic grammar of blocs and groupings has replaced vague culturalist evocations of common roots. In 1910, Pan-Asian solidarity was still mainly based on simplistic arguments drawn from the domain of nativism. Now, Pan-Asianism has become a thoroughly materialist and economically minded form of regionalism.

Still it seems that scientific materialism has been unable to entirely prevent populist idealism from prospering. General MATSUI Iwane (1878-1948), commander in chief of the Japanese expeditional force in Shanghai from 1937 to 1939 and in charge of the troops in Nanjing, referred to the Asians as "brothers within the Asian family" even in 1937. MARUYAMA Masao comments on this event by saying that "the general really believed his talk about brotherly love."[41] In 1940, Foreign Minister Matsuoka declares that the mission of Japan would be to propagate to the world the way of the Tenno. Any earlier idealist, cosmopolitan type of nationalism is definitely abandoned.[42]

It is clear that political cynicism can be developed in the realm of materialism as much as in the realm of idealism. One of the results of the new "geopolitical" approach was that the establishment of the "independent" state of Manchukuo could now be justified in terms of a mutuality of interdependence. The existence of an "annexation" was denied (Miwa 145).

In summary one might say that the above-described "scientific attitude" has been far too shallow. Retrospectively, Japanese geopolitics of the time looks as romantic as its culturalism. Richard Storry is probably right when blaming the "political immaturity of the Japanese people" for such failures as well as the fact that "for any Japanese [it had been] difficult to think in terms beyond those of nationality or of national interest."[43]

In any case, the attempts to create a new form of culturalism, which thinkers like Nishida and Watsuji would subsequently undertake, must be understood within this context. A really scientific theory of Japanese culture had never existed (*had* it existed, things might have developed otherwise). True, Nishida and his pupils overtook much of an organic theory of the state (that was commonplace anyway among intellectuals worldwide); but apart from that, Nishida's idea that the spirit of culture is always something non-material—a nothingness present in a culture—must be designated as an approach distinct from both materialism and idealism.

Notes

1. The Slavophiles were simply not sufficiently known in Czecheslovakia at that time, and especially non-Russian Pan-Slavism has been developed relatively independently by Czech and Slovak scholars. Cf. Milojkovic-Djuric 1994.

2. Cf. Boro-Petrovich 1956, 35. According to MacMaster, also Nineteenth Century historians like H. Rückert, G. Gervinius and C. von Rotteck worked on

lists of civilizations. Robert MacMaster: *Danilevsky: A Russian Totalitarian Philosopher*. Harvard University Press, 1967, 205.

3. Also to mention are the Czechs Frantisek Palatsky, Frantisek Rieger and the Pole Adam Mickievicz. See Hans Kohn: *Pan-Slavism: Its History and Ideology* (Notre Dame: University of Notre Dame Press, 1953).

4. "Evrasijstvo" in *Evrazijskij vremennik* Vol. 4 Berlin 1925, 7, note. The Eurasianists, as Savitzky insists, are not the first people who saw Eurasia as a third continent, but Russian geographers like V. I. Lapansky drew attention to the existence of an autonomous Eurasia in 1892 (6).

5. Cf. Sergei Glebov: "Science, Culture, and Empire: Eurasianism as a Modern Movement" in *Slavic & East European Information Resources* 4: 4, 16.

6. Cf. L. I. Novirkovka and I. I. Sisemskaja: *Россиа между Европой и Азией: Евразийский соблазн. Антология* (Moscow: Nauka, 1993), 13.

7. Sir Halford Mackinder: "The Geographical Pivot of History" in *Democratic Ideals and Reality* [1904] (New York: Norton, 1962), 213ff.

8. I am using this term not necessarily in the Russian sense as an identity-oriented humanistic research but in the German or American sense of Kulturwissenschaften or cultural turn coined in the 1960s. (In Russia culturology is an often compulsory part of university courses that largely replaces the teaching of dialectical materialism).

9. Slavomir Mazurek: "Russian Eurasianism—Historiosophy and Ideology" *Slavic and East European Thought* 54 1-2 March 2002, 120.

10. Vladimir Tikhinov: "Korea's First Encounter with Pan-Asianism Ideology," http://world.lib.ru/k/kim_o_i/ n101.shtml.

11. Cf. Yves Bougon, "Le Japon et le discours asiatiste" in Ph. Pelletier (ed.): *Identités territoriales en Asie orientale*. Paris: Les Indes Savantes, 2004, 241.

12. Cf. W. G. Beasley, 1987. "Japan and Pan-Asianism: Problems of Definition" in Janet Hunter (ed.), *Aspects of Pan-Asianism*. London: London School of Economics, 1987.

13. Prime Minister KONOYE Fumimaro's "New Order in East Asia" proclamation of 1938 propagated the concept of "Greater East Asia Co-Prosperity Sphere" made public by Foreign Minister MATSUOKA Yosuke on 1.8.1940). It was the official name given to the Asian territories that Japan had occupied during and before the Pacific War. While the "Inner" Co-Prosperity Sphere contained only Japan, Manchuria, the Lower Yangtze Region and Maritime Russia, the "Greater" Co-Prosperity Sphere contained East Asia, Australia, India, and the Pacific Islands (cf. Bary, Theodore de, Ryusaku Tsunoda, Donald Keene (eds). 1964. *Sources of Japanese Tradition* (New York: Columbia University Press, 1964), 802).

14. WATSUJI Tetsurō. 1935. 風土 : 人間学的考察 (Fudō: Ningengakuteki kōsatsu; Climate: A Study in Humanities). Tokyo: Chuokoronsha. German transl.: *Fudo: Der Zusammenhang zwischen Klima und Kultur* (Darmstad: Wissenschaftliche Buchgesellschaft 1992).

15. The Pan-European movement was founded in 1923 by Richard Coudenhove-Kalergi and is considered a precursor of the European Union. Coudenhove's writings (see bibliography) manifest amazing parallels with Trubetzkoy's, especially with regard to a "conversionist" conception of culture. This is particularly evident in Coudenhove's concept of "Eurafrica" that Coudenhove sug-

gested in 1923 in his book *Paneuropa* (Wien: Herold, 1966). See also *Europa Erwacht!* Wien: Pan-Europa Verlag, 1934. For Eurafrica see Liliana Elena: "'Political Imagination, Sexuality and Love in the Eurafrican Debate" in *The European Revue of History* 11: 2, 2004; and Charles R. Ageron: "L'Idée d'Eurafrique" in *Revue d'Histoire moderne et contemporaine* 1975.

16. One catalyst for the rapid and widespread development of Pan-Africanism was the colonization of the continent by European powers in the late nineteenth century. The First Pan-African Congress, convened in London in 1900. The congresses were attended by the North American and West Indian black intelligentsia and did not propose immediate African independence; they favored gradual self-government and interracialism. In 1944, several African organizations in London joined to form the Pan-African Federation, which for the first time demanded African autonomy and independence. Pan-Africanism as an intergovernmental movement was launched in 1958 with the First Conference of Independent African States in Accra, Ghana. Ghana and Liberia were the only sub-Saharan countries represented; the remainder were Arab and Muslim. Thereafter, as independence was achieved by more African states, other interpretations of Pan-Africanism emerged, including: the Union of African States (1960), the African States of the Casablanca Charter (1961), the African and Malagasy Union (1961), the Organization of Inter-African and Malagasy States (1962), and the African-Malagasy-Mauritius Common Organization (1964). In 1963 the Organization of African Unity (OAU) was founded to promote unity and cooperation among all African states and to bring an end to colonialism. One of its longest commitments and greatest victories was the end of apartheid and the establishment of majority rule in South Africa. Efforts to promote even greater African economic, social, and political integration led to the establishment in 2001 of the African Union (AU), a successor organization to the OAU modeled on the European Union. Pan-Arabism is a movement for unification among the Arab peoples and nations of the Middle East. It is closely connected to Arab nationalism. Pan-Arabism has tended to be both secular, socialist, and against Western influence.

17. Letter from 1592. Quoted from Stephen Hay: *Asian Ideas of East and West: Tagore and his Critics in Japan, China, and India* (Cambridge: Harvard University Press, 1970), 112.

18. Hay points to the fact that the initial idea of Pan-Asianism might have been developed by Western intellectuals and that the Asians picked these ideas up. Above that, Asianism is certainly also connected to a refusal of Western Yellow-Peril thinking.

19. NOGUCHI Yonejiro: *The Spirit of Japanese Art* (London: Murray, 1915); *The Spirit of Japanese Poetry* (London: Dutton, 1914). It needs to be mentioned that Pan-Asianist ideas existed already in the 1870s and were propagated through UEKI Emori and TARUI Tōkichi (1850-1922) who wanted to unite Japan with China.

20. Simultaneously KU Hung-ming, LIANG Sou-ming, and CHANG Chun-mai attempted to strengthen Confucian traditions while TAI Xu and LIANG Qichao strengthened Buddhist traditions. Baogang He: "East Asian Ideas of Regionalism: A Normative Critique" in *Australian Journal of International Affairs* Vol. 58: 1 March 2004, 107.

21. The Bengali religious leaders Mozoomdar and Vivekananda had visited Japan in the 1880s and 1890s.

22. Hay, 39. Hay's book provides a very detailed account of the Tagore's activities in East Asia.

23. Cf. Rana Mitter: *A Bitter Revolution: China's Struggle With the Modern World* (Oxford: Oxford University Press, 2004), 278.

24. LI Dazhao was one of the founders of the Chinese communist party and was executed in 1927. See Bougon 251.

25. Cf. Christopher Szpilman: "The Dream of one Asia: Ōkawa Shūmei and Japanese Pan-Asianism" in Harald Füss (ed.), *The Japanese Empire in East Asia and its Postwar Legacy.* München: Iudicium, 1998, 55ff

26. *A Plan for the Reorganization of Japan* (*Nihonkaizō hōan taikō* [1919]) has usually been condemned as fascist. Kita considers Japanese social traditions and introduces neo-Confucian elements. In Kita's plan there are suggestions of de-modernization. See George Wilson *Radical Nationalist in Japan: Kita Ikki 1883-1937.* Cambridge, MA: Harvard University Press, 1969, 79.

27. "Introduction" to James White et al. (eds): *The Ambivalence of Nationalism: Modern Japan Between East and West* (Lanham, MD: University Press of America, 1990), 6.

28. Vladimir Lenin: "The Awakening of Asia" in *Collected Writings* Vol. 19 (Moscow: Progress Publishers, 1963), 86. Later on, Stalin would call himself "Asian" in order to assume leadership in Asia. On the first Pan-Asian congress in Bandung, the Soviet Union appeared as the alley of all victims of colonialism and imperialism. Cf. R. Coudenhove-Kalergi: *Weltmacht Europa* (Stuttgart: Seewald, 1976), 52.

29. Albert Altman & Harold Schifferin: "Sun Yat-sen and the Japanese: 1914-16" in *Modern Asian Studies* 6: 4, 1972, 386.

30. Cf. Joseph Kennedy: *Asian Nationalism in the Twentieth Century.* London, Melbourne: Mamillian, 1960), 19.

31. The *Genyōsha* 玄洋社 (Dark Ocean Society) was a nationalist society founded about 1881 with the goal to establish Japanese domination in Asia. In 1901 *genyōsha* leaders founded the "Amur Society" whose purpose was the "heightening of the wisdom and virtue of the Yamato race (1930 document of the Amur Society)." Quoted from Bary et. al., *Sources . . .*, 761. The Amur society cooperated with the nationalist Chinese revolution of Sun Yat-Sen.

32. See MIWA Kimitada. "Japanese Policies and Concepts for a Regional Order in Asia, 1938-1940" in White 1990, 140.

33. *Hakkō ichiu* 八紘一宇 (Chinese pronunciation *bahong yiyū*) signifies in Chinese that all corners of the world can be governed like one's own house. It can be found in the *Nihongi*, and according to the *Kokugo Daijiten* (Ed. Shōgakkan) Emperor Kanmu used it already in the sense of "to unify the country." ŌKAWA Shūmei presents the concept in his *History of Japan from 660 BC.* See also Kennedy 1968, 142 and Mark Peattie: "Though, under the principle of *hakkō ichiu,* the Japanese Emperor will be leader of the East Asian League and eventually the world, Japan itself will not occupy this position." *Ishiwara Kanji and the Japanese Confrontation with the West* (Princeton University Press, 1975), 321.

34. The panoramic perspective can be prolonged: NAKAYAMA Masaru explains how to bring about communitarian social change by concentrating on

agrarian cultural values (140). According to Miwa, this "agrarianist response to the social problems of Japan had become the prototype of the new order to be established in East Asia" by the end of the 1930s (141).

35. Miwa, 136. NAITŌ Konan (1868-1945) explained why a modern Nation State could not be formed there because "in China there are no greater [subjectively] bodily organizations than a village community or an extended family."

36. ISHIWARA Kanji was a Japanese military officer in the Guandong Army. He and ITAGAKI Seishirō were the men behind the Mukden Incident that took place in Manchuria in 1931.

37. Cf. Peattie 333: KITA Ikki's "revolutionary empire" at the center of Asian reform was a notion not unlike Ishiwara's.

38. Japan's leading role in the Pan-Asian cooperation and especially Manchukuo is established in an idealistic way as a "racial paradise" for the various peoples of Manchuria. It is the question of creating a "third civilization," of letting China return to East Asia, and of the foundation of world peace.

39. In 1936, GOTŌ Ryūnosuke, Prince Konoe's close friend, organized the *Shōwa kenkyū-kai* (Shōwa Research Association) to advise the prince on long-range political and economic planning. He invited distinguished scholars, such as the philosopher MIKI Kiyoshi, the political scientist RŌYAMA Masamichi. Cf. Miwa 137 and Ben-Ami Shillony: *Politics and Culture in Wartime Japan* (Oxford: Clarendon 1981), 111.

40. Cf. NOJIMA KATO Yoko: "The Attraction of Regionalism: Japanese Conceptions of Transnational Integration and Chinese Responses 1912-1945" Unpublished paper presented at the Second International Convention of Asia Scholars, Berlin 2001. http://www4.ocn.ne.jp/~aninoji/final.comments.html.

41. MARUYAMA Masao: *Thought and Behaviour Patterns of Japan's Wartime Leaders* [1949] (Oxford University Press, 1963), 95.

42. Cf. UMEGAKI Michio's Epilogue "National Identity, National Past, National Isms" in White 1990: "Little room was left for persons like KIYOSAWA Kiyoshi or the young ISHIBASHI Tanzan to assert any influence on official policy. Their idealistic nationalism—tolerant of others' nationalism and presuming a higher authority regulating the relationships among states—had little chance of survival."

43. Richard Storry: *The Double Patriots: A Story of Japan's Nationalism.* Westport, CT: Greenwood, 1957, 299.

Timeline:
"Philosophical Events in Russia and Japan"

RUSSIA	JAPAN
	7th-8th centuries: Establishment of centralized state
10th-13th centuries: Kievan State	
MONGOL INVASION (13th Century)	
1725 "Modernizer" Peter the Great dies	1716-36: Kyōhō Reforms
1836 Petr Chaadaev "the first original Russian philosopher" (M. Epstein) publishes the "Philosophical Letter"	
1840 First Russian Slavophiles gather in Moscow ("paternalist and conservative")	
1848-49: Revolutions in Prague, Vienna, and Budapest	
1848: First Pan-Slav Congress in Prague	
1850: "Westernizer" Herzen's *From the Other Shore*	
1853-56: CRIMEAN WAR	1853: Perry Expedition
1858: Formal Foundation of Russian Pan-Slav Movement	
1867 Moscow Slav Congress	**1867: MEIJI RESTAURATION**
1860-70 Major Reforms (1861: emancipation of serfs)	1871: Abolition of Feudal Divisions
1871: Danilevsky's *Russia and Europe* (the "Pan-Slavist Bible")	

143

1881 Tsar Alexander II assassinated	
	1887: INOUE Enryō founds the *Philosophical Institute* to promote the study of Buddhism
1888 Solov'ëv, "the first Russian original systematical philosopher" (Lossky) publishes *The National Question in Russia*	
1901: Foundation of the Religious-Philosophical Society of St. Petersburg	
1902: Symposium "Problems of Idealism"	1902: Okakura's *Ideals of the East* inaugurating the "Asian Spiritual Renaissance"
1904-1909: Articles by Symbolist writers appear in *Vesy*, inaugurating the "Russian Religious-Philosophical Renaissance"	
1904-05: RUSSO-JAPANESE WAR	
	1906: KITA Ikki's *Theory of National Polity and Pure Socialism*
	1908-09: "Paternalist, conservative and rational" Chairs in "Colonial Studies" are created at Tokyo and Waseda Universities
	1911: Nishida, "the first original Japanese philosopher" writes *Zen no Kenkyū*
	1911: Sun-Yat sen's Revolutionary Movement in China
1912: S. Trubetzkoy's *Solov'ëv's Worldview*	
RUSSIAN REVOLUTION OF 1917	
	1918 Japanese Radicals around ŌKAWA Shūmei found the Rōsōkai Society
1921: Eurasianist Manifesto *Exodus to the East*	
	1929: Kuki's *The Structure of 'Iki'*
	1931-32: Japan's Takeover of Manchuria
	Round-Table Discussions of right-wing philosophers: "The World-Historical Standpoint and Japan
	1935: Watsuji's *Culture and Climate*

	1935: The Japanese Romantic School begins publishing its journal *Nihon Rōmanha*
	1937: SINO-JAPANESE WAR
1937: Last volume of the *Eurasian Chronicle* appears	
	1941: ATTACK OF PEARL HARBOR
	1942: Conference "Overcoming of Modernity"
	1943: Nishida's *Principle of a New World Order*

Bibliography

Abe, Masao. "Nishida's Philosophy of Place," *International Philosophical Quarterly* (1988): 28: 4.

Areopagite. *The Divine Names and Mystical Theology.* Milwaukee: Marquette University Press, 1980.

Aksakov, K. S. "Über Russlands inneren Zustand," *Östliches Christentum* 1 (1855): 82-120.

Alekseev, Nikolai. "Евразийцы и государство," *Евразийская хроника* 9 (1927) 31-39.

Anno, Tadashi. "*Nihonjinron* and *Russkaia Ideia*: Transformation of Japanese and Russian Nationalism in the Postwar Era and Beyond" in G. Rozman (ed.) *Japan and Russia: The Tortuous Path to Normalization, 1949–1999.* New York: St. Martin's Press, 2000.

Antoshchenko, Alexander. "On Eurasia and the Eurasians: Studies on Eurasianism in Current Russian Historiography" http://petrsu.ru/Chairs/Archiv/BIBLENG.RTF, 2000.

Antonioli, Manola. *Géophilosophie de Deleuze et Guattari.* Paris: Harmattan, 2003.

Altman, Albert & Harold Schifferin. "Sun Yat-sen and the Japanese: 1914-16," *Modern Asian Studies* (1972): 6: 4.

Arima, Tatsuo. *The Failure of Freedom: A Portrait of Modern Japanese Intellectuals.* Cambridge, MA: Harvard University Press, 1969.

Arisaka, Yoko. *Space and History: Philosophy and Imperialism in Nishida and Watsuji.* Riverside: University of California Press, 1996.

Bakhtin, Mikhail M. *Творчество Фурансуа Рабле и народная култура средневековъя и ренессанса.* Moskow: Khudozh. Literatura, 1965. Engl. transl.: *Rabelais and his World.* Cambridge, MA: MIT Press, 1968.

———. "Проблема содержания, материала и формы в словесном художественном творчестве," *Вопросы литература и эстетики. Исслед обвания лет.* Moscow: Khudozh. Litetatura: 6-71, 1975a. Engl. transl.: "The Problem of Content, Material and Form in Verbal Art" in *Art and Answerability.*

————. "Слово в Романе," *Вопросы литература и эстетики. Исслед обвания лет.* Moscow: Khudozh. Litetatura 1975b. Engl. transl.: "Discourse in the Novel" in *The Dialogic Imagination*. Austin: University of Texas Press, 1981.

————. *Проблемы поэтики Достоевского.* Moscow: Sovietskaja Rossija, 1979. Engl. trans. (by Emerson): *Problems of Dostoevsky's Poetics.* Minneapolis: Minnesota University Press, 1984.

————. "Автор и герой в эстетической деятельности," *Работы 1920-х годов.* Kiev: Next, 1994a. Engl. trans.: "Author and Hero in Aesthetic Activity" in *Art and Answerability. Early Essays.* Austin: University of Texas Press, 1990.

————. "Искусство и ответственностъ," *Работы 1920-х годов.* Kiev: Next, 1994b. Engl. trans.: "Art and Answerability" in *Art and Answerability. Early Essays.* Austin: University of Texas Press, 1990.

Bakunin, Mikhail. *God and the State.* New York: Dover, 1870.

Barabanov, E. V. "Russian Philosophy and the Crisis of Identity," *Russian Studies in Philosophy* (1992): 31: 2, 24-51.

Bary, Theodore de, Ryusaku Tsunoda, Donald Keene (eds). *Sources of Japanese Tradition* ["The Rise of Revolutionary Nationalism," 759-805]. New York: Columbia University Press, 1964.

Bastid, Marianne. "Review of Hao CHANG's *Chinese Intellectuals in Crisis: Search for Order and Meaning,*" *Pacific Affairs* 62: 1 (1989): 97-99.

Baudrillard, Jean. *Art and Artefact* in N. Zurbrugg (ed.), *Jean Baudrillard: Art and Artefact.* London, Thousand Oaks, 1997.

Bazhanov, Valentin. "Philosophy in Post-Soviet Russia," *Studies in East European Thought* 51: 3 (1999): 219-241.

Beasley, W. G. "Japan and Pan-Asianism: Problems of Definition" in Janet Hunter (ed.), *Aspects of Pan-Asianism.* London: London School of Economics, 1987.

Beaune, Danièle. "I. M. Grevs, juge de L. P. Karsavin," *Revue des études slaves* 68: 3 (1996).

Belinsky, Vissarion G. *Selected Philosophical Works.* Moscow: Progress, 1956.

Bellah, Robert. "Japan's Cultural Identity: Some Reflections on the Work of Watsuji Tetsuro," *Journal of Asian Studies* 24: 4 (1965): 573-594.

Benl, Oscar. *Seami Motokiyo und der Geist des Nô-Schauspiels. Geheime kunstkritische Schriften aus dem 15. Jahrhundert.* Mainz: Steiner, 1952.

Berdiaev, Nicolai. "Из этюдов о Я. Беме. Этюд 1: учение об унгрундье и свободе" [Studies on J. Böhme. 1. The teaching about the *Ungrund* and freedom] in *Путь* 20 (1930): 47-79.

————. *Aleksei Stepanivitch Khomiakov.* Moscow, 1912.

————. "Духовные задачы эмиграций" *Put'* 1 (1925): 3-8.

————. "Утопический этатизм евразийце," *Путъ* 8 (1927): 141–48.

————. "The Ethics of Creativity" in A. Schmemann (ed.), *Ultimate Questions: An Anthology of Modern Russian Religious Thought.* Crestwood: St. Vladimir's Seminar Press, 1977.

————. *The Russian Idea.* New York: Macmillian, 1948.

Bergson, Henri. *Fichte.* Strasbourg: Presses Universitaires de Strasbourg, 1988.

Berlin, Isaiah. *Russian Thinkers.* London: The Hogarth Press, 1978.

Berque, Augustin and Nys, Philippe (eds). *Logique du lieu et œuvre humain.* Brussels: Ousia, 1997.

Besançon, Alain. "Peut-on intégrer la Russie dans un ordre mondial oligopolaire?" in J. Baechler & R. Kamrane (ed.) *Aspects de la mondialisation politique.* Paris: Académie des sciences, 2001.

Bhabha, Homi. *Nation and Narration.* New York: Routledge & Kegan Paul, 1990.

———. *The Location of Culture.* New York: Routledge, 1994.

———. "Of Mimicry and Man: The Ambivalence of Colonial Discourse," *October 28* (1984): 125-133.

Binswanger, Ludwig. *Grundformen und Erkenntnis des menschlichen Daseins.* Zürich: Niehans, 1953.

Bird, Robert. "Martin Heidegger and Russian Symbolist Philosophy," *Studies in East European Thought* 51: 2 (1999): 85-108.

Bizilli, Pavel M. "'Восток' и 'запад' в истории Старого Света" [East and West in the history of the old world] in *На путях: Утверждение евразийцев.* Moscow & Berlin, 1922.

Black, Cyril (ed.). *The Modernization of Japan and Russia: A Comparative Study.* New York: The Free Press, 1975.

———. 1927. "Два лика евразийства," *Современные записики* (Paris) 31: 421-426.

Böss, Otto. *Die Lehre der Eurasier: Ein Beitrag zur russischen Ideengeschichte des 20. Jahrhunderts* Wiesbaden: Harrassowitz, 1961.

Bobrinskoy, Boris. "L'Icône: Objet d'art ou de culte?" in: Saint Jean Damascène: *L'Icône: Objet d'art ou objet de culte?* Paris: Cerf, 2001.

Bohner, Hermann. *Noh.* Tokyo: Deutsche Gesellschaft für Natur und Völkerkunde, 1959.

Bolshakoff, Serge N. *The Doctrine of the Unity of the Church in the Works of Khomiakov and Moehler.* London, 1945.

Boobbyer, Philip. *S. L. Frank: Life and Work of a Russian Philosopher 1877-1950.* Athens: Ohio University Press, 1995.

Borisov, Vadim, Felix F. Perchenok & Arsenii B. Roginsky. 1993. "Community as a Source of Vernadsky's Concept of Noosphere," *Configurations* 1: 3, 415-438.

Boro-Petrovich, Michael. *The Emergence of Russian Pan-Slavism 1856-1870.* New York: Columbia University Press, 1956.

Botz-Bornstein, Thorsten. *Place and Dream: Japan and the Virtual.* Amsterdam, New York: Rodopi, 2003.

———. (ed. with Jürgen Hengelbrock). *Re-ethnicizing the Minds? Cultural Revival in Contemporary Thought.* Amsterdam, New York: Rodopi, 2006.

———. "All-Unity Seen Through Perspective or the Narrative of Virtual Cosmology," *Seeking Wisdom* 2 (2005).

———. "Virtual Reality and Dream: Towards the Autistic Condition?," *Philosophy in the Contemporary World* 11: 2 (2004): 43-49.

Bougon, Yves. "Le Japon et le discours asiatiste" in Ph. Pelletier (ed.): *Identités territoriales en Asie orientale.* Paris: Les Indes Savantes, 2004.

Bouterwek, Friedrich. *Idee einer Apodiktik,* 2 vols. Halle: Renger, 1799.

Brook, Peter. *The Empty Space.* New York: Touchstone, 1968.

Brown, Delmer M. *Nationalism in Japan: An Introductory Historical Analysis.* Los Angeles: University of California Press, 1955.

Brzezinsky, Zbigniev. *The Grand Chessboard—American Primacy and its Geostrategic Imperatives.* New York: Basic Books, 1997.

Buber, Martin. *Ich und Du* (Werke, Vol. 1). München: Kösel, 1962-64.

Bulgakov, Sergei. "Heroism and Asceticism (Reflections on the Religious Nature of the Russian Intelligentsia)," M. Shatz and J. Zimmermann (eds), *Signposts – vekhi.* Irvine: Schlacks, 23-63, 1986.

———. О рынках при капиталическом производстве [On markets in capitalist production]. Moscow: Kolchugin, 1897.

Burkman, Thomas W. "Nitobe Inazō: From World Order to Regional Order," J. Th. Rimer: *Culture and Identity: Japanese Intellectuals During the Interwar Years.* Princeton: Princeton University Press, 1990.

Bychkov, Viktor. "Russian Religious Aesthetics," M. Kelly (ed.) *Encyclopedia of Aesthetics* Vol 4. Oxford: Oxford University Press, 1998, 195-202.

———. "Die Eigenart des russsischen ästhetischen Bewußtseins im Mittelalter" in *Ostkirchliche Studien* 41: 1 (1992), 22-33.

Bykova, Marina. "Nation and Nationalism. Russia in Search of its National Identity," E. Zweerde & G. Steunebrink: *Civil Society, Religion, and the Nation: Modernization in Intercultural Context: Russia, Japan, Turkey.* Amsterdam & New York: Rodopi, 2004.

Byung-joon, Ahn. "Regionalism in the Asia-Pacific: Asian or Pacific Community?," *Korea Focus* 4: 4 (1996): 5-23.

Calman, Donald. *The Nature and Origins of Japanese Imperialism: A Reinterpretation of the Great Crisis of 1873.* London: Routledge, 1992.

Chaadaev, Petr. *Sochineniia i pismi* 1. Moscow: Mysl, 1913.

Chamberlin, William Henry. *Japan Over Asia* (Boston: Little Brown), 1937.

Chang, Hao. *Liang Ch'i-ch'ao and Intellectual Transition in China: 1890-1907.* Cambridge, MA: Harvard University Press, 1971.

Chari, C. T. "Russian and Indian Mysticism in East-West Synthesis" *Philosophy East & West* 2: 2 (1952): 226-237.

Cheng, François. *Cinq méditations sur la beauté.* Paris: Albin Michel, 2006.

Chernyshevsky, Nikolai G. Что делать? [What is to be done] in Современник (St. Petersburg), 1863.

Christoff, Peter K. *An Introduction to Nineteenth Century Russian Slavophilism. A Study in Ideas,* Vol. 1: A. S. Xomiakov. 'S-Gravenhage: Mouton, 1961.

Coleman, Frederic. *The Far East Unveiled: An Inner History of Events in Japan and China in the Year 1916.* Wilmington: Scholarly Resources Inc., 1973.

Cooper, Simon. "Plenitude and Alienation. The Subject of Virtual Reality" in Holmes, David (ed.) *Virtual Politics. Identity and Community in Cyber-Space.* London: Sage, 1997.

Coudenhove-Kalergi, Richard. *Weltmacht Europa.* Stuttgart: Seewald, 1976.

Dale, Peter. *The Myth of Japanese Uniqueness.* New York: St. Martin's Press, 1986.

Danilevsky, Nicolai. Россия и Европа [Russia and Europe]. St. Petersburg: Obshestvenna Pol'za, 1867.

Deleuze, Gilles. *Différence et répétition.* Paris: PUF, 1968.

Deleuze, Gilles & Félix Guattari. *Mille Plateaux: Capitalisme et schizophrénie 2.* Paris: Minuit, 1980.

Dilworth, D. A. "The Initial Formations of *"Pure Experience"* in Nishida Kitarō and William James," *Monumenta Nipponica* 24 (1969): 93-111.

———. "Nishida's Early Pantheistic Voluntarism," *Philosophy East & West* 20 (1970).

———. "Nishida Kitarō. Nothingness as the Negative Space of Experiential Immediacy," *International Philosophical Quarterly* 13: 4 (1973): 463-485.

———. "Watsuji Tetsurō (1889-1960): Cultural Phenomenologist and Ethician" in *Philosophy East & West* 24: 1 (1974).

———. "The Concrete World of Action in Nishida's Later Thought," in Nitta, U. and Tatematsu H. (eds) *Japanese Phenomenology* (Analecta Husserliana 8). Dordrecht: Kluwer, 1978.

———. "Introduction" to Nishida, *Last Writings. Nothingness and a Religious Worldview.* Honolulu: University of Hawai'i Press, 1987.

———. With V. H. Viglielmo (eds). *Sourcebook for Modern Japanese Philosophy: Selected Documents.* Westport, CT: Greenwood, 1998.

Doak, Kevin Michael. *Dreams of Difference: The Japan Romantic School and the Crisis of Modernity.* Berkeley: University of California Press, 1994.

Durkheim, Emile. *De la Division du travail social.* Paris: Presse universitaire française, 1893.

———. *The Structure of Social Action* (2 volumes). New York: McGraw Hill, 1937.

———. *The Social System.* New York: The Free Press, 1951.

Edie, J. M., J. P. Scanlan & M. B. Zeldin. *Russian Philosophy* (3 Vols.). Chicago: Quadrangle, 1966.

Elena, Liliana. 2004. "Political Imagination, Sexuality and Love in the Eurafrican Debate," *The European Revue of History* 11: 2.

Elias, Norbert. 1978 [1939]. *The Civilizing Process: The History of Manners.* New York: Urizen Books.

Epstein, Klaus. *Die Ursprünge des Konservatismus in Deutschland.* Berlin: Ullstein, 1973.

Epstein, Mikhail. "Response: 'Post-' and Beyond," *Slavic and East European Journal* 39: 3 (1995a): 357-366.

———. *After the Future: The Paradoxes of Postmodernism and Contemporary Russian Culture.* Amherst: Massachusetts University Press, 1995b.

———. "Russian Philosophy of National Spirit from the 1970s to the 1990s" in Th. Botz-Bornstein & J. Hengelbrock (eds.) *Re-ethnicize the Minds? Tendencies of Cultural Revival in Contemporary Philosophy.* Amsterdam: Rodopi, 2006.

Faure, Bernard. "The Kyoto School and Reverse Orientalism" in Heine, Steven and Charles Wei-hsun Fu. 1995. *Japan in Traditional and Postmodern Perspectives.* Albany, NY: SUNY Press, 1995.

Fedotov, Georgy. "Судьба империй," *Новый журнал* 16 (1947).

Fichte, Johann Gottlieb. *Darstellung der Wissenschaftslehre aus dem Jahre 1801.* Berlin: Veit, 1845.

————. *Erste und zweite Einleitung in die Wissenschaftslehre*. Hamburg: Meiner, 1920.

Fink, Hilary L. *Bergson and Russian Modernism 1900-1930*. Evanston, IL: Northwestern University Press, 1999.

Fitzgerald, John. "The Nationless State: The Search for a Nation in Modern Chinese Nationalism," *Australian Journal of Chinese Affairs* 33 (1995): 75-104.

Fletcher, Miles. "Intellectuals and Fascism in Early Showa Japan," *Journal of Asian Studies* 39: 1 (1979) 39-63.

Florensky, Pavel A. *Столп и утверждение истины* [The Pillar and Foundation of Truth]. Moscow: Izdavitel'stvo pravda 1990 [1914]. Engl.: *The Pillar and Ground of the Truth* (Princeton University Press, 1997).

Florovsky, Georgy; P. Savitsky, P. Suvchinsky, and N. Trubetzkoy. *Исход к востоку: Предчуствия и свершения. Утверждение евразийцев* [Exodus to the East: Forboding and events. An affirmation of the Eurasians. Sofia: Balkan, 1921.

————. "Еврасийский соблазн," *Современные записки* 34 (1928): 312-346.

Frank, Semën L. *Душа человека: опыт введения в философскую психологию* (1917) (republished by Nauka, in Moscow: 1995) Engl.: *Man's Soul: An Introductory Essay in Philosophical Psychology*. Athens: Ohio University Press, 1993.

————. *Духовные основы общества: введение в социальную философию.* Paris: YMCA Press (republished in New York, 1988). Engl: *The Spiritual Foundations of Society: An Introduction to Social Philosophy*. Athens: Ohio University Press, 1987.

————. *The Unknowable: An Ontological Introduction to the Philosophy of Religion* (Athens: Ohio University Press, 1983) originally published as *Непостижимое* in *Put'* May/Sept. Nr. 60, 1939.

Fukuzawa, Yukichi. *An Outline of a Theory of Civilization [bunmeiron no gairyaku]*, transl. by D. Dilworth and C. Hurst. Tokyo: Sophia University Press, 1970.

Fustel de Coulanges, Numa Denis. *La Cité antique*. Paris: Hachette, 1880 [1864].

Gadamer, Hans-Georg. *Truth and Method*. New York: Continuum, 1975.

Gaidenko, Piama. "The Philosophy of Freedom of Nicolai Berdiaev" in Scanlan (ed): *Russian Thought After Communism: The Recovery of a Philosophical Heritage*. Armonk, NY: M. E. Sharp, 1994.

Galley, Gregory L. "The Art of Subversion and the Subversion of Art," *Journal of Japanese Studies* 21: 2 (1995): 365-404.

Gentelle, Pierre. 2004. "Chine: Visions de l'autre et visées sur l'autre" in Ph. Pelletier (ed.): *Identités territoriales en Asie orientale*. Paris: Les Indes Savantes.

Gessen, Sergei. "Новыи опыит интуитивной философии," *Severnie Zapiski* April-May (1916): 222-237.

Glebov, Segei. "Science, Culture, and Empire: Eurasianism as a Modern Movement," *Slavic & East European Information Resources* 4: 4 (2003): 13-31.

Gluck, Carol. *Japan's Modern Myths: Ideology in the Late Meiji Period*. Princeton: Princeton University Press, 1985.

Goddard, Jean Christophe. "Une lecture néo-platonicienne de Fichte," *Les études philosophiques* 4 (2001): 465-479.

Gombrich, Ernst. *Art and Illusion: A Study in the Psychology of Pictorial Representation.* London: Phaidon, 1960.

Goto-Jones, Christopher. "Transcending Boundaries: Nishida Kitarō, K'ang Yu-Wei, and the Politics of Unity," *Modern Asian Studies* 39: 4 (2005): 793-816.

———. "If not a Clash then What? Huntington, Nishida Kitarō, and the Politics of Civilizations," *International Relations of the Asia Pacific* 2 (2002): 223-243.

Griffin, Roger. "Europe for the Europeans: Fascist Myths of the New Order 1922-92" (1998) www.alphalink.com.au.

Gurvitch, Georges D. "La philosophie russe du premier quart du XXe siècle," *Le Monde Slave* 8 (1928).

———. *Fichtes System der konkreten Ethik.* Tübingen: Mohr, 1924.

———. *La Vocation actuelle de la sociologie* Vol. II. Paris: Presses Universitaires Françaises, 1969.

Haga, Noburu. "The Fallacy of Fukuzawa Yukichi's Datsuaron," *East West Education* 4: 1 (1983): 31-53.

Halem, Friedrich von. "Die Rechtsansichten der Eurasier—Rechtordnun oder Wertordnung," *Studies in East European Thought* 52: 1-2 (2000): 7-47.

Han, Do-Yun. "Shamanism, Superstition, and the Colonial Government," *The Review of Korean Studies* 3: 1 (2000): 34-54.

Han, Kee-hyung. "Sin Chaeho and Nationalist Discourses in East Asia," *Sungkyun Journal of East Asian Studies* 2: 2 (2006).

Han, Kyu Sun & Tim S. Gray. *A Comparative Study of the Anti-Confucianism of Fukuzawa Yukichi and Yi-Kwang-su.* Brookfield: Ashgate, 2000.

Harootunian, Harry D. *Things Seen and Unseen. Discourse and Ideology in Tokugawa Nationalism.* Princeton: Princeton University Press, 1988.

———. *Overcome by Modernity. History, Culture, and Community in Interwar Japan.* Princeton: Princeton University Press, 2000.

———. with B. Silberman (eds). *Japan in Crisis: Essays of Taishō Democracy.* Princeton: Princeton University Press, 1974.

Harris, Peter. "Chinese Nationalism: The State of the Nation," *The China Journal* 38 (1997).

Hase, Shoto. "The Problem of the Other in Self-Awareness," *Zen Buddhism Today* 15: (1998): 119-138.

Hauchard, Claire. "L. P. Karsavin et le mouvement eurasien," *Revue des études slaves* 68: 3 (1996).

Havel, Vaclav. 1991. "On Home," *New York Review of Books* 3: 20 (December 5), 49.

Havens, Thomas. 1970. *Nishi Amane and Modern Japanese Thought.* Princeton: Princeton University Press.

Hay, Stephen. *Asian Ideas of East and West: Tagore and his Critics in Japan, China, and India.* Cambridge, MA: Harvard University Press, 1970.

Hazegawa, Nyozekan. "The Lost Japan and the New Japan" in R. Tsumoda and Th. De Bary, *Sources of Japanese Tradition.* New York: Columbia University Press, 1964.

He, Baogang. "East Asian Ideas of Regionalism: A Normative Critique," *Australian Journal of International Affairs* 58: 1 (2004): 105-125.

Heim, Michael. *The Metaphysics of Virtual Reality*. Oxford: Oxford University Press, 1993.

———. "Virtual Reality and the Tea Ceremony" in J. Beckmann (ed.): *The Virtual Dimension*. Princeton: Princeton Architectural Press, 1998.

———. *Virtual Realism*. New York: Oxford University Press, 1998b.

Heine, Steven and Charles Wei-hsun Fu. 1995. *Japan in Traditional and Postmodern Perspectives*. Albany, NY: SUNY Press.

Heine, Steven. *A Dream Within a Dream*. New York: Lang, 1991.

Heisig, James. "Non-I and Thou. Nishida, Buber, and the Moral Consequences of Self-Actualization," *Philosophy East and West* 50: 2 (2000).

Henrich, Dieter (ed). *All-Einheit: Wege eines Gedankens in Ost und West*. Stuttgart: Klett-Cotta, 1985.

Herzen Alexandr Ivanovich. *С того берега*. Engl.: *From the Other Shore*. London: Weidenfeld & Nicolson, 1850.

Hirschkop, Ken. *Mikhail Bakhtin. An Aesthetics for Democracy*. Oxford: Oxford University Press, 1999.

Hocking, Ernst. *The Coming World Civilization*. New York: Harper, 1956.

Holenstein, Elmar."Die russische ideologische Tradition und die deutsche Romantik" in Holenstein, Gadamer, Jakobson (eds) *Das Erbe Hegels II*. Frankfurt: Suhrkamp, 1988.

Holtom, Daniel C. *Modern Japan and Shinto Nationalism*. U. of Chicago Press, 1943.

Hosking, Geoffrey. "Empire and Nation-Building in Late Imperial Russia" in G. Hosking and R. Service (eds), *Russian Nationalism Past and Present*. London: School of Slavonic and East European Studies. *Present*. School of Slavonic and East European Languages London, 1998.

Hung, Yok Ip. "The Origins of Chinese Communism: A New Interpretation," *Modern China* 20: 1 (1994): 34-64.

Hunter Janet (ed.). *Aspects of Pan-Asianism*. London: LSE, 1987.

Huntington, Samuel P. *The Clash of Civilizations and the Remaking of World Order*. London and New York: Touchstone, 1996.

Irige, Akira. *Cultural Internationalism and World Order*. Baltimore: Johns Hopkins Press, 1997.

———. *New Order in the Far East 1921-1931*. Cambridge MA: Harvard University Press, 1965.

Ishbolin, Boris. "The Eurasian Movement," *Russian Revue* 5: 2 (1946): 64-73.

Issa. *Oraga Haru* (trans. by Nobuki Yuasa). Berkeley and Los Angeles: University of California Press, 1960.

Ivanov, Vyacheslav V. "The Dominant of Bakhtin's Philosophy: Dialogue and Carnival," *Critical Studies* 3: 2 (1993).

———. "Afterword" in Scanlan, 1994.

Jansen, Marius B. *The Japanese and Sun Yat-Sen*. Stanford: Stanford University Press, 1954.

———. "On Foreign Borrowing" in A. Craig (ed.): *Japan: A Comparative View* (Princeton: Princeton University Press, 1979.

Jullien, François. *Eloge de la fadeur: A partir de la pensée et de l'esthétique de la Chine*. Paris: Livre Poche, 1991.

Jung, Hwa Yol. "Bakhtin's Dialogical Body Politics" in M. Mayerfeld Bell & Michael Gardener (eds) *Bakhtin and the Human Sciences*. London and Thousand Oaks: Sage, 1998.

Kant, Immanuel. *Kritik der Urteilskraft* [Critique of Judgment]. Berlin: Reimer, 1908. Engl.: *Critique of Judgment* (trans. Werner S. Pluhar). Indianapolis: Hackett, 1987.

————. *Zum ewigen Frieden: Ein philosophischer Entwurf*. Leipzig: Reclam, 1881.

Karl, Rebecca E. "Creating Asia: China in the World at the Beginning of the Twentieth Century," *American Historical Review* 103: 4 (1998), 1096-1118.

Karsavin, L. P. "Основы политики" [The Foundations of Politics] in *Evraziiskii Vremennik* 5, 1927.

Kawatake, Toshio. *Japan on Stage: Japanese Concepts of Beauty in the Traditional Theatre*. Tokyo: 3A Corporation, 1990.

Kennedy, Joseph. *Asian Nationalism in the Twentieth Century*. London, Melbourne: Mamillian, 1960.

————. *Patterns of Nationalism*. London, Melbourne: Mamillian, 1968.

Keum, Jang-tae. "Human Liberation in Early Modern Korean Thought," *Korea Journal* 38: 3 (1998): 267-291.

Khoruzhy, S. S. "Диалогическая природа философского творчества карсавина," *Revue des études slaves* 68: 3 (1996).

Kim, Key-Hiuk. *The Last Phase of the East Asian World Order Korea, Japan, and the Chinese Empire*. Berkeley: University of California Press, 1980.

Kimmerle, Heinz and Henk Oosterling (eds). *Sensus communis in Multi- and Intercultural Perspective: On the Possibility of Common Judgments in Arts and Politics*. Würzburg: Königshausen & Neumann, 2000.

Kimura, Bin. 人と人のあいだの病理 (Hito to hito no aida no byorin). Tokyo: Kobundo, 1972. German trans.: *Zwischen Mensch und Mensch Strukturen japanischer Subjektivität*. Darmstadt: Wissenschaftliche Buchgesellschaft, 1995.

————. 分裂病の現象学 (Bunretsubyō no genshōgaku; Symptomatology of Schizophrenia). Toyko: Kobundo, 1975.

————. 時間と自己 (Jikan to jiko; Time and I). Tokyo: Iwanami, 1982.

————. "Signification et limite dans la formation psychothérapeutique" in P. Fedida and J. Schotte (eds). *Psychiatrie et existence*. Grenoble: Million, 1991.

————. *Ecrits de psychopathologie phénoménologique*. Paris: Presses Universitaires de France, 1992.

Kireevsky, Ivan. *Russischer Intellekt in Europäischer Krise*. Köln, Graz: Böhlau, 1966.

————. *Collected Works I*. Moscow: Gerchenzon, 1911.

Kitagawa, Joseph. "A Past of Things Present. Notes on Major Motives of Early Japanese Religions," *History of Religions* 20 (1980).

Kizevetter, Alexandr. "Евразийство," *Русский экономический сборник* 3 (1925): 50–65.

Knauth, L. "Life is Tragic. The Diary of Nishida Kitarō," *Monumenta Nipponica* 2: 3-4 (1965).

Kogan, L. A.. "The Philosophy of N. F. Fedorov," *Soviet Studies in Philosophy* 30: 4 (1992)

Kohn, Hans. *Pan-Slavism: Its History and Ideology.* Notre Dame: University of Notre Dame Press, 1953.

Komparu, Kunio. 1983. *The Noh Theatre: Principles and Perspectives.* New York & Tokyo: Weatherhill.

Konishi, Jin'ichi. "Michi and Medieval Writing" in E. Miner: *Principles of Classical Japanese Literature.* Princeton: Princeton University Press, 1985.

Koo, Jong-suh. "Pan-Asianism: For Primacy of East Asia," *Korea Focus* 3: 2 (1995): 34-41.

Kosaku, Yoshino. *Cultural Nationalism in Contemporary Japan: A Sociological Enquiry.* New York: Routledge, 1992.

Koschmann, Victor. "The Debate on Subjectivity in Postwar Japan: Foundations of Modernism as a Political Critique," *Pacific Affairs* 54: 4 (1982-83).

Koyré, Alexandre. *La Philosophie et le problème national en Russie au début du XIXe siècle.* Paris: Gallimard, 1976.

Kracht, Klaus. "Nishida und die Politik," *Japonica Humboldtiana* 5 (2001).

———. "Nishida as a Philosopher of the State" in Gordon Daniels et. al. (eds), *Europe Interprets Japan.* Kent: Norbury: 198-203 (1984).

Krasteva, Galya Andreyeva. "The Criticism towards the West and the Future of Russia-Eurasia," *The Eurasian Politician* July (2003).

Kullberg, Anssi. "From Neo-Eurasianism to National Paranoia: Renaissance of Geopolitics in Russia," *The Eurasian Politician* 4 (2001).

Kupchan, Charles. *The End of the American Era.* New York: Knopf, 2002.

Kusahara, Machiko. "The Art of Creating Subjective Reality: An Analysis of Japanese Digital Pets," *Leonardo* 34: 4 (2001): 299–302.

LaFleur, William. "Buddhist Emptiness in the Ethics and Aesthetics of Watsuji Tetsurō," *Religious Studies* 14: 2 (1978): 237-250.

———. "A Turning in Taishō: Asia and Europe in the Early Writings of Watsuji Tetsurō" in T. Rimer: *Culture and Identity: Japanese Intellectuals During the Interwar Years.* Princeton: Princeton University Press, 1990.

Laurel, Brenda. "Virtual Reality Design: A Personal View" in S. K. Helsel and J. Roth (eds): *Virtual Reality: Theory, Practice and Promise* Westport, CT and London: Meckler, 1991.

Lavelle, Pierre. *La Pensée politique du Japon contemporain.* Paris: Presse universitaire française, 1990.

Lebra Sukiyama, Takie. "Self in Japanese Culture" in N. R. Rosenberger, *Japanese Sense of Self.* Cambridge: Cambridge University Press, 1992.

Lee, Kwang-rin. "The Rise of Nationalism in Korea," *Korean Studies* 10 (1986).

Lenin, Vladimir Ilitch. "The Awakening of Asia," *Collected Works* Vol. 19. Moscow: Progress Publishers, 1965.

Lensen, George Alexander. "The Russian Impact on Japan" in Vucinich 1972.

Lesourd, Françoise. "Karsavin, historien de la culture," *Revue des études slaves* 68: 3 (1996).

Levenson, Joseph R. "The Suggestiveness of Vestiges: Confucianism and Monarchy at the Last" in Arthur F. Wright (ed.): *Confucianism and Chinese Civilization.* Stanford: Stanford University Press, 1964, 291-314.

Li, Xiaodong. "Aesthetic of the Absent: The Chinese Conception of Space," *Journal of Architecture* 7: 1 (2002): 87-101.

Lin, Fu-Kuo. "The Renewal of Regionalism and an East Asian New Order" in Fu-Kuo Lin & Philippe Régnier (eds), *Regionalism in East Asia. Paradigm Shifting?* New York: Routledge, 2003.

Lloyd, Fran (ed). *Consuming Bodies: Sex and Contemporary Japanese Art.* London: Reaktion Books, 2002.

Lopatin, Lev. "Монос и плюрализм," *Voprosy filosofii i psikhologii* 113: 83 (1913).

Lossky, Nicolas O. *History of Russian Philosophy.* New York: International University Press, 1951.

―――. *Интуитивная философия Бергсона* [The Intuitive Philosophy of Bergson]. Moscow, 1914.

―――. *The World as an Organic Whole.* Oxford: Oxford University Press, 1928.

―――. *L'Intuition. La Matière de la vie.* Paris: Alcan, 1928.

―――. *Handbuch der Logik.* Leipzig: Teubner, 1927.

―――. "Fichtes konkrete Ethik im Lichte des modernen Tranzendentalismus" [review of Gurvitch's book] in *Logos* 2 (1926).

Lotman, Yuri. *Universe of the Mind.* London & New York: Tauris & Co, 1970.

―――. "The Poetics of Everyday Behaviour in Eighteenth Century Russian Culture" in Nakhimovsky, A. D. & A. S. (eds.): *The Semiotics of Russian Cultural History.* Ithaca: Cornell University Press (1985): 165-176.

Luks, Leonid."Der 'dritte Weg' der 'Neo-Eurasischen' Zeitschrift 'Elementy'―zurück ins Dritte Reich?," *Studies in East European Thought* 52: 1-2 (2000): 49-71.

Mackinder, Halford. "The Geographical Pivot of History," *Democratic Ideals and Reality* [1904]. New York: Norton, 1962.

MacMaster, Robert E. *Danilevsky: A Russian Totalitarian Philosopher.* Cambridge, MA: Harvard University Press, 1967.

Malia, Martin. *Russia Under Western Eyes: From the Bronze Horseman to the Lenin Mausoleum.* Cambridge: Cambridge University Press, 1999.

Mancall, Mark. "Russia and China: The Structure of Contact" in Vucinich, 1972.

Maraldo, John. "Translating Nishida," *Philosophy East & West* 39: 4 (1989): 465-496.

―――. with Heisig, James (eds). *Rude Awakenings: Zen, the Kyoto School, and Questions of Nationalism.* Honolulu: University of Hawai'i Press, 1994.

―――. "Tradition, Textuality, and the Trans-lation of Philosophy: The Case of Japan" in Heine, Steven and Charles Wei-hsun Fu (eds), *Japan in Traditional and Postmodern Perspectives.* Albany, NY: SUNY Press, 1995, 225-43.

―――. "The Problem of World Culture: Towards an Appropriation of Nishida's Philosophy of Nation and Culture," *Eastern Buddhist* 28: 2 (1995b).

Maruyama, Masao. *Thought and Behaviour in Modern Japanese Politics.* Oxford: Oxford University Press, 1963.

―――. *Studies in the Intellectual History of Tokugawa Japan.* University of Tokyo Press, 1974 [1952].

Marx, Edward. "What about my Songs: Yone Noguchi in the West" in Y. Hakutani (ed.): *Modernism in East-West Literary Criticism: New Readings.* Madison, NJ: Fairleigh Dickinson University Press, 2001.

Mazurek, Slavomir. "Russian Eurasianism—Historiosophy and Ideology," *Slavic and East European Thought* 54 1-2 March, 2002.

Masaryk, T. G. *The Spirit of Russia. Studies in History, Literature, and Philosophy* (3 Vols.). London: Allen & Unwin, 1955.

Masolo, D. A. "Communitarianism: An African Perspective," in St. Dawson (ed.) *Intercultural Philosophy.* Bowling Green, KY: Philosophy Documentation Center, 2001.

Medvedev, Pavel N. *Формальный метод в литературоведении. Критическое введение в социологическую поэтику.* Leningrad: Priboi, 1928. Engl. trans.: *The Formal Method in Literary Scholarship. A Critical Introduction to Sociological Poetics.* Cambridge, MA and London: Harvard University Press, 1985.

Mehlich, Julia. "Die philosophisch-theologische Begründung des Eurasismus bei L. P. Karsavin," *Studies in East European Thought* 52: 1-2 (2000): 73-117.

Michelis, Panayotis A. *An Aesthetic Approach to Byzantine Art.* London: Batsford, 1964.

Milojkovic-Djuric, Jelena. *Panslavism and National Identity in Russia and in the Balkans 1830-1880: Images of the Self and Others.* Boulder, CO: East European Monographs, 1994.

Miwa, Kimitada. "Japanese Policies and Concepts for a Regional Order in Asia, 1938-1940" in White, James et al. (eds). *The Ambivalence of Nationalism: Modern Japan Between East and West.* Lanham, MD: University Press of America, 1990.

Miller, Roy Andrew. *Japanese Ceramics.* New York: Crown, 1960.

Möhler, Johann A. *Die Einheit der Kirche oder das Prinzip des Katholizismus.* Regensburg: Manz, 1825.

Morris, Ivan. *Nationalism and the Right Wing in Japan.* Oxford: Oxford University Press, 1960.

Morris-Suzuki, Tessa. "The Invention and Reinvention of Japanese Culture," *The Journal of Asian Studies* 54: 3 (1995): 759-780.

Müller, Eberhard. *Russischer Intellekt in europäischer Krise: Ivan V. Kireevskij (1806-1856).* Köln & Graz: Böhlau, 1966.

Muraviec, Laurent. *L'Esprit des nations: culture et géopolitique.* Paris: O. Jacob, 2002.

Naff, William. "Toson's *Before Dawn*: Historical Fiction as History and as Literature" in White, 1990.

Nakamura, Yūjirō. "Nishida, le premier philosophe original au Japon," *Critique* 39 (1983): 32-54.

———. "Logique du lieu et savoir théâtral: Sur la logique du lieu" in Berque and Nys, 1997.

———. "Au delà de la logique du lieu" in Berque, Augustin (ed.) *Logique du lieu et le dépassement de la modernité.* Bruxelles: Ousia, 2000.

Nancy, Jean-Luc. *La Communauté désœvrée.* Paris: Christian Bourgeois, 1986.

Nasagawa, Kunihiko. Das Prinzip des Ich bei Fichte und das Problem des Selbst bei Dōgen, in Dieter Henrich (ed.), *All-Einheit: Wege eines Gedankens in Ost und West*. Stuttgart: Klett-Cotta, 1985.

Nethercott, Frances. *Une rencontre philosophique: Bergson en Russie (1907-1917)*. Paris: Harmattan, 1995.

Nishida, Kitarō. NKZ (NISHIDA Kitarō Zenshū [Complete Works], Tokyo: Iwanami, 1965-66.

———. 善の研究 (Zen no kenkyū; Study of the good) NKZ 1 (1911): 1-200. Engl. transl. by Masao Abe and Charles Ives: *Inquiry into the Good*. New Haven, CT: Yale University Press, 1990.

———. 自覚に於ける直観と反映 (Jikaku ni okeru chokkan to hansei). NKZ 2 (1913-23). Engl. transl.: *Intuition and Reflection in Self-Consciousness*. Albany, NY: State University of New York Press, 1987.

———. 芸術と道徳 (Geijutsu to dōtoku) in NKZ 3 (1921-23): 239-546. Engl. transl.: *Art and Morality*. Honolulu: University of Hawai'i Press, 1975.

———. 場所 (Basho; place) in NKZ 4 (1926): 208-289.

———. 私と汝 (Watashi to nanji; I and Thou). NKZ 6 (1932): 341-427.

———. 哲学の根本問題 (Tetsugaku no konpon mondai; Fundamental problems of philosophy) in NKZ 7 (1933-34): 3-173. Engl. transl: *Fundamental Problems of Philosophy: The World of Action and the Dialectical World*. Tokyo: Sophia University Press, 1970.

———. "歴史的身体" (Rekishiteki shintai) in NKZ 14 (1937): 264-291. Engl. transl.: "The Historical Body" in D. A. Dilworth, V. H. Viglielmo (eds). *Sourcebook for Modern Japanese Philosophy*. Westport, CT: Greenwood, 1998. 37-53.

———. "歴史的世界においての個物の立場" (Rekishiteki sekai ni oite no kobutsu no tachiba; The Position of the Individual in the Historical World) in NKZ 9 (1938): 69-146.

———. 絶対矛盾的自己同一. (Zettai mujunteki jiko tōitsu; Absolute Self-Contradictory Self-Identity) in NKZ 9 (1939): 147-223. Engl. "The Unity of Opposites," *Intelligibility and the Philosophy of Nothingness*. Tokyo: Maruzen, 1958. 163-245.

———. 歴史的形成作用としての芸術的創作 (Rekishiteki keisei sayō to shite no geijutsuteki sōsaku; Artistic creation as Formative Act of History) in NKZ 10 (1941): 177-264.

———. 実在の根底としての人格概念 (Jitsuzai no kontei to shite no jinkaku gainen; The Concept of Personality as the Foundation of Reality) NKZ 14 (1932): 133-174.

———. 世界新秩序の原理 (Sekai shinchitsujo no genri) in NKZ 12 (1943): 426-34. Engl. transl.: "Fundamental Principle of a New World Order" in D. A. Dilworth, V. H. Viglielmo and Augustin Jacinto Zavala (eds). *Sourcebook for Modern Japanese Philosophy*. Westport, CT: Greenwood, 1998: 73-77.

———. 予定調和を手引きとして宗教哲学へ (Yoteishūwa o tebiki to shite shūkyō tetsugaku e) in NKZ 11 (1944a): 114-146. Engl. transl.: "Towards a Philosophy of Religion with the Concept of Pre-established Harmony as Guide," *The Eastern Buddhist* 3(1) 1970: 19-46.

———. 場所的論理と宗教的世界観 (Bashoteki ronri to shūkyōteki sekaikan) in NKZ 11 (1944b): 371-464. Engl. transl.: "The Logic of *Topos* and the

Religious Worldview." Part 1 in Eastern Buddhist 1986, 19(2) 1986: 1-29; Part 2 in *Eastern Buddhist* 1987, 20: 1, 81-119.

———. "哲学論文集第四補遺" (Tetsugaku ronbun shū dai yon hoi; Fourth supplement to the philosophical article) in NKZ 12 (1944c): 397-425. Engl. trans.: "On the National Polity" in D. A. Dilworth, V. H. Vigliel- mo and Augustin Jacinto Zavala (eds) *Sourcebook for Modern Japanese Philosophy*. Westport, CT: Greenwood, 1998, 78-95.

———. "Affective Feeling" (感情). Excerpts from *Ishiki no mondai; Problems of Consciousness*, 1920) in NKZ 3 (1978): 3-232. Engl. transl. by Dil- worth and Vilgielmo in *Analecta Husserliana* 8, 223-247. Dordrecht: Kluwer, 1978.

Nishitani, Keiji. *Nishida Kitarō*. Berkley, Los Angeles, and Oxford: University of California Press, 1991.

———. *Religion and Nothingness*. Berkeley, Los Angeles, and Oxford: Univer- sity of California Press, 1982.

Nitschke, Günter. "From Ambiguity to Transparency: Unperspective, Perspec- tive and Perspective Paradigms of Space," *Supplement of Louisiana Revy* 35: 3 (1995).

Noda, Matao. "East-West Synthesis in Kitarō Nishida," *Philosophy East & West* 4: 4 (1955): 345-365.

Northrop, F. S. C. "The Relation Between Eastern and Western Philosophy" in W. R. Inge et. al. (eds) *Radhakrishnan: Comparative Studies in Philos- ophy Presented in Honour of his Sixtieth Birthday*. London: Allen and Unwin, 1951.

Novirkovka, L. I. & I. I. Sisemskaja (eds). *Россиа между Европой и Азией: Евразийский соблазн. Антология*. Moscow: Nauka, 1993.

Nussbaum, Martha. "Patriotism and Cosmopolitanism" in Joshua Cohen (ed.) *For Love of Country: Debating the Limits of Patriotism*. Boston: Beacon Press, 1996.

Odum, Eugene. *Fundamentals of Ecology*. Philadelphia: Saunders, 1971.

Ōe, Kenzaburō. "Japan, the Dubious, and Myself" in Heine, Steven and Charles Wei-hsun Fu (eds) *Japan in Traditional and Postmodern Perspectives*. Albany, NY: SUNY Press, 1995.

Ohashi, Ryōsuke."Phänomenologie der Noh-Maske," *Japan im interkulturellen Dialog*. München: Iudicium, 1999.

———."Jeu et logique du lieu" in Berque, Augustin (ed.) *Logique du lieu et dépassement de la modernité*. Bruxelles: Ousia, 2000.

———. "Sensus communis in the Context of the Question of a Non-Western Concept of Modernity" in Kimmerle & Oosterling, 2000b, 53-60.

Okakura, Kakuzō. *Ideals of the East*. New York: Dutton, 1905.

Olson, Lawrence. "Takeuchi Yukichi and the Vision of a Protest Society in Ja- pan," *Journal of Japanese Studies* 7: 2 (1981): 319-48.

Onasch, Konrad & Annemarie Schnieper. *Icons: The Fascination and Reality*. New York: Riverside, 1997.

Oosterling, Henk. "A Culture of the 'Inter': Japanese Notions *ma* and *basho*," in Kimmerle & Oosterling, 2000, 61-84.

Panarin, A. S. "Return to Civilization or 'Formal Isolation'?" in *Russian Studies in Philosophy* (1992): 31: 2.

Panofsky, Erwin. *Perspective as Symbolic Form*. New York: Zone Book, 1991.

Parkes, Graham. "The Putative Fascism of the Kyoto School and Political Correctness of the Modern Academy," *Philosphy East & West* 47: 3 (1997): 305-36.

Parsons, Talcott. *The Structure of Social Action* (2 Volumes). New York: MacGraw Hill, 1937.

———. *The Social System.* New York: The Free Press, 1951.

Pearson, Keith Ansell. "Viroid Life: On Machines, Technics and Evolution" in Pearson, *Deleuze and Philosophy.* Routledge, 1997.

Peattie, Mark. *Ishiwara Kanji and the Japanese Confrontation with the West.* Princeton: Princeton University Press, 1975.

Pelletier, Philippe (ed.). *Identités territoriales en Asie orientale.* Paris: Les Indes Savantes, 2004.

Peri, Noël. *Le Nô.* Tokyo: Maison Franco-Japonaise, 1944.

Philonenko, Alexis. *La Liberté humaine dans la philosophie de Fichte.* Paris: Vrin, 1966.

Pierson, John D. *Tokutomi Sohō 1863-1957. A Journalist for Modern Japan.* Princeton: Princeton University Press, 1980.

Pilgrim, Richard. "The Artistic Way and the Religio-Aesthetic Tradition in Japan," *Philosophy East and West* 27/3 (1977).

Piovesana, Gino. *Recent Japanese Thought 1862-1996: A Survey.* Tokyo: Japan Library, 1997.

Pipes, Richard. *Struve. Liberal on the Left, 1870-1905.* Cambridge, MA: Harvard University Press, 1980.

Przebinda, Grzegorz. "Vladimir Solovëv's Fundamental Philosophical Ideas," *Studies in East European Thought* 54: 1 (2002): 47-69.

Raeff, Mark. *Political Ideas and Institutions in Imperial Russia.* Boulder, CO: Westview Press, 1994.

Rhee, Syngman. *The Spirit of Independence: A Primer of Korean Modernization and Reform.* Honolulu: University of Hawai'i Press, 2001.

Rhee, Sang-woo. "Japan's Role in New Asian Order," *Korea Focus* 4: 3 (1996): 22-36.

Rice, Talbot, David and Tamara. *Icons and Their History.* Woodstock: Overlook Press, 1974.

Relph, Edward. *Space and Spacelessness.* London: Pion, 1976.

Riasanovsky, Nicolas V. *Russia and the West in the Teachings of the Slavophiles: A Study of Romantic Ideology.* Cambridge, MA: Harvard University Press, 1952.

———. "Khomiakov on *sobornost'*" in E. J. Simmons (ed.) *Continuity and Change in Russian and Soviet Thought.* Cambridge, MA: Harvard University Press, 1955, 183-196.

———. "Russia and Asia: Two Eighteenth Century Russian Views," *California Slavic Studies* 1 (1960): 170-81.

———. "The Emergence of Eurasianism," *California Slavic Studies* 4 (1967), 39-72.

———. "Asia through Russian Eyes" in Wayne S. Vucinich (ed.): *Russia and Asia: Essays on the Influence of Russia on the Asian Peoples.* Stanford University Press, 1972, 3-29.

Robinson, Michael E. "National Identity and the Thought of Ch'aeho: Sadaejuui and Chuch'e in History and Politics," *The Journal of Korean Studies 5*

(1984): 121-142.

————. "Nationalism and the Korean Tradition, 1896-1920: Iconoclasm, Reform and National Identity," *Korean Studies* 10 (1987): 35-53.

————. "Mass Media and Popular Culture in 1930s Korea: Cultural Control, Identity, and Cultural Hegemony" in Dae-Sook Suh (ed.) *Korean Studies: New Pacific Currents.* Honololu: University of Hawai'i Press, 1994.

Rorty, Richard. *Philosophy and the Mirror of Nature.* Oxford: Blackwell, 1980.

Rozman, Gilbert. "Flawed Regionalism: Reconceptualizing Northeast Asia in the 1990," *The Pacific Review* Vol 5: 1 (1998): 105-124.

————. "Japan and Russia: Great Power Ambitions and Domestic Capacities" in G. Rozman (ed.) *Japan and Russia: The Tortuous Path to Normalization, 1949–1999.* New York: St. Martin's Press, 2000.

Ryan, Marie-Laure. *Narrative as Virtual Reality: Immersion and Interactivity in Literature and Electronic Media.* Baltimore: Johns Hopkins Press, 2001.

Saigusa, Mitsuyoshi. "Henri Bergson and Buddhist Thought," *Philosophical Studies of Japan* 9 (1969): 79-101.

Sakai, Naoki. *Translation and Subjectivity. On Japan and Cultural Nationalism.* Minneapolis: University of Minnesota Press, 1997.

Sakharov, A. N. "The Main Phases and Distinctive Features of Russian Nationalism" in G. Hosking & Robert Service (eds), *Russian Nationalism: Past and Present.* London: SSEES, 1998.

Sato, Kumiko. "How Information Technology has (not) Changed Feminism and Jaânism: Cyberpunk in the Japanese Context," *Comparative Literature* 41: 3, (2004): 335-356.

Savitsky, Petr N. "Два мира," *На путях: Утверждение евразийцев* (1922a): 9–27.

————. "Степь и оседлость," *На путях: Утверждение евразийцев* (1922b): 341–355.

————. "Евразийство," *Евразийский временник* 4 (1925): 5–26.

————. "Хозяии и хозяйство" *Евразийский временник* 4 (1925b): 406–445.

Scanlan, James P. (ed.). *Russian Thought After Communism: The Recovery of a Philosophical Heritage.* Armonk, NY, London: M. E. Sharp, 1994.

————. "Lossky" in *The Routledge Encyclopedia of Philosophy* (ed. E. Craig). London and New York: Routledge, 1998, 833-838.

Schelling, F. W. J. *Philosophie der Offenbarung.* Ed. by M. Frank. Frankfurt: Suhrkamp, 1977.

Schelting, Alexander von. *Russland und Europa im russischen Geschichtsdenken.* Bern: Francke, 1948.

Schinzinger, Robert. "Introduction" to Nishida Kitarō, *Intelligibility and the Philosophy of Nothingness.* Tokyo: Maruzen, 1958.

Schmidt, André. "Rediscovering Manchuria: Sin Ch'aeho and the Politics of Territorial History in Korea," *The Journal of Asian Studies* 56, 1 (1997): 26-46.

Schwartz, Benjamin. *In Search of Wealth and Power: Yen Fu and the West.* Cambridge, MA: The Belknap Press of Harvard University Press, 1964.

Sendler, Egon. *L'Icône: Image de l'invisible. Eléments de théologie, esthétique et technique.* Paris: Desclée de Brouwer, 1981.

Seton-Watson, Hugh. "Russia and Modernization," *Slavic Review* 20: 4 (1961): 583-88.

Sharf, Robert R. "The Zen of Japanese Nationalism," *History of Religions* 33: 1 (1993): 1-43.
———. "Experience" in Mark C. Taylor (ed.): *Critical Terms of Religious Studies*. Chicago: University of Chicago Press, 1998.
———. "On the Allure of Buddhist Relics," *Representations* 66 (1999).
———. "Prolegomenon to the Study of Japanese Buddhist Icons" in R. Sharf and E. Horton-Sharf (eds): *Living Images: Japanese Buddhist Icons in Context*. Stanford: Stanford University Press, 2001.
Shillony, Ben-Ami. *The Jews and the Japanese: The Successful Outsiders*. Tokyo: Tuttle, 1992.
———. *Politics and Culture in Wartime Japan*. Oxford: Clarendon Press, 1981.
Shin, Bok-ryong. "Western Infiltration into Asian Nations and Their Disturbances: An Introduction to the Understanding of Korean Nationalism," *Journal of Social Sciences and Humanities* 45 (1977): 49-73.
Sil, Rudra. *Managing "Modernity": Work, Community and Authenticity in Late-Industrializing Japan and Russia*. Ann Arbor: University of Michigan Press, 2002.
Solov'ëv, Vladimir. *Conscience de la Russie*. Paris: Plon, 1950.
———. *Crise de la philosophie occidentale*. Lille: Aubier, 1944.
———. *Erkenntnislehre. Ästhetik, Philosophie der Liebe*. Freiburg: Wewel, 1953.
Steunebrink, G. "*Sensus Communis* and Modernity as a Common Horizon. A Contribution to the Theory of Intercultural Communication" in Kimmerle & Oosterling, 2000, 31-52.
Stepun, Fiodor. *Das Antlitz Russlands und das Gesicht der Revolution*. München: Kösel, 1961.
Stock, Gregory. *Metaman: The Merging of Humans and Machines into a Global Superorganism*. New York: Simon & Schuster, 1993.
———. "Россия между Европой и Азией," *Новый журнал* 69 (1962): 251–277.
Stone, Jackie. "A Vast and Grave Task: Interwar Buddhist Studies as an Expression of Japan's Envisioned Global Role" in J. Th. Rimer: *Culture and Identity: Japanese Intellectuals During the Interwar Years*. Princeton: Princeton University Press, 1990.
Storry, Richard. *The Double Patriots: A Story of Japan's Nationalism*. Westport, CT: Greenwood, 1957.
Suvchinsky, Pierre. "L'Eurasisme" in Eric Humberclaude: *(Re)lire Souvtchinski*. Paris: La Bresse, 1990.
Suzuki, Daitetz. *Zen and Japanese Culture*. New York: Pantheon Books, 1959.
———. *Japanese Spirituality*. Tokyo: JSPS, 1972.
Szpilman, Christopher. "The Dream of one Asia: Ōkawa Shūmei and Japanese Pan-Asianism" in Harald Füss (ed.), *The Japanese Empire in East Asia and its Postwar Legacy*. München: Iudicium, 1998.
Takeda, Hiromichi. "Nishida's Doctrine of 'Universals,'" *Monumenta Nipponica* 23: 2-3 1968): 497-502.
Takeuchi, Yoshimi. *What is Modernity? Writings of Takeuchi Yoshimi*. Trans. Richard F. Calichman. New York: Columbia University Press, 2005.
Tankha, Brij. *Kita Ikki and the Making of Modern Japan: A Vision of Empire* [contains Engl. translation of Ikki's "The Fundamental Principles of the

Reorganization of Japan" (Kaizo hoan taiko)]. Kent: Global Oriental, 2006.

Tikhinov, Vladimir. "Korea's First Encounter with Pan-Asianism Ideology," http://world.lib.ru/k/kim_o_i/ n101.shtml, 2000.

Tomonaga, Tairako. "Die Grundzüge des japanischen Faschismus und die Kriegsverantwortlichkeit japanischer Philosophen während der Kriegszeit," *Hitotsubashi Journal of Social Studies* 22 (1990): 19-25.

Tönnies, Ferdinand. 1886. *Gemeinschaft und Gesellschaft*. Leipzig: Fuess.

Torbakov, Igor. "From the Other Shore: Some Reflections of Russian Emigré Thinkers on Soviet Nationality Policies 1920s-1930s," *Slavic & East European Information Resources* 4: 4 (2003): 33-49.

Trubetzkoy, Nicolai S. "Об истинном и ложном национализ ме" in Florovsky et al. (eds), *Исход к Востоку*. Sofia (1921): 71-86.

———. "Русская проблем," *На путях: Утверждение евразийцев*. Moscow & Berlin (1922): 294-317.

———. "О Туранском элементе в русской культуре," *Евразийский временник* 4 Berlin (1925): 351-77.

———. 1927. "Общеевразийский национализм," *Евразийская хроника* 9, Paris (1927): 24-31.

———. *The Legacy of Gengis Khan and Other Essays on Russian Identity*. Ann Arbor: Michigan Slavic Publication, 1991.

Tulaev, Pavel. "Sobor and sobornost," *Russian Studies in Philosophy* 31: 4 (1993): 25-53.

Uchida, Michio. "Natsume Soseki in Manchuria and Korea," *Acta Asiatica* 79 (2000): 1-20.

Ueda, Makoto. "Yūgen and Erhabene: Onishi Yoshinis attempt to Synthesize Japanese Western Aesthetics" in T. Rimer: *Culture and Identity: Japanese Intellectuals During the Interwar Years*. Princeton: Princeton University Press, 1990.

Uspensky, Boris. *The Semiotics of the Russian Icon*. Lisse: Peter de Ridder, 1976.

Uspensky, Leonid & Vladimir Lossky. *The Meaning of Icons*. Crestwood: St. Vladimir's Seminar Press, 1999.

Umegaki, Michio. "Epilogue: National Identity, National Past, National Isms" in James White et al. (eds). *The Ambivalence of Nationalism: Modern Japan Between East and West*. Lanham, MD: University Press of America, 1990.

Vernadsky, George. *A History of Russia*. New Haven, CT: Yale University Press, 1929.

———. *The Mongols and Russia*. New Haven, CT: Yale University Press, 1959.

Vernadsky, Vladimir I. *The Biosphere*. New York: Copernicus, 1998.

Vieillard-Baron, Jean-Louis. "Bergson et Fichte," in Ives Radrizziani (ed.): *Fichte et la France*. Paris: Bauchesne, 1997.

Vietroff, J. "L'Influence de la philosophie de H. Bergson," *Mouvement socialiste*, Janvier (1912).

Voloshinov, V. A. Марксизм и философия языка. Основные проблемы социологического метода в научном языке. Leningrad: Priboi, 1929.

Engl.: *Marxism and the Philosophy of Language*. Ann Arbor, New York, and London: Seminar Press, 1973.

———. "Стилистика художественной речи," *Literaturnaja Ucheba* 5 (1930).

Vucinich, Wayne S (ed.). *Russia and Asia: Essays on the Influence of Russia on the Asian Peoples*. Stanford: Stanford University Press, 1972.

Walicki, Andrei. *Russian Thought from the Enlightenment to Marxism*. Oxford: Clarendon Press, 1980.

———. *The Slavophile Controversy: History of a Conservative Utopia in Nineteenth-Century Russian Thought*. Oxford: Clarendon Press, 1975.

Walraven, Boudewijn. "Religion and the City: Seoul in the Nineteenth Century," *The Review of Korean Studies* 3: 1 (2000): 178-206.

Wang, Hui. "Les Asiatiqus réinventent l'Asie," *Le Monde diplomatique* Février (2005).

Wargo, Robert J. *The Logic of Basho and the Concept of Nothingness in the Philosophy of Nishida Kitarō*. Thesis, University of Michigan, 1972.

Watsuji, Tetsurō. 1935. 風土 : 人間学的考察 (Fudō: Ningengakuteki kōsatsu; Climate: A Study in Humanities). Tokyo: Chuokoronsha, 1935. German transl.: *Fudo: Der Zusammenhang zwischen Klima und Kultur* (Darmstad: Wissenschaftliche Buchgesellschaft 1992).

———. 人間の学としての倫理学 (Ningen no gaku toshite no rinrigaku; The significance of ethics for humanities). Watsuji Tetsurō Collected Works (WTZ) Vol. 9 (1937): 1-192. Tokyo: Iwanami. Engl. transl.: *Watsuji Tetsuro's Rinrigaku*. New York: SUNY Press, 1996. Transl. of first Chapter in Dilworth 1998.

———. 族日本精神研究 *WTZ* Vol. 4. Tokyo: Iwanami, 1965 [1935].

———. 封建思想と神道の教義 [Hōken shisō to shintō no kyōgi], 1945.

Weidlé, Vladimir. "Russia and the West [1956]" in A. Schmemann (ed.), *Ultimate Questions: An Anthology of Modern Russian Religious Thought*. Crestwood: St. Vladimir's Seminar Press, 1977, 11-27.

Weinmayr, Elmar. "Thinking in Transition: Nishida Kitaro and Martin Heidegger," *Philosophy East and West*, 55: 2 (2005): 232-256.

Weizmann, Kurt. *The Icon*. London: Evans, 1993.

White, James W. et al. (eds). *The Ambivalence of Nationalism: Modern Japan Between East and West*. Lanham, MD: University Press of America, 1990.

Wiederkehr, Stefan. "Der Eurasismus als Erbe N. Ja. Danilevskijs? Bemerkungen zu einem Topos der Forschung," *Studies in East European Thought* 52: 1-2 (2000): 119-150.

Willock, Hiroko. "Japanese Modernization and the Emergence of New Fiction in Early Twentieth Century China: A Study of Liang Qichao," *Modern Asian Studies* 29: 4 (1995): 817-840.

Wilson, George M. *Radical Nationalist in Japan: Kita Ikki 1883-1937*. Cambridge, MA: Harvard University Press, 1969.

Wong, Young-tsu. "Revisionism Reconsidered: Kang Yuwei and the Reform Movement of 1890," *Journal of Asian Studies* 51: 3 (1992).

Yamazaki, Masakazu. "The Aesthetics of Ambiguity: The Artistic Theories of Zeami" in T. Rimer (ed.): *On the Art of the Nô Drama: The Major Treatises of Zeami*. Princeton: Princeton University Press, 1984.

Yasmann, Victor. "The Rise of the Eurasians," *Radio Free Europe Security Watch*, April 30, 2001.

Yi, Tae-Jin. "Was Korea Really a Hermit Nation?," *Korea Journal* 39: 4 (1998): 5-35.

Yun, Kyong-Ro. "Tosan's Political Philosophy" in Tschung-Sun Kim & Michael Reinschmidt (eds) *Strengthened Abilities: Assessing the Vision of Tosan Chang-Ho Ahn*. Los Angeles: Academia Koreana of Keimyung University, 1998.

Yun, Pyong-sok. "Korea's Independence Movement in the 1910s," *Journal of Social Sciences and Humanities* 46: 1-12, 1977.

Yusa, Michiko. "Nishida and Totalitarianism: A Philosopher's Resistance" in Maraldo and Heisig, 1994.

———. "Nishida and the Question of Nationalism," *Monumenta Nipponica* 46: 2 (1991).

Zavala, Augustin Jacinto. "The Return to the Past: Tradition and the Political Microcosm in the Later Nishida" in Maraldo and Heisig, 1994.

———. "The Bodily Manifestation of Religious Experience and Late Nishida Philosophy," *Zen Buddhism Today* 15 (1998).

Zenkovsky Vasily V. *History of Russian Philosophy* Vol. 2. New York: Columbia University Press, 1995.

Zeami, Makoto. *Kwadensho* or *Fushikaden* (The Book of Flowers) in T. Rimer (ed.): *On the Art of the Nô Drama: The Major Treatises of Zeami*. Princeton: Princeton University Press, 1984.

Zernov, Nicolas. *The Russian Religious Renaissance of the Twentieth Century*. London: Darton, Longman & Todd, 1963.

Zweerde, Evert van der. "What is Russian About Russian Philosophy" in Botz-Bornstein & Hengelbrock (eds) *Re-ethnicizing the Minds? Cultural Revival in Contemporary Thought*. Amsterdam, New York: Rodopi, 2006.

Zwerde, Evert van der and Gerrit Steunebrink (eds). *Civil Society, Religion, and the Nation: Modernization in Intercultural Context: Russia, Japan, Turkey*. Amsterdam & New York: Rodopi, 2004.

Index

About the Author

Thorsten Botz-Bornstein was born in Germany and studied philosophy in Paris and Oxford. As a postdoctoral researcher based in Finland he undertook extensive research on Russian formalism and semiotics in Russia and the Baltic countries. He has also been researching in Japan, in particular on the Kyoto School and on the philosophy of NISHIDA Kitarō. Since 1999 is affiliated with the Centre Japon of the EHESS of Paris from which he received his 'habilitation' in 2000. He has been Professor of Philosophy at Zhejiang University in Hangzhou, China and at Tuskegee University (Alabama), and is now Associate Professor at the Gulf University of Science and Technology in Kuwait. His publications are: *Place and Dream: Japan and the Virtual*; *Vasily Sesemann: Experience, Formalism and the Question of Being* and *Virtual Reality: The Last Human Narrative?*; *Films and Dreams Tarkovsky, Bergman, Sokurov, Kubrick, Wong Kar-wai* (Lexington Books). He is the editor of *Re-ethnicizing the Minds? Tendencies of Cultural Revival in Contemporary Philosophy* and *Culture, Nature, Memes: Dynamic Cognitive Theories*.